BRIDGES OF
OPPORTUNITY

*A History of the
Center for Adult Learning
and Educational Credentials*

This book is dedicated to Cornelius P. "Neil" Turner, whose vision, determination, and commitment made possible today's Center for Adult Learning and Educational Credentials.

TABLE OF CONTENTS

FOREWORD

*T*he history of the American Council on Education's (ACE's) Center for Adult Learning and Educational Credentials is an important part of our nation's history. Ever since its first programs were initiated during World War II, the Center for Adult Learning has been a leader in the adult education movement. Guided by the philosophy that what an individual learns is more important than when, where, and how the individual learned it, the Center has led the movement to evaluate and award credit for learning acquired outside the classroom. As a result of its efforts, the Center has opened the doors of higher education to millions of adults whose academic careers otherwise might have ended after—or even before—high school. One outcome of the Center's efforts has been better jobs and career opportunities for many. But perhaps even more important, the Center has helped generations of adults believe in themselves as lifelong learners.

To fully appreciate the Center for Adult Learning, one must understand something about ACE. ACE was founded in 1918 to coordinate higher education's response to the entrance of the United States into World War I. With the advent of the war, it was determined that colleges and universities needed to form a group to represent higher education before government and to provide concerted effort to meet certain needs during the war—namely, educating troops. Thus, the "Emergency Council on Education"—later, the American Council on Education—was founded. This was the beginning of ACE's long and important relationship with the U.S. military services. Throughout ACE's history, the military has played an integral role in the development of ACE's adult learning programs and, consequently, in the lifelong learning movement.

*T*his history of the Center for Adult Learning tells the story of men and women who recognized the need for national educational advocacy for learners of all ages.

Since its founding, ACE's mission has been to ensure equal educational opportunity for all Americans and high-quality education on the nation's postsecondary education campuses. ACE has approximately 1,600 colleges and universities and 200 higher education associations as members, which it represents before Congress, federal agencies, and the courts. ACE thus unifies the diverse higher education community on education issues of national importance.

Today, ACE's mission of advancing the interests and goals of higher and adult education is more important than ever before. The need for learning continues to grow as the nation's economy becomes increasingly skill-based and knowledge intensive. Despite significant progress during the last century, obtaining a college degree—or even a high school diploma—has remained impossible for too many individuals.

But times are changing. New technologies and new providers are making the dream of access to education anywhere and anytime more and more real. In fact, as the lines separating "traditional" from "nontraditional" learning become increasingly blurry and as we all become lifelong learners, we must question whether the term "adult" education will continue to be used as it has been for decades.

This history of the Center for Adult Learning tells the story of men and women who recognized the need for national educational advocacy for learners of all ages. These leaders' vision and dedication to bring equity and access to higher education have left a lasting legacy. This story helps us comprehend how far lifelong learning has come in America and lays the foundation for what still is to come.

Stanley O. Ikenberry
President, American Council on Education

PREFACE

*T*he Center for Adult Learning and Educational Credentials is a division of the American Council on Education (ACE), a national association of higher education institutions. Home to some of the most widely recognized adult education programs in the United States, the Center has three functional areas: military, corporate, and the General Educational Development Testing Service (GEDTS).

The military group includes the Military Evaluations program, the Military Installation Voluntary Education Review (MIVER), the Army/ACE Registry Transcript System (AARTS), and the Sailor/Marine Corps/ACE Registry Transcript. Corporate programs include the College Credit Recommendation Service (formerly the Program on Non-Collegiate Sponsored Instruction [PONSI]), Credit by Examination program, and the three civilian registries (National Registry of Training Programs, International Registry of Training Programs, and Registry of Credit Recommendations). GEDTS includes Test Development, Program Operations, Partner Outreach, and Special Projects.

*A*mericans need to better understand the origins of the modern-day adult learning movement.

All of these programs have gained wide recognition for the services they provide to millions of adult learners. But it was not the recognition of the Center for Adult Learning's programs that led to the decision to write this history. Rather, it was the important contributions the Center has made to the adult education movement as a whole.

In the not-so-distant past, adult education was the forgotten "other half" of the American education system. Underfunded and undervalued, it too often was neglected in favor of the more traditional education model: four years of high school followed immediately by four years of college culminating in a degree. This undervaluation stemmed from an implicit assumption that all formal education should be acquired in a lock-step progression as "preparation" for a productive adulthood. To do otherwise suggested a lack of ability or motivation. Erroneous as it was, this impression fostered an unreceptive environment for many adult education programs in the United States.

But times are changing. As increasing numbers of adults move with relative ease within and among educational experiences, it no longer can be said that higher education and secondary-level options leading thereto are primarily for the young. Today, adult students, who typically have employment and family responsibilities, account for the majority of enrollments at many higher education institutions across the country. Only 33 percent of college students today are enrolled full time and are under the age of 22 (NCES 1996).

The "traditional" education model is no longer the norm. What historically has been referred to as "adult education" has entered the mainstream as a permanent and important fixture in the American education establishment. The Center for Adult Learning has played an important role in bringing about this transformation.

PURPOSE

Americans need to better understand the origins of the modern-day adult learning movement. People in other countries who are seeking ways to adapt this uniquely American model to meet their own societies' needs can also benefit. This book is intended to fully recount the Center's nearly 60-year struggle to win access to educational opportunities for American adults. Of course, the Center for Adult Learning is not solely responsible for the ensuing victory, but it pioneered the awarding of credit and credentialing for learning acquired outside the traditional classroom setting.

AUDIENCE

The primary audience for this book is college and university presidents and key administrative officials who shape adult education policy and lifelong learning opportunities on campus;

administrators and faculty of adult and continuing education programs; graduate students in schools of education; state directors of adult education; administrators and teachers of GED programs; military educators; educators from other countries who are developing their own adult learning programs and systems; and trainers in business, industry, government, and other employment settings.

ORGANIZATION

This book recounts the history of the Center chronologically, rather than programmatically, because all of the Center's programs stemmed from the same root. To separate the histories of the programs would diminish the common history they all share.

Chapter 1 covers the period from 1942 to 1945, when educators were beginning to prepare for the end of World War II and the influx of veterans returning to civilian life. It was during this time that the seeds of today's GEDTS and the Military Evaluations program were planted.

Chapter 2 traces the development of the Commission on Accreditation of Service Experiences (CASE) and the GED Tests between 1946 and 1950.

Chapter 3 covers the same period of time as Chapter 2—1946 to 1950—but traces the development of the Military Evaluations program and Advisory Service.

Chapter 4 details the events of 1951–55 relating to both the GED Tests and the Military Evaluations program. This period saw the beginning of the Korean War and the realization that the credit practices that had been established for World War II veterans would be equally important for Korean War veterans.

Chapter 5 discusses the first 10 years (1956–66) of Neil Turner's leadership of CASE. It was during these years that the number of civilians taking the GED Tests surpassed the number of veterans taking them.

Chapter 6 covers the events of 1967–74, including Turner's final years as director of CASE; development of the Spanish- and French-language versions of the GED Tests; introduction of the tests in Canada; CASE's opposition to the Community College of the Air Force; the beginning of PONSI; and the evolution of the *Guide to the Evaluation of Educational Experiences in the Armed Services.*

Chapter 7 documents the growing criticism of voluntary military education programs between 1975 and 1985, the growth of PONSI, the evaluation of Military Occupational Specialties, the establishment of the Credit by Examination program and AARTS, and the commission's targeting of diploma mills.

Chapter 8 focuses on the rise of the Center for Adult Learning as a leader in shaping higher education policy during the 1986–95 time period. It also traces the beginnings of the National External Diploma Program, MIVER, and administration of the GED Tests to at-risk, in-school youths; redevelopment of the Spanish-language GED Tests; and the establishment of accommodations for prelingually deaf GED candidates and GED candidates with specific learning disabilities.

Chapter 9 covers the period from 1996 to 2000, including the Center's most recent—and dramatic—reorganization, the decision to keep GEDTS under ACE's leadership, and the decision to sell the National External Diploma Program. It also documents the growth of the programs during this period and summarizes the far-reaching impact of the Center for Adult Learning.

The book's chronological organization has its drawbacks— namely, the confusion that can result from jumping from program to program. The following timeline and leadership summary are intended to help eliminate any such confusion. The timeline highlights the main events in the different programs' histories and documents the programs' name changes. The leadership summary details the tenures of ACE presidents, Center for Adult Learning directors, and commission chairs. Finally, an acronym glossary is provided at the end of the book as an aid for identifying various higher education and government organizations.

ACKNOWLEDGMENTS

*S*pecial thanks to the American Council on Education (ACE) for supporting this project and to Susan Porter Robinson, vice president and director of the Center for Adult Learning and Educational Credentials, for her commitment to seeing it through.

I also am most grateful to Beatrice Wallace of the Center for Adult Learning for her administrative support; Jill Bogard, director of ACE's Library and Information Service, for her help in tracking down numerous hard-to-find texts; ACE's publications department for editing, design, and production; and Deborah Skowronski, Melissa Smith, and Shelley Sanner and for guiding this book through the production process.

The manuscript of this book was reviewed at various stages of the writing process by several people. Many thanks to Andy Anderson, Joan Auchter, Michael Baer, Stanley Ikenberry, Judy Koloski, Jerry Miller, Allan Quigley, Jo Ann Robinson, Gene Sullivan, Doug Whitney, and Bill Xenakis. Without their feedback, this book surely would have been incomplete. Thanks also to Fred Edwards, Dorothy Fenwick, Morris Keeton, and Penelope Suritz for supplying missing details.

Finally, my most sincere thanks go to Susan Porter Robinson, Henry Spille, and David Stewart for their support, guidance, and knowledge. They participated in the writing and editing of this history each step of the way. It would not have been possible without them.

Laura A. Mullane
Author

INTRODUCTION

*T*o understand the development of the Center for Adult Learning, it is important first to understand the historical foundation on which the Center is built.

ADULT EDUCATION FROM POST–CIVIL WAR TO PRE–WORLD WAR I

Prior to the Civil War, postsecondary education comprised low-enrollment, limited curriculum liberal arts colleges. After the war, adults' increased interest in higher education resulted in the beginning of the modern adult education movement. As Malcolm S. Knowles observed, "While the dominating spirit of the adult education movement up to the Civil War had been the diffusion of knowledge, that of the period between the Civil War and World War I might be characterized as the diffusion of organizations" (1977, 36). Specifically, summer schools, evening study, correspondence instruction, noncredit education, and agricultural extension became the venues through which adults' educational needs were met (Harrington 1977, 13, 14–19).

One of the earliest organizations to significantly impact the establishment of adult education programs was the Chautauqua Institution. Founded in 1874, Chautauqua was intended to be a pan-denominational normal school for Sunday school teachers. But the popularity of the summer educational program grew so that Chautauqua began attracting other participants; its offerings subsequently broadened. Fourteen years later, in 1878, "the first integrated core program of adult education organized in this country on a national scale came into being." The Chautauqua Literary and Scientific Circle, or CLSC, was established. A four-year program of home reading in history and literature that operated in connection with local reading circles, the CLSC was one of the first organized ventures into correspondence education. Simultaneous with the beginning of CLSC was Chautauqua's establishment of summer schools (which came to include a Normal School of Languages, a College of Liberal Arts, a School of Speech, a School of Physical Education, a School of Music, a School of Domestic Science, a School of Library Training, a Theater School, and a School of Theology) and the expansion of its informal lecture series, classes, and conferences (Knowles 1977, 37).

But perhaps the most significant contribution of the Chautauqua Institute was its promotion of lifelong learning. As Chautauqua founder John Vincent wrote in his 1886 book *The Chautauqua Movement,* "The principle now so generally accepted, that education is the privilege of all, young and old, rich and poor, that mental development is only begun in school and college, and should be continued through all life, underlies the Chautauqua system" (Grattan 1955, 168, quoting Vincent).

Due in large part to the influence of Chautauqua (Knowles 1977, 47), colleges and universities in the late 1800s began to expand their summer school offerings—previously noncredit courses for undereducated school teachers—and to recognize many of them for regular academic credit. Yet because summer school took place during the day, enrollment usually was limited to teachers or other adults who were able to leave their jobs for several weeks at a time. Evening study and correspondence courses filled the gap left by summer schools by providing educational opportunities for adults who were not able to leave work (Harrington 1977, 14).

Evening study was primarily an urban phenomenon. Begun by institutions in major metropolitan areas in the 1890s, these programs gave adults a chance to pursue an academic degree by taking regular credit courses after their regular workday. Like the majority of today's adult students, most students in these programs were "fully employed adults, enrolled part time and determined to fight their way up the social and economic ladder" (Harrington 1977, 14–15). But the offerings of the first evening schools were limited almost entirely to the basic subjects of the primary grades. It was not until the turn of the century that the curriculum expanded to include vocational courses and an "Americanization" program for immigrants. The latter was an important element of the evening school phenomenon. Prior to the influx of southern and eastern European immigrants between 1903 and 1914, educating immigrants was "not perceived as being critical so long as their number was small and they came overwhelmingly from countries of northern and western Europe." However, as less "familiar" and less educated immigrants began to flood into the country, public concern grew. When Congress added a literacy requirement for naturalization in 1917, it became clear that immigrants had to be educated; evening schools became the place to do it. By the end of World War I, immigrant education had become "the dominant activity of the public evening schools" (Knowles 1977, 55).

Prior to the influx of southern and eastern European immigrants between 1903 and 1914, educating immigrants was "not perceived as being critical so long as their number was small and they came overwhelmingly from countries of northern and western Europe."

—Malcolm S. Knowles

Correspondence instruction, or home study, extended education's reach even further. By giving adults the opportunity to earn academic credit through the mail, people living in remote areas and those with unaccommodating work schedules became able to pursue a higher education. Several institutions became pioneers in the home-study movement. Illinois Wesleyan College, for example, not only offered correspondence courses, but even awarded academic degrees—including the Ph.D.—for coursework completed by mail (Harrington 1977, 14–15).

William Rainey Harper, an early proponent of correspondence instruction, offered the first such course at Chautauqua in 1879. Then a professor of Hebrew at Yale, Harper started an informal "advice by mail" experiment which became so popular that only five years later, several instructors were offering "correspondence" courses. The informal courses became more formal, with regular assignments and a course fee of 10 dollars (Knowles 1977, 39). The success of the correspondence courses led Harper to predict that "the work done by correspondence will be greater in amount than that done in the classrooms of our academies and colleges" (Grattan 1955, 174, quoting Harper). Harper "took home study into the big time" (Harrington 1977, 14) when, as president of the newly founded University of Chicago, he established a correspondence division in the extension department (Knowles 1977, 39). Despite the lack of faculty support, Harper made certain that the university awarded under-graduate credit for correspondence offerings in the liberal arts. In the next decade, state universities joined the growing correspondence field and began offering applied and technological credit and noncredit courses—as well as college and lower-level courses—for "practical-minded adults" (Harrington 1977, 14–15).

The demand for practical courses, as opposed to liberal arts courses, was the impetus behind the "most distinctively American contributions to postsecondary adult education": non-credit agricultural and general extension programs. Agricultural, or cooperative, extension is the consequence of the Morrill Land-Grant Act of 1862, which promised assistance to one or two state colleges or universities in each state if they were willing to offer practical training in agriculture and engineering. Originally intended as a piece of antipoverty legislation, the Morrill Land-Grant Act became a significant landmark in the history of adult education by encouraging coursework designed to meet the needs of working adults (Harrington 1977, 16–17).

However, it soon became clear that few farmers could leave their land to attend classes. So universities began offering winter short courses in the 1880s and even brought education to the public by sending professors around the state to give lectures on crop and soil improvement and plant and animal diseases (Harrington 1977, 16–17). The concept of "in-the-field" teaching was originated by Seaman A. Knapp, who believed that farmers needed to see new techniques demonstrated on their own farms before they could be convinced to change their practices (Knowles 1977, 42). Land-grant institutions' rural adult education programs were extended even further by the Hatch Act of 1887, which earmarked government funds for university experimental farms, and the Smith-Lever Act of 1914, which "permanently tied" agricultural extension to the land-grant system (Harrington 1977, 16–17).

Meanwhile, general extension programs were being developed to meet the needs of adults in nonagricultural fields. British universities had begun to offer extension education in the early 19th century. But the idea did not take root in the United States until Herbert B. Adams, a professor of history at Johns Hopkins University, advocated the development of an American university extension. In 1891, in response to a proposal by Melvil Dewey, then chief librarian at Columbia University, the Regents of the University of the State of New York appropriated $10,000 to establish a university extension and thus sparked the growth of extension programs across the nation (Knowles 1977, 47).

Nevertheless, extension programs at American universities in the late 19th and early 20th centuries typically comprised off-campus adult courses—such as correspondence study, credit and non-credit courses, traveling libraries, lecture series, fine arts presentations, and advisory services—as well as on-campus activities, including lectures, conferences, and workshops and institutes. It was the University of Wisconsin that first established a general extension program that became a model for other institutions. In 1907, President Charles R. Van Hise reorganized the University of Wisconsin's 16-year-old extension division with the intent of drawing "the boundaries of the campus co-terminous with the boundaries of the state" (Harrington 1977, 18, quoting Van Hise). Van Hise encouraged Wisconsin faculty to offer credit courses far from the campus in Madison, and in a broader range of disciplines. In doing so, Wisconsin expanded the purpose of extension "toward an all-embracing concept of the role of the university in serving all people of the state in relation to the full scope of life problems—agricultural, political, social, and moral" (Knowles 1977, 49). The university thus provided short-course training in nursing and other fields, set up vocational schools, organized state conferences for adults, and arranged lectures and concerts across the state. Professors also served as advisors to state officials regarding social legislation (Harrington 1977, 18).

Originally intended as a piece of antipoverty legislation, the Morrill Land-Grant Act became a significant landmark in the history of adult education by encouraging coursework designed to meet the needs of working adults.

Thanks to Van Hise's ingenuity, the University of Wisconsin "integrated its three central functions of culture, vocation, and research into one dominant idea—service." Educating the state's masses was one piece of the university's service mission (Stubblefield and Keane 1994, 140). The "Wisconsin Idea," as it became known, embodied Van Hise's assertion that "the purpose of University Extension [is] to carry light and opportunity to every human being in all parts of the nation: this is the only adequate ideal of service for the university" (141, quoting Van Hise). Although few institutions copied the University of Wisconsin's extension philosophy and practices exactly, the Wisconsin Idea laid the foundation for "the broad view of a university's total responsibility to the adult community"—a concept that gained increasing acceptance in the years leading up to the First World War (Harrington 1977, 19).

WORLD WAR I AND THE NEW SOCIAL ORDER

World War I and its aftermath ushered in a new social order that forced educators and intellectuals "to grapple in thoughtful and disciplined ways with the question of what kind of education adults needed" (Stubblefield 1988, Introduction). World War I also marked the first time that the U.S. military partnered with higher education to train its forces. The foundation of this partnership can be traced to a 1916 provision in the United States Code that reads in part:

> In addition to military training, soldiers while in active service shall hereafter be given the opportunity to study and receive instruction upon educational lines of such character as to increase their military efficiency and enable them to return to civil life better equipped for industrial, commercial, and general business occupations (United States Code 1946, 736).

This commitment to educating military personnel was a contributing factor in the establishment of the American Council on Education (ACE) in 1918. The original objective of ACE—then called the "Emergency War Council"—was to place "the resources of the education institutions of our country more completely at the disposal of the national government." Specifically, the Council sought to augment "the patriotic services of the public schools, professional schools, the colleges and universities;" maintain "a continuous supply of educated men;" and secure "greater effectiveness in meeting the educational problems arising during and following the war" (Dobbins 1968, 3). This partnership between the military and higher education is one of the most important factors in the history of adult education in the United States. Certainly it has been key to the history of ACE and its Center for Adult Learning. Never before had civilian and military educators joined forces on such a grand scale to educate adults. It was a vital partnership. When war was declared in April 1917, the military faced the imposing task of classifying and training soldiers and maintaining morale (Stubblefield and Keane 1994, 181).

This partnership between the military and higher education is one of the most important factors in the history of adult education in the United States. Certainly it has been key to the history of ACE and its Center for Adult Learning.

To address the classification issue, the Secretary of War established the Committee of Classification of Personnel in the Army, under the direction of Robert M. Yerkes. This committee developed and administered intelligence tests to almost 2 million men, ranking them on a competence scale from A to E. The Army used the results to classify recruits and determine who would enter officer training, who would be assigned to trade skills, and who would be discharged (Stubblefield and Keane 1994, 181).

The Committee on Education and Special Training, established by the U.S. War Department, was made responsible for training. Charged with linking the military with colleges and universities (or technical and trade schools) offering relevant skill training for new servicemembers, the committee trained 110,000 soldiers by the end of the war. The military also trained illiterate and non-English-speaking draftees by establishing schools for the teaching of English. The Army adopted the YMCA's English language program and added courses in citizenship, American history, geography, and government. In just a year and a half, almost 25,000 illiterate and non-English-speaking troops received training through this program (Stubblefield and Keane 1994, 181–182).

World War I had a significant impact on the development of adult education; it demonstrated "that adult males could be trained and educated and that they were motivated toward—and had the intellectual ability to benefit from—general education" (Stubblefield and Keane 1994, 187). But there was a negative impact as well. After World War I, the prevailing trend among secondary and postsecondary institutions was to reward returning veterans for their duty and patriotism with "blanket credit"— often a year of credit for every year served, regardless of the academic value of their wartime experience. The effect was disastrous. Large numbers of veterans who were awarded blanket credit were unable to meet the academic demands of college. Many failed and dropped out. Thus, blanket credit became "a dubious kindness to the returning servicemen themselves," in large measure because of "its patent educational unsoundness" (ACE 1943, i). Nevertheless, it was this disastrous legacy of blanket credit that led to some of the most extensive and enduring adult education programs in American history—including those of the Center for Adult Learning and Educational Credentials.

$\mathcal{T}$IMELINE

SUMMARY OF NAME CHANGES

1945–74	CASE (Commission on Accreditation of Service Experiences)
1974–78	OEC (Office on Educational Credit)— ACE staff
	COEC (Commission on Educational Credit)—governing body
1978–87	OECC (Office on Educational Credit and Credentials)—ACE staff
1978–98	COECC (Commission on Educational Credit and Credentials)—governing body
1987–present	Center for Adult Learning and Educational Credentials (Center for Adult Learning; the Center)—ACE staff
1998–present	Commission on Adult Learning and Educational Credentials—governing body

$\mathcal{O}$VERVIEW OF EVENTS

1918

March:
- Emergency Council on Education is formally organized.

July:
- Name changes to the American Council on Education (ACE).

1942

April:

■ ACE calls together a special committee to develop policies and procedures for the evaluation of educational experiences acquired through the United States Armed Forces Institute's (USAFI's) educational programs.

May:

■ Under the leadership of Ralph Tyler, construction of tests to evaluate servicemembers' learning through USAFI's educational programs begins at the University of Chicago. Four types of exams are developed at the college and high school levels: end-of-course tests, field tests, technical competence tests, and general educational development (GED) tests.

■ ACE calls a meeting of regional accrediting associations which recommend that the USAFI examinations be used to measure the knowledge and level of competence of all veterans, not just those who have taken USAFI educational courses.

1943

■ Under the auspices of the University of Chicago, first GED test forms are developed by Everet F. Lindquist at the University of Iowa.

■ First GED norming study is conducted.

■ USAFI establishes the Central Clearing Agency to provide colleges and universities with complete information regarding servicemembers' educational experiences in the armed services.

February:

■ Based on the conclusions of the May meeting, ACE publishes *Sound Educational Credit for Military Experience: A Recommended Program.*

May:

■ National Association of Secondary School Principals forms the Committee on Secondary School Credit for Educational Experience in Military Service.

1944

January:

■ GI Bill of Rights introduced in the House of Representatives.

February:

- In response to the introduction of the GI Bill, ACE calls a conference to devise a plan to assist colleges and universities in awarding credit to returning veterans.

May:

- ACE sponsors *Cooperative Study on Training and Experience in the Armed Services* under the direction of George P. Tuttle at the University of Illinois in Urbana. This study becomes the first *Guide to the Evaluation of Educational Experiences in the Armed Services* (the *Guide*).

June:

- GI Bill of Rights is signed into law by President Franklin D. Roosevelt.

July:

- As a result of the February conference, ACE publishes Bulletin 69, which makes recommendations to colleges for the awarding of credit for military experience.

1945

- ACE establishes the Commission on Accreditation of Service Experiences (CASE).
- ACE establishes the Veterans' Testing Service (VTS) (predecessor of today's GED Testing Service) at the University of Chicago.

September:

- World War II ends.

December:

- Design of the four types of USAFI exams is completed.

1946

January:

- CASE holds its first meeting, with Thomas Barrows as director and Cornelius "Neil" P. Turner as associate director.
- CASE approves the reprinting of the *Guide*.

February:

■ Barrows and Turner set off to visit the secondary and post-secondary education leaders of all 48 states to promote CASE policies for awarding credit to veterans.

April:

■ CASE passes a resolution to request that USAFI make its tests available to civilian education institutions that would operate through a system of controlled testing centers. These became the first GED test centers.

May:

■ Barrows and Turner complete their tours of the states.

August:

■ As a result of Barrows's and Turner's meetings with educators, CASE publishes *Accreditation Policies of State Departments of Education for the Evaluation of Service Experiences and USAFI Examinations*, also known as Bulletin Number 5.

■ The first complete, bound edition of the *Guide* is published by ACE with funding from the Veterans' Administration (VA).

September:

■ Commission approves the VA's request to use secure test forms to test hospitalized veterans.

October:

■ CASE publishes *Accreditation Policies for Peacetime Military Service* which makes explicit CASE's policy that high schools should not award GED diplomas to students prior to the graduation of their class.

1947

March:

■ CASE begins reducing operations as funds decrease.

April:

■ Floydine Miscampbell, head of CASE's Advisory Service, presents at the annual meeting of the American Association of Collegiate Registrars.

May:

■ Thomas Barrows presents on the work of CASE at the ACE annual meeting.

June:

■ Barrows and Turner leave their positions at CASE in response to the reduction in operations. Turner becomes director of the newly established New York High School Equivalency Testing Program.

Fall:

■ New York becomes the first state to enter an informal agreement with ACE to administer the GED Tests to active-duty servicemembers, veterans, and nonveteran adults, including patients and inmates in state institutions.

1948

January:

■ War-Navy Committee of USAFI requests the continued operation of CASE; CASE votes to continue if sufficient funds are secured.

April:

■ ACE signs a contract with USAFI for the continued operation of CASE. Barrows returns as director.

■ VTS administrative functions are transferred to the newly formed Educational Testing Service (ETS).

1950

June:

■ U.S. involvement in the Korean War begins.

1952

■ Veterans' Readjustment Act (1952 GI Bill) becomes law.

1953

March:

■ CASE approves revision of the *Guide*, to include a condensation of the 1946 *Guide* and a supplementary section containing new and modified courses since 1946.

1954

■ Responsibility for distribution of the GED Tests is returned to ACE from ETS.

February:

■ Neil Turner is named associate director of the 1953 *Guide* project and, after the project's completion, associate director of CASE.

March:

■ CASE publishes first issue of the *Newsletter.*

1955

■ Under the auspices of the University of Chicago, second GED test forms are developed at the University of Iowa.
■ Second GED norming study begins, funded by the Department of Defense (DoD).

September:

■ CASE modifies its policy on the administration of high school–level GED Tests to allow for the testing of prisoners and institutionalized patients using secure test forms.

October:

■ CASE approves the evaluation of reservist training for credit recommendations.

1956

May:

■ CASE approves the move of VTS from the University of Chicago to ACE.

July:

■ Neil Turner becomes director of CASE.

1957

May:

■ CASE approves policy to make secure forms of the GED Tests available in federal prisons.

1958

■ CASE approves policy to allow for the testing of foreign nationals and civilians living overseas.

July:
■ VTS moves from the University of Chicago to ACE.

1959

■ For the first time, the number of nonveteran adults taking the GED Tests exceeds the number of veterans taking them.

1961

July:
■ VTS discontinues distribution of the college-level GED Tests.

1963

May:
■ CASE approves the evaluation of high-level service school courses for graduate-level credit recommendations.

July:
■ VTS changes its name to the GED Testing Service (GEDTS).

1964

May:
■ CASE approves the printing of the GED Tests in Braille and large print and recording on records and magnetic tape for the visually impaired.

1965

July:
■ ETS introduces the Comprehensive College Tests to replace the college-level GED Tests. The Comprehensive College Tests later become part of the College Board's College-Level Examination Program.

1966

■ Veterans' Readjustment Benefits Act (1966 GI Bill) becomes law.

1967

■ First GED test forms developed by ETS are introduced.

1968

■ Third edition of the *Guide* is published.

1969

September:

■ First GED Tests are administered in Canada.

1971

■ First GED administrators' conference is held in Washington, DC.
■ The Commission on Non-Traditional Study (or "Gould Commission") is formed under the sponsorship of the College Entrance Examination Board and ETS.

August:

■ First Spanish-language GED Tests are administered.

1972

■ Servicemen's Opportunity Colleges (SOC) consortium is created. (Later renamed Servicemembers' Opportunity Colleges.)

1973

■ The Commission on Non-Traditional Study publishes *Diversity by Design.*
■ California becomes the last state to adopt a uniform acceptance policy of the GED Tests.
■ Community College of the Air Force (CCAF) receives accreditation as an occupational education (non-degree-granting) institution.

May:

■ Jerry Miller becomes director of CASE.

July:

■ The draft is discontinued.

1974

■ Fourth edition of the *Guide* is published and includes for the first time semester-hour credit recommendations for vocational-technical military training; it also marks the beginning of onsite evaluations for all courses and the first computerized, ongoing *Guide* system.

■ ACE Task Force on Educational Credit and Credentials is formed to address issues relating to the educational credentialing system.

March:

■ CASE expands its role to include the evaluation of nonmilitary courses. CASE is renamed the Commission on Educational Credit (COEC); CASE staff is renamed the Office on Educational Credit (OEC).

■ ACE and the New York Board of Regents jointly sponsor the Project on the Evaluation of Non-Collegiate Sponsored Instruction to evaluate nonmilitary, noncollegiate training courses. (Later becomes the Program on Non-Collegiate Sponsored Instruction [PONSI].)

1975

■ Credit by Examination program begins at ACE.

■ Education benefits provided by the GI Bill for new enlistees are eliminated.

May:

■ COEC approves an ongoing evaluation of the Military Occupational Specialty system and publication of credit recommendations in the *Guide*.

1976

■ First edition of the *National Guide to Educational Credit for Training Programs* is published.

June:

■ COEC approves the evaluation of classified military courses.

1977

■ SOC Associate Degree is created.

January:

■ U.S. Commissioner of Education approves CCAF's request for degree-granting authority.

February:

- COEC approves an ongoing evaluation of certain Navy Enlisted Classification systems.

1978

- ACE Task Force on Educational Credit and Credentials publishes *Credentialing Educational Accomplishment.*
- OEC is renamed the Office on Educational Credit and Credentials (OECC); COEC is renamed the Commission on Educational Credit and Credentials (COECC).
- Henry Spille is named director of OECC.
- GEDTS's research capability is established with the hiring of the program's first director of research.
- Developed by ETS, second generation of the GED Tests is introduced.
- Registry of Credit Recommendations begins operation. (Spawns creation of National Registry of Training Programs and International Registry of Training Programs.)
- ACE publishes first *Guide to External Degree Programs in the United States.*

1979

- "Academic Quality Control: The Case of College Programs on Military Bases" by former ACE Vice President Stephen K. Bailey is published.

1981

- ACE establishes the Commission on Higher Education and the Adult Learner (CHEAL).
- For the first time, GEDTS raises the minimum score required for passing the GED Tests.
- First edition of *Guide to Educational Credit by Examination* is published.

1983

- COECC votes to establish OECC as a clearinghouse of accurate information about diploma mills.

1984

- Education benefits for new enlistees are restored.

- Army/ACE Registry Transcript System (AARTS) pilot program is launched.
- CHEAL publishes *Adult Learners: Key to the Nation's Future* and *Postsecondary Institutions and the Adult Learner: A Self-Study Assessment and Planning Guide.*
- ACE assumes responsibility for the development of the GED Tests from ETS, and the test development process is brought in house.

1987

- AARTS implementation is completed.
- OECC changes its name to the Center for Adult Learning and Educational Credentials.
- Center for Adult Learning conducts first "Focus on Adults" workshop based on *Postsecondary Education Institutions and the Adult Learner: A Self-Assessment and Planning Guide.*
- Center for Adult Learning conducts its first workshop for colleges and universities based on *Model Policy on Awarding Credit for Extrainstitutional Learning.*

1988

- Third generation of the GED Tests is introduced, including the addition of a writing sample requirement. This is the first set of test forms developed in house by GEDTS staff.
- *Diploma Mills: Degrees of Fraud* by David Stewart and Henry Spille is published.
- GEDTS develops accommodations for candidates with specific learning disabilities.

March:
- Virginia makes the first official request for an exemption to allow the testing of enrolled, at-risk high school students.

1989

- *Principles of Good Practice for Alternative and External Degree Programs for Adults* is published.
- CHEAL organizes "A More Productive Workforce: Challenge to Postsecondary Education and Its Partners" conference.

P
——

1990

■ Coalition of Adult Education Organizations develops *Bill of Rights for the Adult Learner.*

■ National External Diploma Program becomes part of ACE.

1991

■ Center for Adult Learning wins DoD contract to administer the Military Installation Voluntary Education Review (MIVER) project.

1992

■ MIVER Principles of Good Practice are developed for military installations and institutions serving military installations.

1993

■ GEDTS publishes *GED Technical Manual.*

■ PONSI establishes PONSI State Offices.

1994

■ Center for Adult Learning participates in planning, organizing, and implementing the First Global Conference on Lifelong Learning held in Rome, Italy.

■ Development of the fourth generation of the GED Tests (2002 series) begins.

1995

■ GEDTS develops accommodations for prelingually deaf and hard-of-hearing candidates.

■ PONSI begins ACE National Coordinators program.

■ GEDTS closes its overseas testing centers.

October:

■ Center for Adult Learning participates in Global Alliance for Transnational Education meeting.

1996

■ Center for Adult Learning task force completes *Guiding Principles for Distance Learning in a Learning Society.*

■ PONSI and the Distance Education and Training Council publish *Distance Learning Evaluation Guide.*

- ACE Board of Directors votes to phase out the GED testing program for at-risk high school students over a five-year period.
- Center for Adult Learning participates in the International Council on Distance Education's Standing Committee of Presidents of Open and Distance Learning Institutions.

May:
- Ontario adopts the GED Tests.

October:
- Independent management consulting firm begins review of the Center for Adult Learning.

November:
- Susan Porter Robinson named director of the Center for Adult Learning.

1997
- PONSI changes its name to the College Credit Recommendation Service (CREDIT).
- GEDTS raises the minimum score required for passing the GED Tests for the second time.
- GEDTS resumes overseas testing using secure computer-based testing.

February:
- ACE Board of Directors votes to keep GEDTS as a program of ACE.

1998
- Center for Adult Learning reorganizes.
- CREDIT selected as a Quality Standards System organization by the U.S. Coast Guard.
- GEDTS launches Strategic Training and Resource Specialists (STARS) program.

1999
- Credit by Examination program begins evaluations of the Military Academic Credit Examination.

- GEDTS establishes four expert advisory panels: Psycho-metric, Workplace, Research, and Learning Disabilities.
- GEDTS publishes *Alignment of National and State Standards*.
- GEDTS transfers the application process for specific learning disabilities accommodations to the jurisdictional level.

March:

- Redeveloped Spanish-language GED Tests are administered for the first time across the United States.

October:

- Sailor/Marine Corps/ACE Registry Transcript is launched.

2000

March:

- ACE sells the National External Diploma Program to Madison Area Technical College in Wisconsin.
- ACE Board of Directors votes to continue the GED testing program for at-risk high school students, reversing its 1996 decision to phase out the program.

August:

- The *Guide* goes online.

$\mathscr{L}$EADERSHIP SUMMARY

Presidents of the American Council on Education

Donald J. Crowling	1918–19
Samuel Paul Capen	1919–22
Charles Riborg Mann	1922–34
George F. Zook	1934–51
Arthur S. Adams	1951–61
Logan Wilson	1961–72
Roger Heyns	1972–77
Jack W. Peltason	1977–84
Robert H. Atwell	1984–96
Stanley O. Ikenberry	1996–present

Directors of the Commission on Accreditation of Service Experiences (CASE), the Office on Educational Credit (OEC), the Office on Educational Credit and Credentials (OECC), and the Center for Adult Learning and Educational Credentials

Thomas N. Barrows	1946–47 and 1948–51
Charles W. McLane	1951–56
Cornelius P. Turner	1956–73
Jerry W. Miller	1973–78
Henry A. Spille	1978–96
Susan Porter Robinson	1996–present

Chairs of CASE, the Commission on Educational Credit (COEC), the Commission on Educational Credit and Credentials (COECC), and the Commission on Adult Learning and Educational Credentials

Paul E. Elicker   1946–49
Executive Secretary, National Association of Secondary School Principals

Harry J. Carman   1949–57
Professor of History and Dean Emeritus, Columbia College, Columbia University

Charles E. Bish   1958
Principal, McKinley High School, Washington, DC

John E. Fellows   1959–60
Dean of Admissions and Registrar, University of Oklahoma

John Dale Russell   1961
Director, Office of Institutional Research, New York University

A. J. Brumbaugh   1962
Consultant, Southern Regional Education Board

Earl J. McGrath   1963
Executive Officer, Institute of Higher Education, Teachers College, Columbia University

Frank G. Dickey   1964–65
Executive Director, Southern Association of Schools and Colleges

G. Herbert Smith   1966–67
President, Willamette University

Frank A. Rose   1968
President, University of Alabama

Lewis W. Webb, Jr.   1969
President, Old Dominion College

J. Douglas Conner   1970
Executive Secretary, American Association of Collegiate Registrars and Admissions Officers

Ernest W. Hartung   1971
President, University of Idaho

Walter D. Talbot   1972
State Superintendent of Public Instruction, State of Utah

Frank G. Dickey   1973
Executive Director, National Commission on Accrediting

J. Boyd Page   1974–75
President, Council of Graduate Schools in the United States

Dorothy Arata   1976–77
Assistant Provost, Michigan State University

Samuel B. Gould   1978
Chancellor Pro Tem, Commission for Higher Education

Thurman J. White   1979–80
Vice President for Continuing Education and Public Service,
University of Oklahoma

Elbert W. Ockerman   1981–83
Dean of Admissions and Registrar, University of Kentucky

Verne Duncan   1984–87
State Superintendent of Public Instruction, State of Oregon

Richard T. Doolittle   1988
Executive Vice President, Graduate School of Banking

Marilyn Schlack   1989
President, Kalamazoo Valley Community College

John Yena   1990
President, Johnson and Wales College

C. Wayne Williams   1991
Executive Director, Regents College, The University of the
State of New York

Sister Karen M. Kennelly   1992–93
President, Mount St. Mary's College

Mary L. Pankowski   1994–95
Vice President, North Miami Campus and University Outreach,
Florida International University

Gregory S. Prince, Jr.   1996–97
President, Hampshire College

Leslie N. Purdy   1998–99
President, Coastline Community College

Gail O. Mellow   2000
President, Gloucester County College

CHAPTER 1

Library of Congress

The War Years

1942–1945

THE WAR YEARS, 1942–1945

BORN IN FEAR:
The Legacy of Blanket Credit

*T*he first programs of what is now the Center for Adult
Learning and Educational Credentials were born in fear.
It was 1942; the bitter fighting of World War II was escalating
rapidly. While most Americans were coming to grips with this
reality, American education leaders were already preparing for
the war's end. In particular, they were concerned about the
impact of returning troops on U.S. higher education. As adult education historian Amy Rose
notes, "Looking back on the World War I experience, it was assumed that enrollments would
dramatically increase as those whose educations
had been interrupted or delayed returned to
school" (1990, 33). The exact numbers of men
and women sent home prior to the end of the
war were kept confidential, but educators were
already noticing an increase in the numbers of
veterans returning to school. They expected the
number to continue to increase, and for good
reason. During World War II, approximately
one-third of the men and women in the armed
forces had attended but not graduated from
high school; one-fourth were high school graduates but had not
attended college; one-tenth had attended but not graduated from
college. Given the large number of men and women who had
interrupted their education to join the war effort, it was clear
that the end of the war would bring an influx of young veterans
interested in resuming their educational pursuits (ACE and
NASSP 1943, 2).

*D*uring World War II,
*approximately one-third of the
men and women in the armed
forces had attended but not
graduated from high school;
one-fourth were high school
graduates but had not attended
college; one-tenth had attended
but not graduated from college.*

Educators feared that a grateful nation would force its education
institutions to award blanket credit to veterans, as it had at the
end of World War I. Understanding that schools and colleges
might be tempted by a "competitive urge" to be "liberal under

P
—
1

pressure, legislative and personal" when granting credit, the academic community went on high alert. Part of the reason the blanket credit trend had run rampant after the first World War was because the opposition had been tardy, unorganized, and lacked an alternative proposal. While World War II raged, U.S. education leaders agreed that veterans' experiential learning while in the military should be recognized, but not in a way that would again compromise the integrity of diplomas and degrees (ACE 1943, i, 1, 21) .

LEARNING FROM THE PAST:
Developing Alternatives to Blanket Credit

Not wanting to repeat past mistakes, the academic community was mobilized to establish a viable alternative that would stop blanket credit before it started (ACE 1943, 21). At the request of the United States Armed Forces Institute (USAFI),[1] the American Council on Education (ACE) called together a special committee on 6 April 1942 to develop policies and procedures for the evaluation of educational experiences of men and women in the armed forces. This would be the first of many important partnerships between ACE and the military in the development of ACE's adult education programs. Over the next six months, ACE, in cooperation with the U.S. War Department, formulated a plan for awarding credit to returning veterans. The committee began by studying USAFI's educational program. USAFI offered correspondence courses to servicemembers all over the world, enabling them to enhance their academic skills and knowledge while in the military and, consequently, facilitating the continuation of their education after the war.

The need for such a correspondence program was obvious. In World War II, the U.S. armed forces were considered the most educated in American history, with the educational median at the 10th-grade level, compared to the sixth-grade level during World War I (Rose 1989, 18). Further, because World War II lasted much longer than World War I, the war effort was carried forward by the first group of servicemembers to interrupt their education (or to have it interrupted by the draft) on such a grand scale. The military knew that it could not take 13 million men

and women out of school to fight a war and then "suddenly release them to civilian life without their having had any contact
during those years with interests of their past life." It was crucial
that servicemembers be given the opportunity to participate in
academic courses that would enable them to continue their education after the war (Turner 1945, 2–3).

When the ACE committee reviewed USAFI in 1942, it endorsed the program but "recommended that USAFI develop a
testing program that would allow schools to objectively evaluate
learning . . . rather than an evaluation of the 'curriculum, the
number of lessons, and the instructor'" (Rose 1989, 19–20, quoting the ACE Special Committee on the Army Institute). ACE
and others wanted to be sure that veterans were awarded credit
on the basis of what they knew, not what they were supposed to
have learned. Educators recognized that the content of most military training did not correlate precisely with that of academic
courses, even if the subjects were related. For
example, a soldier taking a radio mechanics
course might learn a lot about electricity but
nothing about mechanics, heat, light, or sound,
which a student in a high school or college
physics class would learn (Turner 1945, 5).

As a result of ACE's recommendations, the U.S.
War Department contracted with the University
of Chicago's Board of Examinations to prepare
tests that would evaluate servicemembers' learning through USAFI's educational programs.
Ralph Tyler, then university examiner, became
director of the examinations staff and, consequently, a fixture in the adult education landscape for most of the next half century. The test
construction project began 1 May 1942 (Tyler Undated, 5); by
December 1945, Tyler and his staff, with the help of the staff at
the University of Iowa, had developed four types of exams: The
first were end-of-course tests that evaluated how well a student
mastered the specific requirements of a particular USAFI course.
The second were field tests that measured servicemembers' competence in a subject field (such as English or physics). The third

*T*he military knew that
it could not take 13 million
men and women out of school
to fight a war and then
"suddenly release them to
civilian life without their
having had any contact
during those years with
interests of their past life."

—Cornelius P. Turner

were technical competency tests in specific, highly technical military courses. The fourth set of exams were the Tests of General Educational Development (the predecessor of today's GED Tests) that determined the level of educational attainment at both the high school and college levels (Tyler Undated, 5-6).

When the USAFI testing program was first established, there were no plans to create the GED Tests. Before long, however, the USAFI Advisory Committee and the Subcommittee on Education of the Joint Army and Navy Committee on Welfare and Recreation indicated "a growing concern for satisfactory means by which appropriate educational credit could be given and proper placement in civilian education life" could be made. Committee members realized that the end-of-course, subject, and technical examinations would not meet this need. In fall 1942, the Subcommittee on Education appointed Everet F. Lindquist, Ralph Tyler, and Edmund G. Williamson to a special committee to "suggest some means for a more comprehensive appraisal of the educational attainments" of servicemembers (Tyler Undated, 7). The result was the development of the GED Tests by Lindquist at the University of Iowa for the University of Chicago. To develop the GED series, Lindquist used five existing examinations of the Iowa Tests of Educational Development and restandardized them "under military auspices on a nationwide basis" (Lindquist 1968, 24). Ultimately, these tests became the most important in the USAFI battery. Originally, the USAFI GED Tests were cited as particularly useful for servicemembers who "have been out of school for a while, but who have had a good many educational experiences since leaving school" (NASSP 1943, 19).

At the secondary level, the general educational development tests measured skills in five areas: correctness and effectiveness of expression; ability to interpret reading materials in social studies and the natural sciences, as well as literary materials; and general mathematical ability (NASSP 1943, 19). At the college level, the tests measured skills in the same areas, with the exception of general mathematical ability. A survey conducted while the tests were being developed revealed that colleges rarely offered general education mathematics courses. Rather, they offered courses in college algebra, trigonometry, analytical geometry, and differential and integral calculus. Because subject area tests had already been constructed for each of these fields of mathematics, it was determined that veterans who wanted to demonstrate competence in college-level math could take those tests (Tyler Undated, 30).

PRESERVING CONTINUITY:
Sound Educational Credit for Military Experience

Beyond evaluating USAFI's education programs and developing tests for its participants, the awarding of credit for *other* learning acquired through military experience was of primary importance. Educators recognized that even those veterans who did not take USAFI courses would have received valuable military training worthy of academic credit.

To address this issue, ACE called a meeting on 28 May 1942 of representatives of all the regional accrediting associations: the North Central Association of Colleges and Secondary Schools, the New England Association of Colleges and Secondary Schools, the Middle States Association of Colleges and Secondary Schools, the Southern Association of Colleges and Secondary Schools, and the Northwest Association of Secondary and Higher Schools. The group unanimously endorsed the educational soundness of USAFI's programs and recommended that colleges use USAFI's examinations to evaluate the knowledge and level of competence of *all* veterans. Thus, the testing program originally developed for servicemembers who had participated in USAFI's correspondence courses was extended "to include measurement of all educational experience in the armed forces, with the objective of assisting schools and colleges at the time of readmission" (ACE 1943, 11–12).

ACE also urged institutions to "go *publicly on record as soon as possible* . . . opposing indiscriminate blanket credit for military experiences." Institutions also were asked to approve the tentative procedures for evaluating military experience that ACE's special committee had developed. Secondary and postsecondary schools were encouraged to inform students of the educational opportunities available through USAFI and of the plans "to measure and grant credit for any increased educational competence, however acquired during service, upon the student's return to school or college, and thus preserve an educational continuity which might otherwise be lost" (ACE 1943, 21–22).

These recommendations were published in February 1943 in ACE's *Sound Educational Credit for Military Experience: A Recommended Program.* More than 34,000 copies were printed and distributed to colleges and universities across the country. At a meeting of the Education Advisory Council of the Joint Army and Navy Committee on Welfare and Recreation on 20 May 1943, it was reported that more than 500 colleges and universities had developed and approved a "sound basis for granting educational credit" (Tyler Undated, 3).

ZEALOUSLY GUARDED:
Maintaining the Rights of Higher Education
Acceptance of the policy on educational credit for learning acquired in the military was widespread, largely because of ACE's insistence that its recommendations be only recommendations. In his foreword to *Sound Education Credit for Military Experience,* George Zook, then president of ACE and former U.S. Commissioner of Education, recognized how strongly "the individual school and college zealously guards its right to determine all matters pertaining to credit" (ACE 1943, ii). Zook stated "most emphatically . . . that neither the Council [ACE] nor the armed forces . . . has any intention or desire to impose an external program on American education . . . . The suggested procedures should be regarded solely as an attempt to provide *valid records and measures* of educational attainment and competence" to the individual institutions for their own use "in determining the amount of credit to be granted" (2–3). By recommending rather than imposing a policy, ACE remained true to its mission: to act as a representative of higher education's interests and as an information clearinghouse, not as a centralized controlling agency.

With the publication of *Sound Educational Credit for Military Experience,* ACE, the War Department, and the regional accrediting bodies created the first systematic, unified policy regarding the awarding of credit for learning acquired outside of the traditional classroom. It was the beginning of a new era of adult education.

NEW CHALLENGES, COMPLEX SOLUTIONS:
Secondary Education and the Military

While ACE was solving the potential problems of veterans returning to college, the National Education Association's National
Association of Secondary School Principals focused on issues
related to veterans returning to high school to earn their diplomas. This was a new challenge for high schools. During World
War I, young men had not been drafted from secondary schools
in large numbers. But in World War II, the draft age was dropped
to 18; 17 was designated the upper limit for voluntary enlistment;
16-year-olds could enlist with their parents' permission. Thus,
many young men and women left high school to join the war effort, posing a much greater problem for high schools than what
they had faced during and after World War I (NASSP 1943, 5).

Like colleges and universities, high schools had to contend with
the issue of blanket credit. A 1943 National Association of
Secondary School Principals' survey of
American high schools' credit granting policies found that as many as five states were permitting the award of blanket credit for the
entire senior year, either by legislation or state
department of education resolution. Six others
were proposing the award of blanket credit for
the last semester of high school. One state
granted a "war emergency diploma" to students who left school early for service. These
findings, coupled with the increased frequency
of letters from servicemembers asking how
they could secure their diplomas, made it clear
that neither blanket credit nor the existing "tight and precise
educational accounting system" was going to help. An alternative plan had to be developed (NASSP 1943, 5–6).

*Many young
men and women left high
school to join the war
effort, posing a much
greater problem for high
schools than what they had
faced during and after
World War I.*

Influenced by the work of ACE and colleges, the National
Association of Secondary School Principals formed the
Committee on Secondary School Credit for Educational
Experience in Military Service. The committee met in
Cleveland, Ohio, in May 1943 to consider problems relating to
the evaluation of the educational competence and attainment of

servicemembers. The committee reviewed the educational opportunities offered in the armed forces and identified three main
types of educational programs: specialized and technical training
programs for officers and enlisted personnel; off-duty education
through voluntary group classes, correspondence, or self-teaching texts, often through USAFI; and "informal educational experiences of military life which may, in some instances, have little
in common with the formal patterns of schooling, but which, in
this global war, will most likely influence greatly the maturity
and development of the men and women who are in the
Service" (NASSP 1943, 4, 7, 9–10).

The National Association of Secondary School Principals determined that off-duty education was particularly valuable, in part
because it demonstrated a strong interest in continuing one's education. Also, in some cases, courses offered by USAFI were specifically for servicemembers who had not completed high school but
wanted to advance their academic career in certain subjects, such
as English, foreign languages, mathematics, science, social studies,
and business and vocational subjects. Even better, the National
Association of Secondary School Principals and the academic
community as a whole were convinced that the "natural inclina-
tion and the counsel of the Institute [USAFI] and field guidance
officers will encourage the individual who seeks a secondary
school diploma for purposes of college admission to give appropriate attention to these standard secondary school subjects"
(NASSP 1943, 11).

In addition to USAFI's correspondence and self-study courses,
the military also offered voluntary group classes, or "locally organized class instruction," organized by an officer-supervisor to
provide instruction in fields of interest. Mathematics, physics,
shorthand, and English were particularly popular subjects. In addition to providing classroom instruction in remote areas that
saw little military action, off-duty education fulfilled "a very real
need in the lives of men and women who find themselves in a
strange environment and who feel the need for the inspiring effects" of education. These educational centers soon were given
informal names, such as the "University of Dutch Harbor" and
"Kodiak College" (NASSP 1943, 14).

After reviewing the educational opportunities offered in the armed services, the National Association of Secondary School Principals developed a policy recommendation for awarding secondary education credit based on military service, stating that agreement on an acceptable policy would "undoubtedly maintain and strengthen the public confidence in our schools that is so necessary in these trying times." However, the association did not stand entirely firm against the pressure to grant blanket credit. It outlined 12 guidelines to help secondary schools grant credit to returning servicemembers, including a recommendation that no more than one semester of credit be granted to "anyone merely for being in the Army or the Navy," and that any credit beyond that maximum "should be dependent upon evidence of educational attainment and competence resulting from military experience." Such evidence was to include servicemembers' scores on the tests developed by Ralph Tyler and his staff at the University of Chicago (NASSP 1943, 7, 23).

PUTTING THE CART BEFORE THE HORSE: USAFI and the Central Clearing Agency

As both ACE and the National Association of Secondary School Principals developed credit recommendation procedures, it became clear that the tools for evaluation at both the secondary and postsecondary levels were limited. The task was to determine how to measure educational attainment and competence that was equivalent to the graduation or credit requirements of servicemembers. To do this, a factual, official report of educational achievement of military personnel was needed. Thus, a clearinghouse of veterans' military education was established within USAFI. Named the Central Clearing Agency, it provided complete (or as near to complete as possible) information regarding service schools attended, results of special examinations, correspondence courses, off-duty voluntary classes, service jobs satisfactorily performed, and other pertinent data (NASSP 1943, 24).

To establish the Central Clearing Agency, USAFI first had to design and distribute an application for servicemembers. Rather than publicize the service and await requests, applications were sent to USAFI students who had completed only three years of high school before entering the service and training in one or more service schools. Only 800 of the 30,000 servicemembers enrolled in USAFI courses met this criterion. Shortly after the applications were mailed, completed forms began flowing back to USAFI. But USAFI did not have a single description of any training program conducted in any branch of the service. The Central Clearing Agency quickly established channels through which it could retrieve course descriptions from the Army, Navy, Coast Guard, and Marine Corps. This took time. Once received, the descriptions needed to be "translated" from military to academic terminology. The result was a significant delay in the functioning of the agency. Nevertheless, by December 1945, more than 3,000 descriptions of military training conducted by all branches of the military during World War II were on file. These descriptions proved invaluable when ACE compiled its first *Guide to the Evaluation of Educational Experiences in the Armed Services* (the *Guide*) (Turner 1945, 8–9).

The Central Clearing Agency's sole purpose was to supply the available data; the education institution retained full responsibility for evaluating the information and data in terms of credit.

Once the Central Clearing Agency was operational, it was able to provide accurate information regarding servicemembers' military training and education. But this was all it provided. USAFI did not recommend the amount of credit that should be awarded to any given veteran. The agency's sole purpose was to supply the available data; the education institution retained full responsibility for evaluating the information and data in terms of credit (Turner 1945, 5).

THE SEARCH FOR UNIFORMITY:
Translating Military Learning into Academic Credit

The commitment to leave full responsibility for awarding credit with individual education institutions resulted in great discrepancies. Colleges and universities "had no basis upon which to judge how such training as that taught in Navy aviation machinist mate school, an Army radio operators school, a Coast Guard diesel engine school, or a Marine Corps amphibious school could be correlated with or evaluated in terms of the ordinary subjects taught in academic high schools." As a result, institutions granted veterans credit in civics, history, English, mathematics, science, physical training, or a lump sum of credit for their training. High schools granted anything from no credit to two-and-a-half years of credit for the same type of training (Turner 1945, 9–10).

This lack of uniformity threatened a repeat of the inequities of the blanket credit policy enacted after World War I. If one veteran received no high school credit for 16 weeks of Navy storekeepers school while another veteran in a neighboring town received credit for four senior courses for the same training, "educational chaos throughout the country" would ensue. As after World War I, veterans returning to school might be placed well above or well below their educational level. This would adversely effect veterans' educational success and, in turn, the school's academic reputation. The political ramifications of such inconsistencies in the evaluation of military training also were not lost on educators. High school principals quickly realized that if one of them awarded more credit to former students than another, charges of unfairness—and possible political retribution—could ensue.[2] It was evident that education institutions needed an established policy, in addition to the services of the Central Clearing Agency, for evaluating military training and awarding credit (Turner 1945, 10–11).

It was evident that education institutions needed an established policy, in addition to the services of the Central Clearing Agency, for evaluating military training and awarding credit.

To address this need, ACE in 1944 sponsored *Cooperative Study on Training and Experience in the Armed Services* under the direction of George P. Tuttle, registrar of the University of Illinois, and subsidized by the various accrediting agencies. The primary purposes of the study were to develop a guide that would describe the training programs in the various branches of the military; to identify the equivalence of these programs to subjects typically taught in both secondary and postsecondary institutions; and to "suggest the approximate equivalents in terms of credits." In addition to making credit recommendations on the basis of military training, the guide also would make specific recommendations on the basis of test performance. Thus, schools and colleges would have their choice of two credit-granting tools, one of which would be the indirect and subjective evaluation of group training experiences and the other, the direct and objective determination of individual competence as evidenced by performance on examinations. The result of this study was the creation of the *Guide*, informally known as the "Tuttle Guide" (Lindquist 1944, 361, 372).

But a single guide was not enough. As new military courses were developed and as servicemembers and veterans continued to return to college, the need for ongoing advice on credit recommendations and the development of appropriate policies under changing conditions became apparent. In fall 1945, the Joint Army-Navy Committee on Welfare and Recreation and the USAFI Advisory Committee recommended that an organization be established to coordinate the activities of education institutions, associations, and organizations related to the evaluation of military training and experience. The Carnegie Corporation awarded ACE a $75,000 grant to help create such an organization: the Commission on Accreditation of Service Experiences, or CASE (Barrows 1947, 1).[3]

A NEW URGENCY:
Establishing a Formal Evaluation Policy

As the war drew to a close, the need to establish a formal credit recommendation policy for all education institutions became more urgent. This urgency was heightened by the introduction of the Servicemen's Readjustment Act of 1944, popularly known as the GI Bill of Rights. Introduced in the House and Senate in January 1944 and unanimously approved and signed into law in June, the GI Bill promised fully subsidized education or job training for 7.8 million veterans (Bennett 1994, 8). Educators were bracing for the impact, and heightened organization was key.

National Association of Secondary School Principals Publishes
"Earning Secondary School Credit in the Armed Forces"
In March 1944, the National Association of Secondary School
Principals printed and distributed "Earning Secondary School Credit
in the Armed Forces." The result of the National Association of
Secondary School Principals' November 1943 conference in
Madison, Wisconsin, the pamphlet reiterated that "service school
training represented educational achievement worthy of high school
credit even though the training was not conducted in a high school
classroom." However, it also acknowledged that very little service
school training correlated directly with formal high school curricula,
so it could not be evaluated in terms of high school subjects. The
National Association of Secondary School Principals therefore recommended that no more than four credits be awarded for the successful
completion of 13 weeks of basic training or 12 weeks of service
school training. The recommendations were approved by every state
department of education in the country (Turner 1945, 13–14).

ACE's Bulletin 69 for Postsecondary Institutions
Meanwhile, postsecondary institutions similiarly became aware of
the need to formalize policy for evaluating military experience and
awarding credit. In February 1944, ACE called a conference in
Madison, Wisconsin, to devise a plan to assist colleges and universities. The result was the publication in July of Bulletin 69. Like the
National Association of Secondary School Principals' "Earning
Secondary School Credit in the Armed Forces," Bulletin 69 recommended that no more than one-half semester of credit be awarded
for basic training; that credit for service school training be granted as
appropriate; and that credit be granted for the satisfactory completion of USAFI courses as indicated by performance on standardized
exams and for USAFI courses offered through cooperating colleges
and universities. ACE's Bulletin 69 was readily adopted by the higher
education community. But it was not its acceptance that made
Bulletin 69 so revolutionary. Rather, "its value [lay] in the fact that
it openly proclaimed to colleges that they could grant credit toward
a degree for work accomplished outside of a college classroom." But
cause for caution remained: Although most colleges had established
policies to evaluate military training, there were no guarantees
that they could meet the challenges that accompanied the return of
veterans (Turner 1945, 14–17).

SETTING THE STAGE

Today, it is difficult to conceive just how revolutionary the actions of ACE, the National Association of Secondary School Principals, USAFI, the U.S. War Department, and the military services were. That secondary and postsecondary education institutions chose to award credit for learning acquired outside of a traditional classroom was a significant development. Many have attributed this and other practices that emerged from the World War II era as the beginning of the modern adult education movement—or, at the very least, a blueprint for future civilian adult education efforts. Regardless, adults' participation in education skyrocketed in the post-war years.

Some had made predictions about the impact of World War II on adult education. For example, in the 1947 book *The Armed Services and Adult Education,* commissioned by ACE's Commission on Implications of Armed Services Educational Programs, Cyril O. Houle, Elbert W. Burr, Thomas H. Hamilton, and John R. Yale predicted:

> Only yesterday high school was attended by the few; now it is attended by the many. Similarly adult education even yet is for the few; it is reasonable to suppose that, as a result of broad social forces and an increasing individual realization of the values of learning, it will become the concern of the many. Even as three-fourths of all young people of high school age are now in high school, so perhaps in another 25 years, three-fourths of all mature people will likely be engaged in conscious learning programs of some sort.

> In the future it is likely that the Army and Navy off-duty programs will be considered to have been among the first of the large-scale adult educational activities (227).

NOTES
[1] USAFI was formerly the Army Institute.
[2] Colleges and universities stood to lose as much as high schools. However, because 90 percent of all applications were for high school credit, high school principals were the most vulnerable.
[3] For the next three decades, CASE would oversee the tremendous growth of the GED Tests and the Military Evaluations program. Chapter 2 details CASE's early years.

CHAPTER 2

Library of Congress

Coming of Age

CASE and the
GED Tests
1946–1950

COMING OF AGE:
CASE AND THE GED TESTS, 1946–1950

WEALTH OF POSSIBILITY:
The End of the War and the Beginning of CASE

*W*ith the end of World War II, educators found themselves face to face with the challenges they had been anticipating since 1942. As they had expected, an influx of young veterans returned to civilian life eager for the jobs, families, and schools they had left behind. Although the academic community was ahead of many other sectors in terms of preparing for the reentry of so many veterans, the GI Bill made the challenge even more daunting.[1] Indeed, "from 1946 until the early 1950s, higher education was completely preoccupied with the problem of accommodating the veterans" (Rose 1990, 32).

Accreditation Policies of States

On 7 January 1946, the American Council on Education's (ACE's) Commission on Accreditation of Service Experiences (CASE)[2] held its first meeting in Washington, DC. Thomas N. Barrows, former president of Lawrence College, served as director of the commission, and Cornelius P. "Neil" Turner, a former lieutenant in the U.S. Navy Reserves and former Chief of Accreditation at the United States Armed Forces Institute (USAFI), served as associate director. The commission soon sensed the urgency of the situation not only for high schools and colleges, but for other nonacademic education programs as well. As William F. Patterson, director of the Department of Labor's Apprentice-Training Service, lamented, "We are struggling with the problem of credit on apprenticeship for the many returned veterans who are now electing that kind of training under the GI Bill" (1946). All facets of education were affected.

In an effort to respond to the growing crisis, Barrows recommended that CASE organize "field trips" where staff would meet with state departments of education, college and university

groups, and other education leaders "to make known the problems and procedures of accrediting service experiences." The
field trips also would enable CASE staff to inventory states'
credit-granting practices and policies at the secondary and postsecondary levels. The commission approved Barrows's proposal
and launched the CASE staff of two on a whirlwind tour of the
country (CASE 1946b, 1).

Barrows and Turner set off in February to visit the secondary and
postsecondary education leaders of all 48 states, with Turner taking all states east of the Mississippi River and Barrows traveling to
those to the west (Turner 1986b, 4). By the time they had completed their tours four months later, the two men had conducted
72 meetings with state department of education officials, secondary school educators, and college officials
across the country (CASE 1946a, 2). The result
of these meetings was the publication in
August 1946 of *Accreditation Policies of State
Departments of Education for the Evaluation of
Service Experiences and USAFI Examinations,*
also known as Bulletin Number 5.

*We are struggling with
the problem of credit on
apprenticeship for the many
returned veterans who are
now electing that kind of
training under the GI Bill.*
— William F. Patterson

Bulletin Number 5 was the first publication
to include concise descriptions of every
state's policies regarding the evaluation of
military learning and the awarding of credit.
As such, it was a significant step toward the
establishment of guidelines for the awarding of credit for nontraditional learning. It also demonstrates ACE's—and CASE's—
continued role as a facilitator rather than dictator of policy. In
the foreword to Bulletin Number 5, ACE President George
Zook writes: "The policies set forth [by the states] reflect the
considered judgment and determination on the part of the educators of this country to help the veteran readjust himself to
civilian life" (CASE 1946a, 2). The bulletin was distributed to
high schools (via state departments of education), colleges and
universities, the military branches, and the Veterans'
Administration (VA). By March 1947—only seven months after
it was published—40,000 copies had been distributed (CASE
1947a, 2).

But gathering information for publication in Bulletin Number 5 wasn't the only purpose of Barrows's and Turner's trips; the trips also were a significant lobbying effort. CASE knew that all of its work would be for naught if high schools and colleges did not accept the principle that credit should be awarded for learning acquired through military training and education. Barrows and Turner used their meetings to explain the credit recommendation process and to gauge how willing institutions might be to award credit. These conversations later gave Neil Turner the idea to target the 48 state departments of education (rather than the thousands of principals and college presidents) in an effort to win support for acceptance of the GED Tests as a basis for awarding a high school credential. His idea was that if a state department of education supported the tests as a basis for awarding a high school diploma, then a state policy to that effect would be established. The plan was dismissed as farfetched at the time, but it became reality over the next 30 years (Turner 1986b, 4).

Barrows and Turner used their meetings to explain the credit recommendation process and to gauge how willing institutions might be to award credit.

CASE Reduction

Although the work at CASE was just beginning, it was decided at the 7 March 1947 meeting that the commission[3] would reduce its operations and meet less frequently. The reason for the reduction was simple: CASE was originally intended to operate for only two years, from January 1946 until January 1948. The funds contributed by the Carnegie Corporation were drying up and could no longer support a full staff. The only staff member to continue would be Floydine Miscampbell, who had been hired to oversee the commission's advisory service, which assisted colleges and universities that used the commission's credit recommendations (see Chapter 3). So Barrows and Turner prepared to give up their positions by January 1948, though they were willing to continue to work with CASE as consultants without compensation. Because January fell in the middle of the academic year (which meant that jobs in education would be harder to find), Barrows and Turner decided to wrap things up before the end of summer 1947 (CASE 1947b, 5; Turner 1947, 1).

In June, Thomas Barrows returned home to California, where he later took a position at the University of California at Berkeley. The following month, Neil Turner left the commission to become director of the newly established New York High School Equivalency Testing Program, a joint project of ACE and the New York Department of Education[4] (Turner 1947, 2). As New York's Commissioner of Education, CASE member Francis Spaulding had convinced the state's association of high schools to issue high school equivalency certificates based on GED test performance—making New York the first state in the country to do so (see page 24). He made the decision to hire Neil Turner to direct the effort (Turner 1986a, 11).

Meanwhile, CASE had to continue its role as policy maker and adviser to the education community. To ensure that this was done expeditiously—despite the infrequent meetings—an executive committee was appointed comprising Paul E. Elicker, executive secretary of the National Association of Secondary School Principals and chairman of CASE; A. J. Brumbaugh, vice president of ACE; and Francis T. Spaulding, New York State's Commissioner of Education (CASE 1947b, 5).

The Rebirth of CASE

The cutback at CASE was short-lived. At the 16 January 1948 meeting, Chairman Paul Elicker read a motion passed by the War-Navy Committee of USAFI that requested the continued operation of CASE, as it was "essential to the effective operation of the Education Programs of the Armed Forces." It further suggested that "arrangements should be made to encourage and support the continuation of the commission" (CASE 1948, quoting USAFI War-Navy Committee).

R. R. Vance, director of the Tennessee State Department of Education's division of high schools, proposed that because "the functions of this commission as originally defined are destined to change," the commission should "be discontinued after the remainder of the original grant of $75,000 [from the Carnegie Corporation] has become depleted" (CASE 1948). A lengthy discussion ensued, with the result that Vance withdrew his motion and instead proposed that "the present commission be continued until 1 July 1949, if sufficient funds can be found to continue its operation" (CASE 1948, 2).

The motion was passed (CASE 1948), with agreement that the executive committee should begin immediate negotiations with military officials for a contract "in accordance with the recommendation of the USAFI Committee and the action of the Commission on Accreditation" (CASE 1949a, 4). Had Vance's original motion to discontinue CASE passed, the administration of the GED Tests and the evaluation of military experience would have been markedly different; at worst, they would have ceased to exist entirely.

With the immediate future of CASE decided, the executive committee set out to find funds. In spring 1948, USAFI appropriated $25,000 for the continued operation of the commission from April 1948 to April 1949.[5] Thomas Barrows returned as director, and Floydine Miscampbell continued to oversee the advisory service and other operations.

At the next CASE meeting on 10 May 1949, the commission decided to recommend to ACE that it "be reconstituted and its membership be put on a rotating basis." It was also agreed, in a motion proposed by E. G. Williamson of the University of Minnesota, that representation of colleges on the commission be increased (CASE 1949b). Although seemingly small decisions, these two motions marked a coming of age for the commission. By recognizing the need to "reconstitute" itself and continue, CASE acknowledged that it had a future. It was no longer serving a temporary function.

CREATING OPPORTUNITY:
The GED Tests and the VTS

Under the guidance of CASE, the GED Tests came of age during the post-war years. Because so many men had been drafted before they had graduated from high school, demand for the GED—particularly the high school–level tests—far exceeded that for the others in the battery offered by USAFI. The GED Tests provided those men and women who had left high school to join the service a promising opportunity for future education.

Sorting Out the Forms

At the end of the war, the GED Tests were part of the battery of USAFI tests administered by the Veterans' Testing Service (VTS), predecessor of today's GED Testing Service. Established by ACE in 1945, VTS operated under a contract with the University of Chicago, where it was based, and was responsible for test development and administration. The University of Chicago provided space, equipment, staff (including Director Lily Detchen) and bill payment services, for which ACE reimbursed the university each quarter. However, the university did not oversee the policies or practices of VTS; as an agency of ACE, VTS was under the purview of CASE (Dobbins 1968, 56; Barrows 1948).

The GED Tests came of age during the post-war years . . . providing those men and women who had left high school to join the service a promising opportunity for future education.

Initially, only two forms of the high school– and college-level versions of the USAFI tests existed: Forms A and B. Form A, "the secret military form," was originally distributed solely by USAFI for the purpose of testing men and women while they were still in the service. ACE's Cooperative Test Service and Science Research Associates distributed Form B to colleges so they could acquaint themselves with the test materials and test their own students to "establish institutional norms" for evaluating test performance. Postsecondary institutions thus could determine their own passing scores based on the performance of their "typical" students (ACE 1954, Exhibit A).

But the large numbers of tests being administered threatened to invalidate Form B as a credit-granting tool (CASE 1946c). To provide a more accurate standard of measurement, ACE asked USAFI to make Form A available to colleges. Yet because Form A previously had been administered only to service personnel through USAFI and was *the* test used by VTS to determine whether a credential would be issued, the security of the tests was of paramount importance.

Concern about test security increased after the 1946 publication of Albert Crawford and P. S. Burnham's article "Forecasting

College Achievement." In it, they asserted that they had "confidential evidence . . . [that] the GED Tests have not always been administered under standardized conditions and that candidates have sometimes been 'helped' to obtain higher scores" (CASE 1946d, Exhibit E, quoting Crawford and Burnham). The commission responded immediately by asking Crawford for a confidential report on their evidence so CASE "could follow up as we have in all other reports of violation, to protect the security of the tests" (CASE 1946e, 5–6). CASE knew that the validity of the GED Tests was dependent in part upon their security. So when ACE recommended to USAFI that Form A be made available to civilian institutions for norming purposes, it made it clear that institutions would be required to establish security measures adequate to protect the testing materials before they could receive them. Then, colleges could administer Form A to their own students to determine the proper credit awards for veterans applying to their institutions (ACE 1954, Exhibit A; Detchen 1947, 479).

USAFI and ACE also were concerned that many men and women would not fully comprehend the importance of continuing their education—and thus would not take the USAFI exams—until after they left the service (ACE 1954, Exhibit A). VTS had to find new ways to accommodate these veterans who were seeking educational credit for their military learning.

Expanding Access: The First Test Centers
When CASE held its second meeting on 6 April 1946, two new forms of the test, Forms C and D, were being compiled. The commission unanimously passed a resolution to request that USAFI make Form C available immediately upon its completion to civilian education institutions that would operate in partnership with ACE through a system of controlled testing centers[6] (CASE 1946c). These centers would be official VTS agencies that would operate under contract with civilian education institutions and systems that were approved and supervised by the state departments of education (CASE 1947b, 3). Thus, VTS—not USAFI—would administer the tests, giving veterans who had not been tested while in the service a second chance to take them. This resolution resulted in the creation of the first GED test centers.

The new test centers gave adults unprecedented access to the GED Tests, but the tests still did not reach all veterans. At CASE's September 1946 meeting, the VA inquired about the possibility of testing hospitalized veterans. The commission recommended that the VA, through CASE, enlist the cooperation of the state departments of education in a program that would use existing VTS agencies to administer Form C tests to these individuals. To do this, the commission approved an exception that would permit VTS agencies to remove the tests from their sites in order to administer them on site to hospitalized veterans. In every other instance, VTS agencies were strictly prohibited from removing the tests off site (CASE 1946e, 2).

By June 1947, "conservative estimates" indicated that between 600,000 and 700,000 men and women had taken the high school–level tests, and that number was expected to increase dramatically.

The value of administering tests through the VTS centers was increasingly apparent. In less than a year, approximately 300 official VTS agencies were created across the country (CASE 1947b, 2). By June 1947, "conservative estimates" indicated that between 600,000 and 700,000 men and women had taken the high school–level tests, and that number was expected to increase dramatically. As Thomas Barrows conservatively speculated, "We expect, therefore, that this testing program for veterans will probably continue to expand for another two or three years" (1947, 4). Because the test centers were so successful, VTS stopped accepting individual applications for testing—referred to as VTS Plan I—as of 30 June 1947. All testing now had to be administered by approved Official VTS Plan II agencies, where applicants were tested under the supervision of a VTS agent and the results were sent by the agent to a school official (VTS 1947).

But as long as VTS administered the tests, this was a "post-war program" designed specifically for veterans; as such, it was only temporary. If the GED Tests were to serve a wider population, a more permanent design would be needed. This was provided in fall 1947 when New York became the first state to enter an informal agreement with ACE to administer the tests to active-duty servicemembers, veterans, and nonveteran adults. New York would be responsible for test supervision and test center inspection according to ACE's established guidelines; ACE would be responsible for collecting fees. This agreement demonstrated ACE's commitment to grant the states autonomous, but guided, control of the testing process (Quigley 1991, 33–34).

This policy of shared responsibility was critical in convincing states to adopt the GED Tests. During Turner's 1946 tour of the states, he talked extensively with education officials, asking what their states would require in order to adopt the GED Tests—for veterans and civilians alike. In most cases, the answer was administrative control. In a 1986 interview, Turner recounted a particular meeting with an educator from South Carolina who would not even consider adopting the GED Tests. Turner "could never get to first base with him." So he made a proposal: "I said to him, 'Now, if you can have the tests to administer at centers that you select, and you score your own tests, will you accept the program?'" The answer was "absolutely" (Turner 1986b, 5). It was clear that the most successful operational model for the GED Tests would include centralized quality control by ACE and decentralized administration through the states. The ACE–New York State partnership cemented that.

This agreement demonstrated ACE's commitment to grant the states autonomous, but guided, control of the testing process.

Servicemembers, veterans, and nonveteran adults were not the only populations given the opportunity to take the GED Tests in New York in 1947. The state also permitted the testing of patients and inmates in state institutions, as well as prisoners and civilians confined to hospitals. New York thus opened "the back door of GED expansion into the civilian world" and set a bold standard that all citizens deserved a second chance to obtain a high school credential (Quigley 1991, 34).

The ETS Switch

Just as VTS was establishing itself, ACE released it to become part of the newly formed Educational Testing Service (ETS). Established on 1 January 1948, the purpose of ETS was to centralize the nation's myriad credentialing examinations.

Many—including CASE—supported the move. In a January 1948 letter to ACE President Zook, CASE Director Barrows recommended that the "preparation of the [GED] tests, the establishment of agencies within the framework of policies determined by educators, and other administrative procedures, should, I believe, quite properly be turned over to ETS, which I judge was established for just such purposes" (Barrows 1948). By April, VTS's administrative functions were transferred to ETS, where they remained until 1954. Meanwhile, the test development process for the GED Tests continued at the University of Iowa (Dobbins 1968, 62).

VTS's change in affiliation received little fanfare. In a 10 April 1948 circular, VTS informed agencies of the change but reassured them that it "should make no difference in our operational scheme here and probably will make no difference for some time to come, if at all." The only major change was the letterhead, which now read "Veterans' Testing Service of the Educational Testing Service" (VTS 1948).

THE ROAD TO ACCEPTANCE:
Expansion of the GED Tests

The most notable evidence of CASE's accomplishment during the first years following the war was institutions' rapid and widespread acceptance of the high school–level GED equivalency diploma as a measure of academic achievement.[7] In December 1945, only 11 state departments of education had adopted policies that approved the granting of high school diplomas or equivalency certificates based on successful completion of the GED Tests (Turner 1945, 25); by March 1947, that number had quadrupled to 44 states and the District of Columbia. Maine and New York soon added their names to the list. (Although New York was the first state to administer the tests [see page 24], its Department of Education had not adopted a formal policy.) Massachusetts and New Jersey were the only states that had no provision for issuing diplomas or equivalency certificates based on the GED Tests.[8] Of the 44 states already accepting the GED, 10 and the District of Columbia had "broadened their policies" to allow nonveteran adults to receive a high school diploma or equivalency certificate based on their performance on the GED Tests, and roughly 20 other states expressed an interest in doing the same (CASE 1947b, 2).

Acceptance through Standardization

The widespread acceptance of the high school–level GED Tests can be attributed both to high demand and to ACE's strong commitment to high quality standards. As the GED Tests were being developed, CASE and VTS recognized that the success of the tests would be linked inextricably to their validity and reliability. This meant not only that the tests' security would have to be maintained, but also that educators would have to be assured the tests were a valid and reliable measure of competence.

The most basic issue of test validity then (as now) was how the tests were standardized. In 1943, the tests were administered to more than 33,000 graduating seniors in more than 800 high schools across the country, making for "an unusually representative nationwide standardization program" (Lindquist 1944, 369). Based on those students' scores, ACE recommended that an acceptable passing score be a minimum standard score of 35 on each of the five GED Tests or a minimum average standard score of 45 for all five tests.[9] If this recommendation had applied to those high school seniors who were tested, 20 percent would have failed (Detchen 1947, 471).

But when the tests were initially administered to the adults who had not completed high school, the pass-fail ratio was significantly different. Between September 1945 and June 1947, approximately 17,500 veterans took the tests. The rate of failure for this group began at only 7 percent and increased gradually to 15 percent over the next year and a half. With this higher-than-expected pass rate, educators worried that students admitted on the basis of their performance on the GED Tests would not perform adequately at the postsecondary level. Yet there was no evidence that GED students were performing at lower levels than other college students. On 2 May 1947, at ACE's annual meeting, Thomas Barrows discussed the pass-fail ratio and noted, "To date, not a single institution [among the 85 percent that accept the results of the GED Tests] has reported that these tests are proving unsatisfactory as predictors of college success" (Barrows 1947, 3).

Later that year, Barrows received a letter from Commissioner E. G. Williamson reporting that he had received "comments and criticisms from high school principals and superintendents concerning the GED Tests . . . such as they are too easy and so forth" (Williamson 1947). Neil Turner replied for Barrows (who had already left for California because of the staff reduction at CASE), writing:

> Those who have operated the GED testing program on a limited basis complain that the tests are too easy since everyone meets the recommended scores of the Council . . . . The fact remains, however, that they have not tested a sufficient number to find out whether the tests are a valid measure or not. In practically all cases thus far, only those who ask to be tested have been tested. It takes courage for an individual without a high school diploma to approach a formal educator and ask to have a battery of mysterious tests administered to him . . . . His courage to make application is usually backed up by confidence in his ability to pass the tests . . . . When [testing is administered to all eligible veterans], there is no question but what the percentage of failures will be pretty high and quite likely will approximate those found in the original standardization program.

He also made it clear that it had "always been recommended, even from the beginning of the GED Tests, that individual institutions, school systems, or states standardize the tests with their own students" (Turner 1947, 2, 3). Although all examinees had to meet the passing standard established by ACE in order to qualify for a diploma, a state could—and still can—establish a higher minimum score based on its own norming study. Turner's prediction that the number of veterans failing the GED Tests would increase over time was accurate. By 1953, the failure rate (based on ACE's recommended scores) among servicemembers had increased to 21 percent (CASE 1954b, 3).

Avoiding "Competition" with High Schools

Another concern was potential misuse of the GED Tests. Specifically, educators—and CASE—wanted to be sure that servicemembers did not take the tests as a way of "skipping" regular school. From the beginning, the commission adhered to the philosophy that "systematic education normally is best obtained by regular attendance in high school." In fact, this philosophy was made into policy when the commission passed a resolution at its October 1946 meeting that "the GED Tests not be administered or recognized as a measure of high school equivalence until after the class of which the man [or woman] was a member has been graduated" (CASE 1955c, 3). This resolution inadvertently established the first policy regarding age requirements.[10]

DEEP AND WIDE:
The Lasting Impact of CASE

The first years after the war were a time of rapid change for CASE, the GED Tests, and the evaluation and advisory service for military experience (see Chapter 3). In just a few short years, the commission and the testing program went from relative obscurity to being fixtures in the national adult education community. CASE's impact was deep and wide—but still new enough to not be fully recognized. As Colonel Walter E. Sewell, chief of the Army Education Branch of the War Department, wrote in a letter to commission chairman Paul Elicker:

> I believe that the commission's contribution to education in this country is far more profound than is at present realized. It is my hope that in the not too distant future, the work of the commission can be expanded into an adult education project, which will revitalize that phase of education in this country (1947).

Little did he know how prophetic his words were.

NOTES

[1] In 1947, veterans accounted for 49 percent of all college enrollments in the United States (Bennett 1994, 10).

[2] The term "accreditation," as used by CASE and educators during the war and post-war years, differs considerably from today's usage. Today, "accreditation"

typically refers to the process of determining the quality of an education institution or program, whereas during the war and post-war years, "accreditation" usually referred to the process of evaluating and determining credit recommendations for non-academic training and experience.

[3] The terms commission and CASE are used interchangeably.

[4] Neil Turner was director of the New York High School Equivalency Testing Program until July 1949, when he left to become deputy director of USAFI (Turner 1986a, 13).

[5] The contract was renewed for the same amount for the year 1 April 1949 through 31 March 1950.

[6] Form C became the property of ACE. All other test forms belonged to USAFI.

[7] The college-level GED Tests had less of an impact on the education community for two primary reasons: First, because most veterans were interested in receiving a diploma that would allow them to get a job or gain admission to college, the demand for the college-level tests was much less than that for high school–level tests. Second, most colleges required that students take their own placement exams and therefore did not accept as readily the results of the college-level GED Tests (Tyler Undated, 31).

[8] California's policy had been to allow the governing boards of local school districts to decide whether to issue a high school equivalency diploma based on the GED Tests. This was true until 1973, when California became the last state to adopt a policy of statewide acceptance (see Chapter 6).

[9] The standard score is obtained through equating. According to *The Tests of General Educational Development Technical Manual*, equating is "the process of performing mathematical adjustments to raw test scores [the number of correct answers] so that the level of performance indicated by a particular scaled score is consistent over time, and from form to form" (GEDTS 1993, 25).

[10] Current policy stipulates that the GED Tests may not be administered to anyone under 16 years of age. Individual jurisdictions can set their own age requirements within the confines of this policy.

CHAPTER 3

Coming of Age, Part Two

THE EARLY
MILITARY
EVALUATIONS
PROGRAM
1946–1950

COMING OF AGE, PART TWO:
THE EARLY MILITARY
EVALUATIONS PROGRAM, 1946–1950

WIDESPREAD ACCEPTANCE:
The Evolution of the Guide

he high school–level GED Tests was not the only program of the Commission on Accreditation of Service Experiences (CASE) to expand during the post-war years. In 1944, publication of the *Guide to the Evaluation of Educational Experiences in the Armed Services* (the *Guide*) dramatically changed the way colleges and universities awarded credit for learning acquired in the military. The *Guide* was prepared under the sponsorship of the American Council on Education's (ACE's) Committee on Measurement and Guidance by a staff of civilian educators directed by George P. Tuttle, registrar of the University of Illinois. The success of the *Guide* was unprecedented. A 1948 study of academic deans revealed that 97 percent of their institutions accepted the *Guide*'s credit recommendations (Rose 1990, 39). This confirmed what Thomas Barrows and Neil Turner had learned during their conferences with education officials in the 48 states. At the second meeting of CASE, Turner reported that "[on] every hand . . . [the] *Guide* is looked upon as an invaluable instrument" in evaluating and awarding credit (CASE 1946c, 2). According to Floydine Miscampbell, who would later oversee the project, "Probably no single educational achievement in our times has met with such universal approbation and acceptance" (1947, 472).

The First Complete Guide
Despite widespread acceptance of the *Guide*, it had been an emergency measure; as such, it had been published in a manner befitting an emergency. The *Guide* was actually a series of pamphlets, not a single resource, and it was not widely distributed. Most colleges purchased the *Guide*, but only 4,000 of the country's 22,000 high schools bought copies. This severely limited its reach (Barrows 1947, 1). For these reasons, CASE Director

Barrows recommended at the first CASE meeting on 7 January 1946 that the commission approve a reprinting of the Tuttle *Guide* in a single, bound volume and distribute it at no cost to every high school and college in the country (CASE 1946b, 1). The commission accepted the recommendation.

At CASE's second meeting, ACE President George Zook told the commission that George Tuttle had returned to his full-time duties at the University of Illinois in Urbana, leaving the *Guide* project without an administrator. Zook thus recommended, and CASE approved, that responsibility for the *Guide* be transferred from the "Tuttle Committee" in Urbana to the commission (CASE 1946c, 3). This substantial undertaking was made even more substantial at the third CASE meeting in May 1946, when the commission also agreed to accept responsibility for evaluating future military course materials, thrusting CASE into the credit recommendation business. In addition, the commission would continue the advisory service of the Tuttle Committee. This service enabled colleges and universities to write to the committee for advice about how to apply credit recommendations or how to locate unpublished recommendations. Another responsibility that came with the shift from Urbana to CASE was the distribution of the *Guide* by ACE's publications department (CASE 1946d, 1). With these commitments, all aspects of the *Guide* project were left in the hands of the commission.

A 1948 study of academic deans revealed that 97 percent of their institutions accepted the Guide's credit recommendations.

It was clear that more funds would be needed to support such a large undertaking, and CASE was not about to accept the new responsibilities without some acknowledgment of that fact. So the commission added the provision that it be permitted, "if necessary," to adjust its budget to allow for the additional expense of continuing the *Guide* project (CASE 1946d, 1). Considering that this commitment included the costly proposal of distributing the *Guide* free to every secondary and postsecondary institution in the country, the financial burden was heavy. To offset the expense, CASE arranged for the Veterans'

Administration (VA) to purchase and distribute 25,000 copies of the *Guide* at a cost of $70,000 (Miscampbell 1947, 472).[1] Funds also would come from copies bought by the military services and individual subscribers, who paid five dollars to receive the *Guide* and its updates. The plan succeeded. In August 1946, the first complete edition of the *Guide* was published and distributed (ACE 1974, xiii).

The Failed Supplement and the Statement of Policy
for Peacetime Military Service

Despite the success of the *Guide*, there was talk of change at the September 1946 meeting of CASE—only one month after the *Guide's* distribution. The impetus for the discussion was the *Guide's* lack of "numerous and important" recommendations for service school training. Most of these "missing" recommendations were for courses that had been classified during the war, thus restricting civilian evaluations. With the war over, however, many of these courses had been declassified but remained without recommendations. To remedy this, it was proposed that a supplement to the *Guide* be published. In addition to including the missing service schools, the supplement would include additional training courses that had not been listed in the *Guide*, a description of the VA hospitals' education program (which included the GED Tests), the United States Armed Forces Institute (USAFI) Peacetime Program, off-duty classes, and the commission's statement of recommended *Accreditation Policies for Peacetime Military Service.*

How to fund the printing and distribution of the supplement was a concern. Because the supplement was to be distributed to those who had received the complete *Guide*, CASE again faced a large financial burden that its budget could not support. At the September commission meeting, Barrows proposed that the remaining funds, which had been earmarked by the VA for distribution of the complete edition of the *Guide*, be used to print and distribute the supplement. Barrows also suggested that the military branches be asked to purchase their own copies of the supplement at cost since they had paid less than the regular price for their copies of the *Guide*. By doing this, the commission was able to approve the free distribution of the supplement to individual subscribers and the inclusion of the supplement with future orders of the *Guide* (CASE 1946e, 3-4).

The work to compile the supplement began with a request by CASE to the military branches to provide descriptions of all service school programs not included in the *Guide*. As it turned out, the unevaluated courses were not as numerous as originally believed. At the March 1947 meeting, Barrows reported that CASE had received only about 400 program descriptions; most were small modifications of courses already included in the *Guide*, such as a change in a school's location. Of the 400 descriptions, only 50 were from important service schools that had not been evaluated during the war because their courses had been classified (CASE 1947b, 4).

Awarding credit on the basis of evaluations and recommendations was a new practice for colleges and universities—not to mention CASE—and it was not always easy.

As CASE staff began looking closely at these changes, they became concerned that if a supplement including only these 50 schools were published, educators would think that programs at schools not listed in either the *Guide* or the supplement were not recommended for credit. They also were concerned that the 50 service schools included in the supplement would be of interest only to colleges and universities, not secondary schools. For these reasons, the staff determined that the supplement would likely be more confusing than beneficial. The commission agreed, and decided it would be better to evaluate the new service schools and make the recommendations available through the advisory service than through a published supplement (CASE 1947b, 4).

Nevertheless, the commission agreed that one component of the planned supplement was important enough to print. On 19 October 1946, CASE published *Accreditation Policies for Peacetime Military Service*, the primary purpose of which was to explicate CASE's policy that the credit-granting procedures of high schools "should not permit men who leave the institution before graduation to obtain their diplomas before such time as they would have by normal attendance." The bulletin also stated CASE's change in policy to no longer recommend credit toward a high school diploma for basic or recruit training for service-members who entered the service after the war (CASE 1946f, 2). This change was in response to an increasing number of complaints from secondary school educators that recruiters were using the credit recommendations for basic training as a way of luring young people away from high school to enlist. According to reports, some students were being told that they would receive two units of high school credit for basic training and thus would be able to graduate with or ahead of their regular class. Credit recommendations for basic training during the war were made because so many young men were drafted before graduating from high school. To deny them appropriate credit for basic training would have been perceived as unfair. With the end of the war, however, this practice could no longer be justified; CASE changed its policy accordingly (CASE 1955b). This change in policy again reflected the commission's—and ACE's—commitment to have its programs enhance servicemembers' education. The programs never were intended to be a quick alternative to a traditional high school education.

DEFINITE CHANNELS:
The Advisory Service of CASE

By agreeing to take over the responsibilities of the Tuttle Committee, CASE took on more than just publication and distribution of the *Guide*; it also agreed to continue the advisory aspect of the committee. The need for this service was clear. Awarding credit on the basis of evaluations and recommendations was a new practice for colleges and universities—not to mention CASE—and it was not always easy. Institutions needed help finding credit recommendations for unlisted courses and understanding how to apply the recommendations. To meet these needs, the CASE advisory service was established.

The purpose of the advisory service was to counsel institutions on how to apply credit recommendations based on servicemembers' military education. The service required a significant amount of work and a highly organized and responsive leader. Floydine Miscampbell, who had been hired in March 1946 as

CASE's administrative assistant and who by mid-1947 had become assistant director, proved to be that leader. Miscampbell
was renowned not only for her success in building and manag-
ing the advisory service, but also for her quick wit and straight-
shooting manner; these qualities served her well in a profession
dominated almost entirely by men. While the responsibilities and
files were being transferred from Urbana to Washington, DC,
Miscampbell learned that E. J. Smith, executive secretary of the
Tuttle Committee, had asked Robert Quick, manager of ACE's
publications, whether Floydine Miscampbell was a Mr., Mrs., or
Miss. She responded,

> Incidentally, I think Bob Quick told you that I am Mrs.
> Miscampbell . . . . I am sorry that this was not clear from
> my letter, but after all, Floydine is a little flowery for a
> male, and you should know that any woman over 16
> cursed with a maiden name of Miscampbell would do
> anything to change it, and it would naturally follow that
> most females with such a name would only hold onto it
> as a part of the marriage contract.

She then chided Smith for his plans to forward unanswered
queries regarding credit recommendations to her. She wrote, "I
can't say that I am enthusiastic about your idea of sending on
100 unanswered cases. Seriously, that's not an even trade for your
advice, that's usury" (Miscampbell 1946).

The advisory service was a significant undertaking. At CASE's
7 March 1947 meeting, Miscampbell outlined the functions of the
advisory service. First, she explained that new and updated course
outlines were kept on file to serve as a reference in determining
the amount of credit to be recommended for training. Second, the
advisory service had oversight of the evaluation of new courses by
the same consultants who did evaluations for the Tuttle
Committee. Third, and perhaps most important, she explained that
the advisory service had worked diligently in establishing "definite
channels . . . with the training divisions of the various branches of
the services to secure needed additional information concerning
service training"—a critical function if the advisory service was to
be of any use to postsecondary institutions (CASE 1947b, 3).

The advisory service, like the GED Tests and CASE itself, was assumed to be temporary. The commission thought that demand
for the service eventually would wane, as would the number of
veterans returning to college (Miscampbell 1947, 476). Yet this
did not prove to be the case. As the number of veterans returning to college continued to increase, so did the number of institutions needing assistance and the volume of work for the
advisory service.

WHAT'S THE SHOOTING ABOUT:
The Marine Corps Institute and Policies and Procedures Relating to Accreditation

As acceptance of CASE's credit recommendations grew, the need
for set standards of measurement of learning became clear. At the
November 1949 CASE meeting, questions about the evaluation
of Marine Corps Institute and Maritime Institute courses were
raised. Unlike USAFI courses, which were evaluated based on
end-of-course exams created by civilian educators, credit recommendations for Marine Corps Institute and Maritime Institute
courses were made based on examinations developed by the
Marine Corps Institute staff itself (CASE 1949c, 1). This disparity threatened the validity of the commission's recommendations.
If courses were evaluated by different standards, how could educators be sure they were valid and reliable? Also, credit recommendations based on the military's own evaluation of its courses
were sure to be resisted by the civilian academic community.

Harry J. Carman, dean of Columbia College (the undergraduate
college of Columbia University) and the new chairman of CASE,
therefore proposed that "the commission set forth a set
of principles as a yardstick for accreditation by which this and all
other programs could be considered." The commission
concurred, and a special committee was appointed to draft a statement (CASE 1949c, 1). On 20 December 1949, the committee—
which included George Tuttle as chairman, A. J. Brumbaugh of
ACE, Paul Elicker of the National Association of Secondary School
Principals, John Dale Russell of the U.S. Office of Education, and
Thomas Barrows—wrote the "Report of a Subcommittee to the
Commission on Accreditation of Service Experiences on Policies
and Procedures Relating to Accreditation."

The three-paragraph policy included the purpose of CASE, which was to:

evaluate and make credit recommendations to civilian education institutions for educational attainment of members of the Armed Forces on active duty, achieved through correspondence courses, voluntary classes, and independent study, provided the educational policies of these programs are determined with the advice of a committee of competent civilian educators, such as the Committee on the Armed Forces Educational Program.

It further stated that these courses would be evaluated only when validated by end-of-course tests approved by the commission. Approval was based on three conditions: First, the exam "must have been prepared by educators who have had extensive experience in preparing and administering examinations of the same type and at the same educational level in recognized civilian institutions"; second, the exam "must be of a nature that permits reasonably objective scoring"; and third, the minimum passing score must be based on "adequate norms," meaning that the norms had to be based either on the "actual performance of representative groups of regular civilian students of the level to which the test applies" or on "judgment by civilian educators [who are] competent in the specific subject matter fields [and] who are not otherwise connected with the military services" (CASE 1949d, 1).

In addition to specifying the requirement for end-of-course examinations, the policy also stated that the commission would evaluate only those courses that had an academic counterpart at accredited civilian institutions. Credit recommendations would be made only for training programs at the conclusion of which students adequately demonstrated achievement and accomplishment (CASE 1949d, 2).

Thomas Barrows submitted the draft policy statement first to President Zook, asking for his input and requesting permission to conduct a mail vote of the commission rather than waiting for the next CASE meeting. Barrows explained that, if adopted,

the policy would not change the existing evaluation and recommendation procedures of USAFI; nor would it change recommendations relating to the GED Tests or the evaluation of
formal service schools. Rather, it would involve "minor but reasonable changes in procedures of the Marine Corps Institute;"
and, because the Maritime Institute program did not fit the requirements laid out in the new policy, its courses would no
longer be evaluated (1949). Zook approved the statement and
the request for a mail vote. By February 1950, the commissioners had approved the statement. Little did they know what trou-
ble it would cause.

The Marine Corps Institute saw the changes as anything but
"minor but reasonable." In a three-page letter to Barrows,
General C. B. Cates, commandant of the Marine Corps, emphatically argued several points of CASE's policy statement, asserting that it violated the USAFI contract. He wrote, "Since the
Marine Corps is governed by the contract between USAFI and
the American Council on Education, it is considered that acceptance of any policy statement is contingent upon its con-
formity with that contract. Study of the proposed statement . . .
indicates disparity with the governing contract." Specifically, he
took issue with the commission's statement that credit recommendations would be made based on the "*educational attainment
of members* of the Armed Forces on active duty" (Cates 1950,
quoting CASE). General Cates argued that this statement "would
violate the terms of the contract by evaluating individual
achievement rather than program or course methodology and
content." He also wrote that CASE's policy would require multiple changes in the Marine Corps Institute's existing policies
and procedures—policies that had been developed during the
Institute's 30 years of operation. "They should not," Cates
warned, "be supplanted without mature deliberation" (1950).

Cates also stated that the commission's policy to evaluate only
those courses intended for active-duty servicemembers was "un-
acceptable" given that members of the Marine Corps Reserve
were eligible for Institute courses. He asserted, "It would not be
equitable to deny to the reserve Marine recommended accredi-

tation of his work while simultaneously granting that courtesy to the regular Marine" (1950).

But the most contentious issue was the role of civilian educators in the development and administration of courses and examinations. To the commission's requirement that military education programs be governed by a committee of civilian educators, Cates rebutted, "As it has for 30 years in the conduct of its educational program, the Marine Corps will continue to seek the advice of civilian educators. However, the Commandant of the Marine Corps expects also to continue to make the final determination of policies affecting that program." Likewise, to the commission's requirement that the norms for end-of-course exams be based on representative groups of civilian students or the judgment of civilian educators, Cates wrote that the Marine Corps "is not prepared to concede that a criterion group need be *civilian*. Neither will it accept norms 'set on the basis of judgment by civilian educators' when more valid criteria are available." He continued, "[This] Headquarters is unalterably opposed" to the commission's requirement that these civilian educators be "not otherwise connected with the military services." Cates argued that the Armed Forces "contain a significant number of individuals who have had the benefit of considerable training and experience in the field of education .... Moreover, highly qualified civilian educators are permanently employed by the military departments" (1950).

The most contentious issue was the role of civilian educators in the development and administration of courses and examinations.

These were only some of the issues General Cates raised. It was clear that the Marines were not pleased—a fact best summed up in a handwritten note from President Zook to Thomas Barrows that was attached to the letter, stating simply: "What's the shooting all about?" Several meetings and discussions ensued in which CASE and the Marine Corps sought to iron out their differences and create a mutually agreeable policy. The final document actually contained very few changes. The only major change was the elimination of the requirement that civilian educators involved

with the Marine Corps Institute exams not be "otherwise connected with the military services" (CASE 1950). It was a small
concession. As Barrows wrote in a letter to committee member
John Dale Russell,

> As you know, some of the boys in the Marine Corps mis-
> interpreted the intent of some of the statements . . . . They
> started out with a terrific blast but after a couple of con-
> ferences have completely accepted the intent but have
> suggested some minor changes, not one of which affects
> the policy a whit. However, I think they would be hap-
> pier if we restate some phrases so that they cannot misin-
> terpret the intent.

Barrows was not entirely ungracious, though. He conceded, "In a
couple of spots I think the changes actually improve and strengthen
our position" (1950). With that, the commission had survived its
first significant challenge to the ACE-military partnership.

GETTING THE WORD OUT:
Campaigning for the Acceptance of Military Learning

The campaign to ensure the acceptance of credit recommendations by colleges and universities was ongoing. All of CASE's
policies and actions were driven by the acknowledgment that
without universal acceptance, its efforts would be fruitless. The
credit recommendations themselves—their validity and applica-
bility to academic courses—were the main factor in gaining acceptance. But beyond the credit recommendations was a public
relations issue. To be accepted by the academic community,
CASE had to increase awareness of its work. The *Guide* was
CASE's most effective public relations tool. By distributing
copies free to every high school and college, CASE was sure to
increase its visibility. But the *Guide* was also limited as a tool because it did not address educators' specific concerns. Conferences
proved to be an excellent venue for doing just that.

In addition to Barrows and Turner's initial conferences in 1946
with educators in the 48 states, CASE made a concerted effort
to reach out to other education organizations of importance. For

example, Floydine Miscampbell presented on the commission's advisory service at the annual meeting of the American Association of Collegiate Registrars[2] in April 1947 (CASE 1947b, 4). Registrars were an important audience given that they were responsible for interpreting and applying the *Guide's* credit recommendations. Miscampbell reiterated that CASE advocated "complete institutional autonomy" with regard to the granting of credit; the purpose of the commission was to recommend policy, not dictate it (Miscampbell 1947, 472).

But Miscampbell did not use her time before the registrars merely to build confidence in CASE and its recommendations. She also expended considerable effort instructing registrars in how to properly use the service. Given that the advisory service was being "extensively used by nearly 200 institutions" and that it maintained hundreds of service school training files, the original materials of the Tuttle Committee, USAFI's outlines and card catalogs, and the syllabuses of nearly 500 course revisions or new courses, Miscampbell and the CASE staff had an interest in receiving as complete information as possible from institutions requesting credit recommendations for courses not listed in the *Guide*. She described how CASE often received "wholly inadequate information" from colleges and universities. "It is no exaggeration," she explained, "to say we have received a discouraging number of letters something like this: 'We have a veteran who completed an eight weeks' course at Miami Beach, Florida. How much college credit should be allowed for this course?'" To discourage such requests, she presented a form that CASE had developed for its own use but which since had been used by a number of colleges and universities contacting the commission. She went through the form line by line, explaining just what information was needed to accurately identify a training course (1947, 473–75).

It is uncertain whether the institutions followed Miscampbell's detailed instructions. But it was clear that CASE's public relations effort to encourage acceptance of its recommendations was successful. Four years later, in a survey of 153 institutions, 95 percent reported that they granted credit toward a bachelor's degree for completion of service school courses—with most granting an average of 30 semester hours per student (CASE 1951b, 4–5).

CASE also had an interest in establishing its role at the highest administrative levels in higher education. One month after Miscampbell spoke at the American Association of Collegiate Registrars meeting, Thomas Barrows presented to college and university presidents at ACE's annual meeting. If ever there was a time to win support for the commission's activities, this was it. This was the second time Barrows spoke to the ACE membership. The previous year, he had presented only "a brief report on the early activities" of CASE. But the commission was now a full-fledged operation in its own right, and it differed significantly from ACE's other programs. Barrows thus began his presentation by stating that the commission was "unique among the projects" of ACE. "Most committees and commissions of the Council," he explained, "are engaged in making educational studies, conducting research, or formulating policies. This project [CASE] differs in that its activities are operational and are devoted to coordinating and implementing programs of the Council and other educational groups." He described the GED Tests and the *Guide* project, emphasizing the commission's commitment to ensuring institutional autonomy in awarding credit and reiterating its position that no veteran be awarded undeserved credit or be encouraged to leave classroom studies early because of the alternatives CASE's programs presented (Barrows 1947, 6).

The implications in the wartime programs of education, training, and testing, as they may apply to adult education, are manifest. I sincerely hope that these permanent implications will be adequately explored while our experiences are still fresh in our minds.
—Thomas N. Barrows

But Barrows went beyond the standard pitch by ending his speech with that which had never before been stated publicly: that the commission's activities were not temporary. He noted how "educators have increasingly recognized that the measurement of general educational development and competence by examination, such as the GED Tests, may be equally valid and applicable to nonveteran adults." He continued, "The implications in the wartime programs of education, training, and testing, as they may apply to adult education, are manifest. I sincerely hope that these permanent implications will be adequately explored while our experiences are still fresh in our minds" (Barrows 1947, 6). Whether this plea would be received favorably remained to be seen.

CONFLICT ANEW:
The Beginning of the Korean War

The commission did not have to wait long to see whether its programs would be continued as options for nonveteran adults. In June 1950, North Korean troops crossed the 38th parallel into South Korea, and U.S. involvement in the Korean War began. This new conflict ensured the enlistment and return of another wave of servicemembers, many of whom would seek to further their education. Passage of the Veterans' Readjustment Assistance Act of 1952, which paid veterans up to $110 a month for school and living expenses, made this even more certain (Montgomery 1994, 50). War again became an important stimulus to the adult education movement of the 20th century.

NOTES
[1] Because of the Veterans' Administration's assistance, the first complete edition of the *Guide* was commonly referred to as the "VA edition."
[2] The American Association of Collegiate Registrars would later become the American Association of Collegiate Registrars and Admissions Officers.

CHAPTER 4

Special Collections, University of Maryland Libraries

The Emerging Leader

1951–1955

THE EMERGING LEADER, 1951–1955

A NEW PHASE:
The Impact of the Korean War

𝒰 S. involvement in the Korean War made it clear to the academic community that accommodating veterans was not a temporary problem. As Ralph Tyler, director of the Veterans' Testing Service (VTS), observed, "With the prospect of a long period of international tension and a correspondingly long period of partial military mobilization, every able-bodied youth can expect a period of military service." Like those who were drafted or who joined the war effort in World War II, few of these men and women would make their careers in the military. Educators continued to be concerned that the years these adults spent in the military would "dim educational goals, cause loss of interest in further education, and result in loss of habits and skills required for effective study" (Tyler Undated, 1).

The Commission on Accreditation of Service Experiences (CASE) continued its work in the early 1950s to ensure that veterans could more easily continue their education upon returning to civilian life. But it also undertook a more concerted effort to use alternative methods of measurement, such as the GED Tests, to help nonveteran adults further their education. The commission's work was entering a new phase.

INTERNAL AFFAIRS:
The Dressel–Schmid and Ralph Tyler Studies

In 1951, Arthur Adams, former president of the University of New Hampshire, became president of the American Council on Education (ACE); Charles W. McLane became the new director of CASE; and Cornelius "Neil" Turner again began attending commission meetings, this time as deputy director of the United States Armed Forces Institute (USAFI). The first meeting of the new year was held at ACE's new offices at 1785 Massachusetts

Avenue, former home of the Mellon family. CASE vacated its
small office on K Street and for the first time joined the other
ACE departments under the same roof.

The same year, Paul Dressel, director of the Cooperative Study
of Evaluation in General Education for ACE, and John Schmid,
assistant professor on the Board of Examiners at Michigan State
College (now Michigan State University), published *An
Evaluation of the Tests of General Educational Development* for
ACE's Committee on Measurement and Evaluation. This report was the first extensive study of the tests. In addition to
outlining the tests' purpose and detailing their use, it correlated
success on the GED Tests with college achievement. The study
concluded that the high school–level GED Tests "met ad-
mirably the purposes for which they were intended" and
"should be continued in essentially the same manner" as long
as "the exigencies of war and the immediate postwar period
were such that the GED Tests were as satisfactory a solution to
the problem as anything they can now envisage" (1951, 49).

However, Dressel and Schmid were less supportive of the testing
of civilians. The GED Tests were a good alternative for veterans
during the "exigencies of war," but Dressel and Schmid asserted
that the tests should not be administered to civilians in non-
emergency situations. They wrote, "Assuming peacetime conditions and extensive development of adult education programs,
there does not appear to be the need for haste, the necessity for
the lower standards, nor the restriction of testing techniques
characteristic of the GED program." They therefore recommended first that the tests include "some written materials to be
considered by a committee of judges on the basis of certain standards insuring a minimum mastery of writing skills."[1] Second,
they suggested that passing standard scores be adjusted so "the
minimum for a diploma awarded by examination would corre-
spond to an 'average high school graduate' or above rather than
the 20th percentile." Third, they recommended that a program
be developed that would limit the tests' availability to specified
times. Last, they proposed that the tests be broadened "in both
techniques and in content so as to cover other educational objectives." Implementing these recommendations "would insure

more all-around performance and would obtain greater prestige and security" for the program (1951, 50).

Although there was "some evidence" to indicate the "later success" of students who were awarded credit based on their performance on the college-level exam, Dressel and Schmid stated that the college-level tests' effectiveness was limited due to infrequent use and the absence of data to demonstrate a link between success in college and performance on the GED Tests. Rather, they believed the most important contribution of the college-level GED Tests was their help in focusing "some attention on the policy of granting credit by examination." They doubted that "any widely acceptable program of granting college credit can be developed by an approach analogous to the college-level GED Tests" (51).

Despite Dressel and Schmid's concerns, they concluded their study with an endorsement of the entire GED testing program. "There can be no question," they wrote, "that the total effect has been beneficial both in terms of immediate results and in terms of developments on which to build for the future" (52).

Ralph Tyler conducted an important fact-finding study of USAFI's testing program in the early 1950s. Initiated in 1952 at the request of USAFI, this project aimed "to study objectively the effectiveness of the various education programs conducted by the Armed Forces" (CASE 1951a, 1). The report was completed in 1954 and was disseminated widely to secondary and postsecondary education institutions.

Unlike Dressel and Schmid's study, Tyler's looked at USAFI's entire testing series, not just the GED Tests. Intended as a follow up to W. W. Charters's 1951 publication, *Opportunities for the Continuation of Education in the Armed Forces,* Tyler's fact-finding study was intended not to make recommendations for improving the tests, but to answer questions raised by USAFI and the Armed Forces Education Program Committee and to present the findings to ACE, "who in turn will examine the facts and make recommendations regarding the steps that should be taken to strengthen the testing program as a part of the total educational program available to men in the armed service" (Tyler Undated, 1–2).

But Tyler's findings made it clear that the GED Tests were serving their purpose. For example, with regard to the success of GED test takers in business and industry, he noted no significant differences between traditional high school graduates and those who had obtained an equivalency diploma via the GED Tests (Tyler Undated, 36). Tyler also answered the question of how "GED graduates" compared to high school graduates in terms of success in college: Of 5,990 college students who had been admitted based on their performance on the GED Tests, 53 percent had achieved average grades at or above the minimum required for graduation, compared to 59 percent of traditional high school graduates (40).

Of 5,990 college students who had been admitted based on their performance on the GED Tests, 53 percent had achieved average grades at or above the minimum required for graduation, compared to 59 percent of traditional high school graduates.

Upon review and extended discussion of Tyler's report, a CASE committee recommended to the commission that the GED Tests continue to be used "as a valid basis for the issuance of a secondary school credential." The committee asserted that "studies relating to the performance in college of students who are admitted on the basis of the GED Tests" support the conclusion that a "large number" of these students "succeed reasonably well academically . . . . [T]here is sufficient evidence from all of the available studies to justify the continued use of the GED Tests as one criterion for admission to college in lieu of the requirement of a high school diploma" (CASE 1956a, 5).

CONTINUING GROWTH:
The CASE Programs

Advisory Service

From February 1951 through January 1952, the CASE Advisory Service answered and initiated more than 4,500 queries regarding the evaluation of service experiences. In the month of May 1951 alone, the Advisory Service received requests from colleges and universities in 43 states, the District of Columbia, and Alaska asking for the evaluation of anywhere from one to 50 courses per institution (CASE 1952a, 2). This number continued to increase. In 1954, Miscampbell, who had resigned as assistant director and become a part-time consultant for CASE, reported that in only six months, the Advisory Service compiled more than 3,000 letters and reported credit recommendations for more than 3,300 servicemembers (CASE 1954c, Tab C).

As demand on the Advisory Service increased, the need to expand outreach among colleges and universities became more apparent. At the 5 November 1954 commission meeting, the staff reported that a group of registrars and admissions officers from colleges and universities in California had requested a workshop on military evaluations and credit recommendations. Although the CASE staff had made a definitive effort to increase awareness and understanding through national conferences, they learned that many of the smaller institutions were unable to send representatives to the conferences and thus were unable to access important information about the service. Even larger institutions typically sent their registrars or directors of admissions, who had little to do with day-to-day admissions counseling, so many of the admissions officers were not fully aware of ACE's credit recommendations or the CASE Advisory Service. CASE staff made arrangements to conduct two one-day workshops in northern and southern California—one at the University of California at Berkeley, the other at the University of Southern California. The purpose of the workshops was not only to teach the techniques and procedures for evaluating specific training programs, but also to educate attendees about the work of the commission and its philosophy and goals (CASE, 1954c, Tab C).

The workshops were a success. The colleges and universities were grateful for the help, and CASE had found another way to increase awareness of its programs. Shortly after the California workshops, the commission began receiving requests for similar workshops in New England (CASE 1955a, 3).

The *Guide*

Meanwhile, the number of evaluations of military courses continued to increase. Between February and December 1951, the commission prepared evaluations for 100 military training programs, USAFI courses, and Marine Corps Institute courses, as well as an estimated 160 courses that had been submitted to consultants (CASE 1952a). This increase again brought to the fore consideration of publishing a revised edition of the *Guide to the Evaluation of Educational Experiences in the Armed Services* (the *Guide*).

At the 26 September 1952 commission meeting, it was suggested that a study be conducted to gauge demand for a revised *Guide*. Three hundred colleges, universities, secondary school principals, and state department of education officials were surveyed as to whether the 1946 edition of the *Guide* was still useful; whether they thought an updated supplement would be helpful; and, if a supplement were published, whether the CASE Advisory Service should be continued. Of the nearly 250 responses, 91 percent reported that the 1946 edition of the *Guide* was still useful; 87 percent thought an updated supplement was necessary; and 84 percent said the Advisory Service should continue even if a supplement were published. Most of the negative responses came from secondary school principals and state departments of education, both of which indicated that they had little use for the *Guide* since diplomas and equivalency certificates were issued on the basis of results on the GED Tests[2] (CASE 1953a, Tab B).

Former CASE director Thomas Barrows had accurately suggested in his 1947 speech to college and university presidents that the GED Tests "may be equally valid and applicable to nonveteran adults."

The overwhelming support for a supplement confirmed the commission's belief that it was indeed time for a new edition. Anecdotal evidence made this even more clear. For example, the commission learned of "an enterprising admissions officer in California who had prepared and distributed to his friends a compilation of credit recommendations in a document titled 'Summary of letters from Mrs. Miscampbell of the American

Council on Education evaluating educational experiences in the armed services which are not included in the *Guide* of 1946.'" Everyone agreed that "no time be lost in getting started" (CASE 1953a, Tab B).

The revised *Guide* would include a condensation of the current *Guide* and a supplementary section containing new and modified courses since 1946. Fifty thousand copies would be printed and distributed to each secondary and postsecondary institution in the United States. The projected cost of the project was $83,000. As with the first edition, the military agreed to fund the project,[3] and George Tuttle agreed to direct it on a part-time basis (CASE 1953a, Tab B; CASE 1953b, 2).

The revision was important not only because it marked the growing importance of CASE's credit recommendations, but also because it brought Neil Turner back to the commission as associate director of the project. But that was not all. Having approved Turner's appointment to the *Guide* project, the selection committee subsequently recommended to ACE President Adams that Turner be named associate director of CASE upon completion of the project. Adams agreed. On 1 February 1954, Neil Turner again became a member of the CASE staff, where he would remain for the next two decades (CASE 1953b, 1).

Of the 42,141 adults who took the high school–level GED Tests in 1954, 65 percent were veterans while 35 percent were—remarkably— nonveteran adults.

Due in large part to Turner's leadership, the revised *Guide* was completed ahead of schedule and was distributed in September 1954 (CASE 1954d, 2).

Veterans' Testing Service and the GED Tests
As with the Advisory Service and military course evaluations, demand for the GED Tests continued to grow. A 1954 survey of VTS agencies revealed a 9 percent increase in the number of high school–level GED Tests administered between 1952 and 1953; between 1953 and 1954, the number increased another 35 percent. Of the 42,141 adults who took the high school–level GED Tests in 1954, 65 percent were veterans while 35 percent

were—remarkably—nonveteran adults (CASE 1955a, 2). Former CASE director Thomas Barrows had accurately suggested in his 1947 speech to college and university presidents that the GED Tests "may be equally valid and applicable to nonveteran adults" (6).

The number of testing sites was also increasing significantly. By fall 1954, VTS had 580 agencies in 44 states, Hawaii, Guam, Puerto Rico, and Mexico—"the largest number of agencies in the history of our program." Sixteen of the 28 private VTS agencies—"those limiting their testing to their own school systems"—had agreed to expand operations and offer the GED Tests "to all well-qualified applicants in their area, thus affording the GED benefits to an increasing number of deserving persons" (CASE 1954d, Tab D).

But the most significant event for VTS and the GED Tests during the early 1950s was the return of test distribution responsibility from the Educational Testing Service (ETS) to ACE. Early in 1954, ACE learned that ETS had discontinued distribution of the college-level Form B exam (given to colleges and universities to establish institutional norms) and was considering discontinuing the high school–level Form B exam as well. According to a 1986 interview with Neil Turner, the reason for the discontinuations was that ETS was not generating a profit from the tests. ACE was understandably concerned. Because "there was still sufficient demand" for the high school–level exam, "it was felt that distribution of this test should be continued." Meetings between ACE and ETS resulted in agreement that "it would be advisable for one agency to distribute both levels" of the Form B test. "Since ETS had definitely discontinued distribution of the college-level tests and would prefer to discontinue distribution of the high school–level tests," the organizations decided that beginning 1 April 1954, "future distribution be made through Veterans' Testing Service" (ACE 1954).

Once back in the hands of VTS, it continued to extend the tests' reach. In the first year following VTS's resumed distribution of the tests, it leased approximately 2,800 batteries and more than 70,000 answer sheets of the high school–level Form B GED Tests to more than 325 approved testing sites and agencies in 40 states, the District of Columbia, and six foreign countries. It also leased more than 2,500 separate test booklets and 6,700 answer sheets of the college-level Form B exam in less than a year. "This is especially gratifying," VTS staff wrote in the *Annual Statistical Survey*, "since before any [Form B tests could be leased], it was first necessary to make educators aware that the Form B college-level GEDs were again being distributed to aid their educational programs" (CASE 1955a, 4).

THE COMMUNICATIONS PUSH:
CASE's Public Relations Campaign

At its 26 January 1951 meeting, the commission had its first formal discussion about what would now be called an extensive public relations campaign. "It was the unanimous judgment of the commission," recount the minutes, "that every attempt should be made to have appropriate articles published in educational journals of national and regional organizations and associations and in popular magazines having wide public distribution." The commission "further agreed that members of the commission should assist in obtaining invitations for members of the staff and USAFI to appear at meetings of educational groups and organizations." The chair of CASE therefore wrote letters to various associations "pointing out the timeliness and importance of accreditation of service experiences and offering the services of staff members for their meetings" (3).

The following year, the commission staff reported attending meetings of the Armed Forces Education Program, the Marine Corps Institute Board of Visitors, and the Association of Collegiate Registrars and Admissions Officers, where CASE director Charles McLane delivered the general address, "A Professional Approach to Accreditation of Service Experiences." The commission also printed and distributed three bulletins "through military and civilian channels" and was preparing to distribute three more (CASE 1952a, Tab A, 2).

In September 1952, CASE's public relations effort was further expanded when its new director, Ernest Whitworth, recommended that CASE staff again conduct meetings with state departments of education in order to maintain relations with "civilian accrediting authorities on the local, state, regional, and national levels in geographic areas of the country" (CASE 1952b, 3, Tab F).

CASE's efforts to inform and influence through personal contacts paid off—at both the policy level and the programmatic level. At the 2 April 1954 commission meeting, Miscampbell remarked on the benefits of establishing personal ties with colleges and universities. She explained how "school officials do not fully understand accreditation policies and often too, they have accepted the program somewhat reluctantly." The reason, she hypothesized, is "that in many cases [the school officials] have had these policies passed down to them from 'higher up' with little explanation of the program." The solution to this information gap was the establishment of traditional outreach efforts, including workshops for admissions officers and registrars (see page 53) and personal relationships. As Miscampbell explained:

> We feel that handling the correspondence of the Advisory Service calls for more than providing a cut and dried answer to a letter to report a credit recommendation. We look on the Advisory Service as a public relations medium. In other words, through correspondence we do make many personal contacts with school officials that we can never hope to meet (CASE 1954c, Tab C).

One of the commission's most successful communications efforts was the CASE *Newsletter*, a four-page, biannual, text-only update on CASE's activities and policies (CASE 1954a, 1). First published in March 1954, the *Newsletter* was an instant hit. Its second issue began with a vow to continue publication and cited "the numerous letters received from secondary school and college officers commending the publication and urging that additional issues be forthcoming" (CASE 1954e, 1). By the third issue— only one year after its beginning—the *Newsletter* was being distributed to 25,000 secondary schools, 2,625 postsecondary institutions, the military branches, the Veterans' Administration (VA), and other interested groups. It was an invaluable communications tool for the commission (CASE 1955a, 3).

THE LONG ARM OF EDUCATION:
Expanding Access to the GED Tests

As mentioned before, sufficient numbers of nonveteran adults were taking the high school–level GED Tests to cause CASE and VTS to reconsider the tests and their purpose. But testing civilians was not the only way CASE and VTS expanded access. Throughout the early 1950s, several other issues concerning the testing of men and women who did not fit the "typical" model of the GED examinee came to the fore, inspiring a rethinking of the tests in an unprecedented way.

Women Recruits

One issue pertained to enlistment requirements for women. Unlike men, women who wanted to enlist in the armed services had to already possess either a high school diploma or equivalency certificate (such as the GED credential). However, because most states required that GED examinees be veterans, active-duty service personnel, or at least 20 years old to qualify for a high school equivalency certificate, the majority of these young women were prohibited from taking the tests (CASE 1952b, Tab A). Without the tests or a diploma, women could not enlist.

In response to this, CASE surveyed the state departments of education in 1952, asking if they would "be willing, for recruitment purposes, to give the examinations to young women under 21 if a state had a minimum age requirement of 21, or willing to administer the tests to nonveterans if the state limited the use of the test to veterans or service personnel." Recognizing that this could be a highly political issue in many states, CASE emphasized "that no attempt or suggestion was being made to induce any state department of education to change its policies

Throughout the early 1950s, several other issues concerning the testing of men and women who did not fit the "typical" model of the GED examinee came to the fore, inspiring a rethinking of the tests in an unprecedented way.

with regard to age or other individual requirements set up in connection with the granting of a high school diploma or equivalency certificate" (CASE 1952b, Tab A).

Survey responses indicated that states were willing to be flexible, but within certain limits. Of the 35 states that responded, 18 indicated that they would be willing to administer tests to women and report results to the recruiting offices for examinees who were at least 19 years of age and whose test application had been approved by their high school principals. A majority also would require a letter from the recruiting office, addressed to the testing agency, stating that the applicant would be accepted to the services provided she could pass the GED Tests. Only eight states said they did not approve the administration of the tests for recruitment purposes to those below the minimum age requirement. The remaining nine states had other special requirements (CASE 1952b, Tab A, 2).

The commission did not make a formal recommendation. It used its survey merely to increase awareness of the issue and to suggest alternatives that would allow women seeking to enlist the opportunity to take the tests. The states' favorable responses made it apparent that they were willing to open the doors of opportunity a little farther.

Correctional and Health Institutions

The testing of prisoners and VA hospital patients proved to be one of the most significant issues relating to the expansion of the GED Tests during the early 1950s. The issue was first raised in earnest at the March 1953 commission meeting. Prisons and VA hospitals had been using the unrestricted high school–level form to test their inmates and patients. Increasingly, states were becoming "more and more reluctant to accept the results of Form B for the purpose of awarding a high school diploma or certificate of equivalency" because they were not secure; thus inmates' and patients' test results were, for the most part, useless. Edward Belknap proposed that the VA be given access to the secure forms of the GED Tests to administer to patients. He argued, "The medical rehabilitation of veterans is being impeded because of the inability to use a GED test or similar instrument in order to stimulate and motivate the patient and assist him in getting out of the hospital and back into civilian life" (CASE 1953a, 2).

The commission did not immediately embrace the idea. Ralph Tyler explained that the "rather rigid standards for the administration of the tests [were] to insure that education institutions would have confidence in the results." Releasing a secure test form to non–VTS agencies could heighten concerns about the tests' reliability and validity. To address this complex issue, a committee composed of Commissioners Charles E. Friley and Galen Jones, CASE Director Ernest Whitworth, and Ralph Tyler was appointed to deliberate on the matter and report back to the commission (CASE 1953a, 2).

The committee met in Chicago in August 1953 to discuss alternatives. During the meeting, it was revealed that USAFI had recently indicated that the secure Form A of the GED Tests had "outlived its usefulness in the military" due to the large number of tests being administered and thus had been withdrawn as of July. Although Form A was no longer useful to USAFI, the VA was happy to use it. So the committee unanimously agreed that CASE should recommend to USAFI that the VA's educational therapy division, physical medicine division, and rehabilitation service be allowed to purchase copies of Form A for use in VA hospitals under procedural guidelines approved by the commission. The committee also proposed that Form A tests be used in prisons. It recommended that USAFI loan copies of the high school–level Form A exams to VTS, which would lease the tests to its agencies, approved by the state departments of education, "for use in Penal Institutions and other State Institutions where inmates or patients are either not able or not permitted to visit an official Testing Center." The commission and USAFI accepted the committee's recommendations. The VA began using USAFI's copies of Form A in May 1954. USAFI also agreed to make its Form A tests available to state governments for the testing of inmates and institutionalized patients. However, some questions remained as to whether USAFI could authorize use of its materials by state government officials, so implementation was delayed (CASE 1953b, Tab A, 1; 1954c, Tab A).

The issue of testing prisoners and institutionalized patients was so important that the CASE policy committee voted in September 1955 to modify the commission's policy on the administration of high school–level tests to ensure that inmates and other wards of the state were given equal opportunity to take the tests. Previously, CASE policy had stipulated that secure forms of the high school–level GED Tests remain on the premises of the official testing agency. This policy was modified so as to allow for the testing of patients and inmates in state institutions and to allow officials of state departments of education to adapt the GED testing program to "conform to administration of other comparable secure testing programs conducted within the state by the state department when there is proper justification." To stave off abuse of this more liberal testing policy, the committee further voted that "authorization for these modifications be granted only in individual cases after the staff of the commission has personally investigated" and approved "the procedures planned by the particular state department of education" (CASE 1955c, 12).

Each of these efforts to expand test delivery evidenced an ongoing balancing act between equal opportunity and test security. The commission was committed to finding alternatives that would satisfy the needs of both adults and the education institutions that served them.

A SECOND LOOK:
Re-norming the GED Tests

As administration of the GED Tests continued through the years, the academic community became increasingly concerned that the original standardization norms of 1943 were no longer valid. Its concern was reasonable. In the 12 years since the first standardization study, there had been changes in high school curricula, population shifts, and other factors that might affect test scores. The call for another standardization study—re-norming—grew. But a standardization study would be costly and time-consuming, and the commission was not going to rush into it (CASE 1954d, Tab A, 1).

First, it was suggested that an exploratory study be conducted using existing data at the University of Chicago. CASE made the proposal to Benjamin Bloom, the University of Chicago's new university examiner. At the 5 November 1954 meeting, CASE Director Ernest Whitworth shared Bloom's response. Bloom wrote that an exploratory study would be conducted using data that were not "obtained under the same conditions as the original set of norms, and it would be very difficult to come to any very definitive conclusions." He suggested that the approximate $5,000 cost of the exploratory study would be better spent on a full-fledged standardization study (CASE 1954d, Tab A, 1).

The commission was committed to finding alternatives that would satisfy the needs of both adults and the education institutions that served them.

A new study, Bloom explained, would involve the administration of Form A of the GED Tests to a random sample of approximately 9,000 high school students in the six regions of the country at a cost of $20,000. The results from each region would be combined with the "proper weighting of the schools, by states and by regions, in order to get the final set of norms." Bloom hypothesized that the results would differ little from the first standardization study completed in 1943. He expected that "certain portions of the country, particularly the South, and to some extent the West, will have risen somewhat in quality of instruction, which should be reflected in the performance of the students on the GED test" (CASE 1954d, Tab A, 1–2). By identifying regional differences, the study would help states set adjusted passing scores that would reflect the relative levels of achievement of the state's high school graduates[4] (Whitney 2000b, 3). But Bloom expected "the results from the other parts of the country to remain constant." For this reason, he admitted "difficulty in deciding whether the study is really worth the time and effort required to do it and the financial investment." Still, Bloom understood—as did the commission—that a new study would "give various users of the test somewhat more confidence in the results than may now be the case." CASE unanimously voted to seek financial support for the study (CASE 1954d, Tab A, 1–2).

The Department of Defense again provided financial support, and the 1955 GED Normative Study was begun. Bloom reported on the study's progress at the 18 May 1955 CASE meeting, telling commissioners that work had begun at the end of February so testing would be completed before the senior class graduated. More than 900 schools agreed to participate, with the result that more than 42,000 students—almost 10,000 more than the original sample in 1943—would be tested. It was clear that this standardization study would be sufficiently comprehensive to allay any fears about its validity (CASE 1955a, 7).

The 1955 sample of seniors actually achieved somewhat higher scores on the GED Tests than had those students tested in 1943, with the greatest increase in mathematics and the slightest change in social studies. In 1943, 50 percent of graduating seniors exceeded the national median standard score of 50 on all five tests; in 1955, approximately 55 percent exceeded the standard score. Despite this increase, the commission felt that it was "not sufficiently significant to warrant a change in the minimum recommended scores" (CASE 1956a, 3). However, the norming study did result in a slightly more difficult test by requiring GED examinees to earn a higher raw score (by answering more questions correctly) to achieve the same minimum standard score[5] (Whitney 2000b, 3–4). The 1955 GED Normative Study also satisfied educators' questions about and reinforced the validity of the tests. In a sense, the study was a $20,000 insurance policy; to the commission, it was worth every penny.

FINDING COMMON GROUND:
Credit for Basic Training

Another important issue during the early 1950s was credit recommendations for basic or recruit training. In 1946, the commission passed a resolution recommending that high school credit no longer be granted for basic or recruit training completed in peacetime. At the 26 January 1951 meeting, the commission restated this policy, but changed it somewhat by unanimously recommending that basic training "be accepted *in lieu* of the mandatory high school requirement of physical education and hygiene or health and physical education" and "be accepted as meeting the requirements in physical education, hygiene, and military training at the freshman and sophomore college level" (CASE 1951a, 1).

The recommendation seemed innocuous but raised some concerns among physical and health educators. At the January 1952 commission meeting, representatives from the American Association for Health, Physical Education, and Recreation, the College Physical Education Association, and the College Committee on Physical Education and Athletics were invited to share their concerns. Professor D. Oberteuffer, chairman of the College Committee on Physical Education and Athletics, spoke for the group, telling the commission that its new recommendation regarding basic training "is not consistent with the best principles and practices in college physical education." He said the policy assumes "identity between the kind and quality of physical education received in the service and that received on college campuses, and urged the commission to re-study its recommendation . . . and to hold in abeyance the present policy until a new one had been developed and adopted" (CASE 1952a, 2).

In the ensuing discussion, Francis Brown of ACE explained that the policy was adopted "in recognition of the total physical education training received in basic military training and throughout military service." He added that CASE "had not assumed identity of the kind or quality of subject matter or teaching method" but that the policy expressed the commission's belief "that the end result was probably equivalent to that of many college physical education programs." CASE agreed to review the policy but denied Oberteuffer's request to rescind its recommendation. Rather, the existing recommendation would stand "until a revised policy may be developed and adopted" (CASE 1952a, 3).

At the 20 March 1953 meeting, the CASE chairman appointed a committee composed of representatives from both CASE and the physical education groups to study the matter. The committee reported its recommendation at the commission's October

1953 meeting. Essentially, all parties were "not so much concerned with the completion of basic military training as they were the total physical education experiences the veteran had while in the service." With this in mind, they changed the policy so "that the physical education experiences during military service of at least six months be accepted in lieu of the mandatory high school requirement of physical education or hygiene and health education." The college-level policy was changed to recommend that military service in its entirety (including the completion of basic training) be accepted as meeting college-level requirements for military training specifically, rather than physical education in general. The commission recommended that to meet a college's physical education or hygiene requirement, "the applicant's military service [be] of at least six months' duration." The specification of the longer length of service assured physical and health educators that the veterans' experience would be sufficiently substantial to warrant the granting of credit (CASE 1953b, Tab B). Physical education representatives were pleased with the new policy, and the commission was satisfied that veterans would continue to be awarded the appropriate amount of credit for their experiences.[6]

The commission was satisfied that veterans would continue to be awarded the appropriate amount of credit for their experiences.

ENHANCING AND ENCOURAGING EDUCATION:
Credit for Reserve Training

One of CASE's biggest policy changes between 1951 and 1955 was the addition of the evaluation of reservist training. At the 5 November 1954 commission meeting, Whitworth reported that the number of requests from civilian education institutions for the evaluation of military reserve training was increasing. Since its inception, CASE had made it clear that it only evaluated and made credit recommendations for "those training programs completed by military personnel on active duty." However, given the country's continued involvement in international conflict, the number of reservists had increased considerably and was expected to continue to do so. The commission was asked whether CASE "should extend its functions to include the evaluation of reserve training programs." Whitworth responded that "no solution to this problem was being proposed since it was one that required serious thought and study." As with most other important issues, a committee was appointed to evaluate the pros and cons and to make a recommendation to the commission (CASE 1954d, 3–4).

Before making its recommendation, the committee surveyed 149 civilian education institutions of varying sizes to determine educators' opinions about credit recommendations for reserve training. Of the 143 that replied, 48 percent reported that they received requests to grant credit for off-campus reserve training; 46 percent said they believed credit should be granted for reserve training; and 57 percent said that "the commission should evaluate Reserve programs" (CASE 1955d, 2). Thus, the committee recommended—and the CASE policy committee and the commission approved—that the commission evaluate and make credit recommendations for reserve training programs, with the following restrictions: The programs had to be full time, not less than three weeks long, and "with a minimum of 30 clock hours of classroom instruction per week." The commission recognized that "the proposal is a compromise between the positions of not evaluating any Reserve programs and, on the other hand, of evaluating all Reserve training." Still, CASE staff believed that the new policy provided "careful safeguards against an indiscriminate extension of the policy of accrediting service experiences." But at the foundation of the policy change was the belief that the reserve training programs were an important part of the nation's defense. "Therefore," the policy committee wrote, "the commission in recognizing the basis of such training will enhance that training and encourage its development" (CASE 1955c, 8–9). This represented a milestone for the commission, which had grown from a small, crisis-driven operation to one capable of "enhancing" and "encouraging" the military's education programs.

GROWING INFLUENCE

The early 1950s were not as turbulent for CASE as World War II and the post-war years had been. Although the United States still was engaged in military conflict, the commission had moved out of its "emergency" mode of operation and had established its programs as ends in and of themselves. That 35 percent of GED examinees were not veterans was the greatest indication that CASE's programs were fulfilling a need beyond the commission's original intentions. As the programs expanded, so did the commission's influence on the national adult education landscape. Over the next 10 years, CASE would see this influence spread even further and solidify the commission's newfound role as a national leader in adult education.

NOTES

[1] A writing sample requirement was added to the GED Tests in 1988.

[2] This was one of the first indications of what later would become a clear trend: use of the *Guide* by colleges and universities and use of the GED Tests by secondary schools. Gradually, the *Guide* and the GED Tests came to serve separate populations.

[3] The first edition of the *Guide* was funded by the Veterans' Administration, whereas the second edition was funded by the Department of Defense.

[4] There is no indication that states with high-achieving seniors raised their GED minimum scores to reflect the regional differences. States with lower achievement results could not lower their minimum score below the standard set by ACE (Whitney 2000b, 3).

[5] In a restandardization study conducted by ETS in 1977, high school seniors scored markedly lower than their counterparts a decade earlier. Although the minimum passing score did not change, the format, length, and content of the tests did. As a result, "many observers judged them to be easier than the earlier tests . . . . In fact, they were easier because the 1977 standardization sample" did not perform as well as its 1967 predecessor (Whitney 2000b, 6).

[6] This issue was raised again in the 1970s (see Chapter 7).

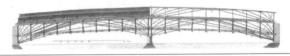

CHAPTER 5

Archives of Labor and Urban Affairs/Wayne State University

*Beginning of the
Turner Era
1956–1966*

BEGINNING OF THE
TURNER ERA, 1956–1966

PRIDE AND HUMILITY:
Director Turner

*O*n 1 July 1956 something happened to the Commission on Accreditation of Service Experiences (CASE) that would have a greater impact on its future than perhaps any other event since World War II: Cornelius "Neil" Turner became its director. Though Turner had been associate director of the commission in 1946, he had left to become director of the New York High School Equivalency Testing Program when the Commission on Accreditation of Service Experiences (CASE) staff was reduced in 1947. In 1951, Turner resumed his relationship with CASE when he became deputy director of the United States Armed Forces Institute (USAFI); two years later, he was again named associate director of the commission. Although he had a long history with CASE, Turner did not treat his appointment as director lightly. In a letter to outgoing Commission Director Charles McLane, Turner wrote:

> Dear Mac:
> Last Monday, May 28th, became a very important day in my life and for my family, when Dr. Adams [president of the American Council on Education (ACE)] appointed me Director of the Commission on Accreditation . . . .

> I can't tell you how deeply pleased I am at my appointment and how grateful and proud I am to know that I have the support and confidence of you and the members of our commission in undertaking the directorship. I feel highly honored, but at the same time I accept the position with a sincere feeling of humility, as I appreciate the magnitude and the importance of the work of the commission.

> It is my sincere hope . . . that I may carry on the work of the commission with the same high degree of success as my predecessors (1956).

Under Turner's direction over the next 18 years, CASE in fact would experience unprecedented success.

NOT JUST FOR VETERANS ANYMORE:
The GED Tests

Unparalleled Growth

In the first 10 years of the Turner era, the GED Tests saw more growth than at any other time in CASE's history. In 1956, 52,522 people—the majority of whom were servicemembers or veterans—took the GED Tests. Within 10 years under Turner's direction, that number had more than tripled to 183,000—and the majority of examinees were civilians. In 1956, there were 601 GED testing centers; by 1966, there were 1,031, an increase of 72 percent (CASE 1957a, 2; 1967, 3). In 1956, only six state departments of education tested individuals in prisons and other institutions; by 1966, 38 states and the District of Columbia did so (CASE 1957d, 2; 1966d, 4).

Part of this meteoric growth was the result of the Veterans' Testing Service's (VTS's) move from the University of Chicago to ACE. Turner, then associate director, was concerned that the GED testing program was not being supervised adequately in Chicago. But ACE President Arthur Adams opposed the idea of moving VTS. According to Turner, "I said to Dr. Adams . . . 'They're not taking care of the tests out there. It's going to blow apart someday if we don't take— and keep—control'" (Turner 1986b, 7). At its May 1956 meeting, the commission unanimously approved the move (CASE 1956b, 10).

The actual move did not take place until 1 July 1958, when VTS moved into the basement of ACE's building on Massachusetts Avenue (CASE 1958a, 4). The move was expensive, costing more than $3,500 and leaving VTS with a cash balance of only $7,500 (CASE 1959a, 7). The move was followed by a name change in July 1963, from the Veterans' Testing Service to the GED Testing Service (GEDTS). With the number of civilian examinees now exceeding the number of veteran examinees, VTS was no longer an appropriate program descriptor.

The growth of GEDTS during Turner's early years as director also can be attributed to increased access to the tests, not only by civilians but by other, typically underserved populations as well. In addition to the increased number of states testing prisoners and patients in state institutions, testing in Veterans' Administration (VA) hospitals was becoming more common. In 1956, 2,000 hospitalized veterans took the GED Tests. It was clear that the tests were facilitating the patients' rehabilitation. In one hospital, 16 of the 19 patients who passed the tests reported that the certificates had helped them get into training programs or schools, or secure a job (CASE 1956c, 7). The increasing numbers of VA patients taking the tests resulted in the commission's approval in 1962 of civilian restricted forms being administered in VA hospitals (CASE 1962, 13).

With the number of civilian examinees now exceeding the number of veteran examinees, VTS was no longer an appropriate program descriptor.

There were other important expansions of access to the GED Tests. In 1957, at the request of the U.S. Department of Justice, the commission approved a policy that would make secure forms of the GED Tests available in federal prisons (CASE 1957b, 13). The following year, the commission approved a policy that would allow for the testing of foreign nationals and civilian citizens living overseas (CASE 1966b, 7). But perhaps the most significant advance between 1956 and 1966 was the modification of secure test forms for persons who were visually impaired.

In 1964, CASE approved a policy that allowed one of the civilian restricted high school–level GED test forms to be printed in Braille and large print and recorded on records and magnetic tape (CASE 1964b, 12). This effort required time and money, so the tests initially were made available only in large type and on magnetic tape without the usual rental fee. Soon after the tests became available, the commission received letters about men and women whose lives had been changed by the tests. One woman, who had acquired her academic knowledge solely through tutoring, passed the tests and was "anxious to continue her education at a higher level through correspondence courses in Braille and through talking books" (CASE 1966a, 2). Once again, the commission learned of the real impact of the GED Tests on people's lives—an impact that fueled Turner's push for universal acceptance of the program during his tenure as director.

USAFI's Study of the GED Tests

As the program grew, so did criticisms of it. The program enjoyed wide support overall, but many questioned its validity in evaluating learning and predicting future success (CASE 1958b, Tab B). For this reason, Darrell Inabnit, deputy director of USAFI, announced at the November 1957 CASE meeting the undertaking of an exploratory study of the GED Tests by the University of Chicago, in accordance with the university's contract with USAFI. Specifically, the study was to determine the effectiveness of the tests and whether other testing procedures would be more effective than existing GED testing techniques. Inabnit reported that the University of Chicago already was in the process of preparing its initial report.

The commission responded to this surprise announcement with apprehension. According to the meeting minutes, the commissioners, consultants, and Turner expressed "deep concern" that such a study would be undertaken without prior coordination with ACE or CASE. Given the results of the 1955 Normative Study and of Ralph Tyler's fact-finding study of USAFI, the commission disputed the need for another evaluation of the GED Tests. Further, commission members worried that the proposed study, "unless carefully coordinated, planned, and controlled, might place the GED testing program in jeopardy." When USAFI officials heard the commissioners' concerns, they volunteered to put the study on hold until "proper coordination had been effected with the commission" (CASE 1957c, 12–13).

At the next meeting, in May 1958, Turner reported that the University of Chicago study had been terminated. He made clear that CASE welcomed "the continual appraisal of the GED Tests and the program" but emphasized the need to coordinate with ACE and the commission before embarking on such studies. The commission therefore recommended that the president of ACE appoint a committee when "any interested agency" presents "sufficient evidence of a need for revision of the GED Tests" to explore the case and formulate recommendations. With this declaration, the commission guaranteed ACE's leadership in decision-making efforts pertaining to the GED Tests (CASE 1958b, 13–14).

Following the May commission meeting, Turner met with representatives from the Office of Armed Forces Information and Education and USAFI to further discuss the commission's actions and "other matters which have a bearing on the accreditation aspects of the educational programs of USAFI and the services." The meeting was successful—everyone reached "complete agreement on all matters discussed"—and went a long way toward mending the relationship between the two agencies and CASE. USAFI even agreed to comply with a long-standing request that it provide CASE with the passing scores from its end-of-course tests (Turner 1958a). In a memo to ACE President Arthur Adams, Turner reported that the commission was "now receiving splendid cooperation" from the Office of Armed Forces Information and Education and USAFI. Indicating just how strained relations had been, Turner concluded, "I know that you will be pleased, as we are, at this change in attitude, and I believe that we can now proceed in complete cooperation with the Office of Armed Forces Information and Education and USAFI to make needed improvements in the off-duty military education program" (Turner 1958b).

> *I know that you will be pleased, as we are, at this change in attitude, and I believe that we can now proceed in complete cooperation with the Office of Armed Forces Information and Education and USAFI to make needed improvements in the off-duty military education program.*
> –Neil Turner

USAFI's Subject Standardized Tests

At the same meeting at which USAFI announced the review of the GED Tests by the University of Chicago, Inabnit announced a study being conducted by Ohio State University that would review the USAFI subject examinations and make recommendations concerning the future use of those tests and the need for revision and restandardization.[1] The following May, USAFI reported the findings of the Ohio State University study—most notably, the recommendation to abolish the existing dual system of subject exams and end-of-course exams and develop instead a single system of subject matter tests that would measure learning acquired through USAFI high school– or college-level courses. The commission agreed, adding that the new tests should be standardized and broader in scope than the existing end-of-course exams. The result was the USAFI Subject Standardized Tests[2] (CASE 1958b, 9; 1959a, 11).

One of CASE's biggest concerns about construction of the new tests was the level of involvement of civilian educators. Past subject examinations and end-of-course tests had been constructed internally by USAFI, but continuation of this practice threatened the tests' acceptance by the academic community. Knowing that civilian educators would have to be highly involved in test construction, the commission stipulated that USAFI would not construct any tests internally, except for those already in process. The commission instead compiled a list of "pre-approved" institutions and agencies with which USAFI could contract to develop the tests (CASE 1959a, 9, Tab A).

Despite agreeing that the Subject Standardized Tests should be developed, the commission had not yet decided to stop distributing the old subject examinations. At the November 1959 meeting, the commission appointed a committee to study the subject tests and determine their fate. In May 1960, the committee presented its report, ultimately recommending—with the commission agreeing—that distribution be discontinued no later than 1 July 1961 (CASE 1960b, 5). Given that the two forms of the subject tests were virtually obsolete, having been constructed and standardized between 1942 and 1945, the recommendation was not surprising.

College-level GED Tests

While CASE worked with USAFI to resolve the issue of the new Subject Standardized Tests, another significant change in the use of USAFI tests began to take shape. As acceptance and usage of the high school–level GED Tests continued to grow, the comparatively minimal use of the college-level GED Tests was becoming increasingly evident. In 1956, VTS administered only 1,676 college-level GED batteries. Although this was nearly three times the number of tests administered the previous year, the number was still small enough to warrant concern (CASE 1957b, 9). By 1958, the number actually decreased by more than half, to 808 (CASE 1959c, 1). The reason for the decrease was unclear, though it seemed due in part to colleges' and universities' shift from general to subject-specific courses. This shift made the college-level tests' general education focus somewhat obsolete. In November 1960, the commission appointed a committee to study whether the college-level GED Tests should be renormed or discontinued. The following May, the committee reported that, generally, colleges no longer granted credit based on these tests, but that to eliminate the tests entirely would be a mistake. The military relied on the college-level tests to measure educational development in its servicemembers. To completely discontinue the tests without providing an adequate replacement would leave the "several services . . . definitely handicapped." As a compromise, the committee recommended that VTS discontinue distribution of the college-level GED Tests as of 1 July 1961 but that USAFI continue to distribute them for administration to military personnel on active duty until the USAFI Subject Standardized Tests were available. The tests would be a stop-gap measure until the Educational Testing Service (ETS) had the opportunity (per its own suggestion) to develop new college-level GED Tests. CASE accepted the recommendations, and VTS ceased to administer the college-level GED Tests (CASE 1961, 6, Tab B).

The tests that ETS developed became known as the Comprehensive College Tests, which later would become part of the College Board's College-Level Examination Program (CLEP).

The tests that ETS developed became known as the Comprehensive College Tests, which later would become part of the College Board's College-Level Examination Program. The program comprised two types of exams: general exams and subject exams. The general exams consisted of a battery of five tests and were intended to provide a comprehensive measurement of the first two years of undergraduate achievement in English, composition, humanities, mathematics, natural sciences, and social sciences and history. The subject exams were end-of-course tests that covered analysis and interpretation of literature, general chemistry, introductory calculus, introductory economics, tests and measurements, and western civilization[3] (CASE 1964c, 1–2).

As when USAFI developed the first series of tests, the commission knew that to be successful, this new set of tests would need the support of civilian education organizations. But because CASE itself did not develop the tests, it did not have the authority to enlist support. CASE therefore voted in November 1963 to ask members of the ETS Interim Council to present a resolution to the regional accrediting associations asking them to "consider the increasing need for a program of continuing education for adult citizens" and to evaluate the Comprehensive College Tests in terms of granting academic credit and advanced standing. Basically, CASE wanted to do what former ACE President George Zook had done during World War II when he secured the cooperation of the regional accrediting associations in developing the military's off-duty education programs. At the time, Zook had convinced the accrediting associations to recommend to its member institutions that credit be granted for service school and USAFI training, that high school certificates be awarded based on adequate performance on the GED Tests, and that advanced standing be granted based on adequate performance on the college-level GED Tests. Support from the regional accrediting associations had proved effective then, and CASE was betting that it would be so again (CASE 1963c, 8–10).

CASE was right. Soon thereafter, the Federation of Regional Accrediting Commissions of Higher Education evaluated the Comprehensive College Tests and passed a resolution to recommend that its members and, through them, higher education institutions, exercise "responsible experimentation with these tests in connection with the increasing need for a program of continuing higher education for adult citizens and particularly as a basis for granting advanced standing or academic credit or both to qualified adults." Another endorsement came from a special committee appointed to consider the suitability of CASE's use of the tests. Composed of representatives from national and regional higher education commissions and other agencies, this committee reaffirmed the federation's resolution, noting that it was "impressed by the evident care with which the tests have been developed, both as to content and technical concerns." Further, this committee declared it appropriate for CASE to accept the Comprehensive College Tests for use in evaluating military experiences. To do this, the committee recommended the appointment of a subcommittee "to work with representatives of appropriate organizations and agencies to determine specific evaluations which should be recommended on the use" of the tests (CASE 1964c, 2).

The fact that few institutions were granting credit or advanced standing based on examinees' test results was a concern.

CASE did this, and at the November 1964 meeting, the subcommittee presented its recommendations. First, it recommended that for the general examinations, institutions grant credit and advanced standing for each of the five tests—not to exceed a total of 30 hours of credit—when the examinee (civilian or military) achieved a score at or above the 25th percentile on each test. Second, for the subject tests, the committee again recommended that credit be awarded only to those examinees who scored at or above the 25th percentile. Regarding the amount of credit granted, the committee suggested that institutions award the same amount of credit hours for each exam as were normally given for completion of the corresponding course. The commission approved the committee's plan, giving CASE yet another set of credit recommendations to include in the *Guide to the Evaluation of Educational Experiences in the Armed Services* (the *Guide*) (CASE 1964c, 1–2).

The Comprehensive College Tests were introduced on 1 July 1965 when USAFI administered the general examinations to military personnel for the first time (CASE 1965, 4). Between July 1965 and September 1966, USAFI administered almost 200,000 tests and mailed the official test results for 1,675 examinees to 279 different colleges and universities. Already, the Comprehensive College Tests were being used by many more adults than had the college-level GED Tests. But the fact that few institutions were granting credit or advanced standing based on examinees' test results was a concern. The commission's interest in the success of the program surpassed the mere development of the tests. Rather, CASE saw the Comprehensive College Tests as a "natural supplement" to the GED Tests.

The commission therefore agreed that "effective action should be taken to encourage colleges and universities to experiment with the tests, to establish local norms, and to adopt the tests as a means for granting advanced standing and credit." CASE once again took on the role of advocate. The commission felt strongly that the Comprehensive College Tests would allow those adults who had acquired knowledge through nontraditional educational experiences the chance to earn credit for it (CASE 1966b, 8–9).

CASE's advocacy role was pivotal for both ACE and the commission, and it proved a contributing factor in the development, in the late 1970s, of the Credit by Examination program (see Chapter 7). For the first time, CASE was asking institutions to use exams developed outside of its or the military's purview to award credit. As Douglas Whitney, later director of the GED Tests, explained, "CASE now was both the advocate of the use of a series of exams and the evaluator on behalf of higher education" (2000b, 4). This shift was important and laid the foundation for much of ACE's future work.

NARROWING AND BROADENING SCOPE: *Military Evaluations and the Advisory Service*

Steady Growth

The number of evaluations of military courses increased steadily during Turner's first 10 years as director but did not skyrocket as the number of examinees taking the GED Tests did. Nevertheless, the introduction of nuclear weapons training and other technological advances contributed to the ongoing need for new and revised evaluations (CASE 1960a, 4). Between 1956 and 1966, the commission evaluated and made credit recommendations for more than 600 USAFI and Marine Corps Institute courses.[4] In addition, the advisory service—under the direction of CASE's new administrative assistant, Shirley Lanham—initiated or answered approximately 5,000 letters each year, most from colleges and universities trying to determine how much credit to award veterans (CASE 1966c). CASE's evaluations and credit recommendations had become an indispensable tool for both the military and the academic community.

Narrowing the Scope: Extension Course Institute Courses

Between 1956 and 1966, changes in CASE policy simultaneously narrowed and widened the scope of evaluations. The narrowing came in 1958 when the commission received a letter from the Extension Course Institute of Air University asking for an evaluation of its courses. The courses had never been evaluated because completion was not validated by an examination. However, the Air Force had begun using a qualification test as an end-of-course exam for Extension Course Institute courses, making the courses a candidate for evaluation. A committee was appointed in December 1958 to examine the issue and to make a recommendation to the commission (CASE 1958c, 12). In May 1959, the committee made its report, recommending not only that CASE *not* evaluate correspondence and informal Extension Course Institute courses, but that it also stop evaluating new or revised Marine Corps Institute courses and that it no longer recommend credit for Navy and Coast Guard training courses.

Justification for these recommendations was based on the committee's review of the policy regarding the types of courses CASE would evaluate; policies and procedures related to the development of new USAFI Subject Standardized Tests; and the commission's "long-standing recommendation that civilian academic credit for service experiences be granted only upon the basis of demonstrated competence." When the committee evaluated these issues, it determined that the commission's policy on the types of courses it evaluated should be "revised and expanded as it applies to the accreditation of all correspondence courses, self-teaching courses, and informal education and training in the Armed Forces." The revision simplified the policy but restated that CASE would review only those courses that measured educational achievement through examinations constructed by "qualified civilian education institutions and agencies approved by CASE." Under this revised policy, Extension Course Institute courses, Marine Corps Institute courses, and Navy and Coast Guard training courses did not qualify for evaluation (CASE 1959a, Tab D).

This policy had serious implications. CASE credit recommendations had become a useful recruiting and morale tool for the

armed forces—and they did not take the loss of recommendations lightly. John E. Fellows, chair of the commission, asked the
Office of Armed Forces Information and Education and each of
the military services for their reactions to this policy change.
The Marine Corps Institute, which had fought hard to have its
courses evaluated in 1950, was the only service that said the new
policy would adversely affect its educational programs. Stating
that the change would "not impair the effectiveness" of its
courses, the institute nevertheless feared that it might have "some
psychological effects on the Marines themselves." Ultimately,
CASE accepted the committee's recommendations at its
November 1959 meeting and consequently narrowed the scope
of course evaluations (CASE 1959b, 9).

Broadening the Scope: Graduate and Foreign Service Institute Evaluations

This narrowing was offset by two other policy changes between
1956 and 1966 that allowed for the evaluation of previously in-
eligible courses. In 1962, the issue was raised as to whether
CASE should evaluate high-level military training for graduate
credit. Turner told the commission how the graduate school at
George Washington University had established graduate programs at the Army War College, the Air War College, and the
Industrial College of the Armed Forces, and other graduate
schools were interested in launching similar programs. CASE's
involvement seemed appropriate, but the commission urged caution. A committee was appointed to explore the issue with invited graduate deans and presidents of colleges and universities
(CASE 1962, 11).

At the committee's February 1963 meeting, Colonel Josephus A.
Bowman of the Office of the Deputy Assistant Secretary of
Defense explained how all of the services were putting an increased emphasis on the educational attainments of their personnel and that the Department of Defense as a whole was
recognizing the need for a better educated military force. He
added, "I don't need to tell all of you gentlemen that the military technology, the military problems being faced by this nation,
are changing so rapidly that we need educated people that can
cope with these problems" (CASE 1963a, 16–17). The military
knew that better educated servicemembers made better leaders,

and evaluating high-level courses for graduate credit would encourage both.

In the end, the committee recommended that high-level courses be evaluated, but only by a group of consultants selected from the faculties of graduate schools. Universities could use the evaluations and descriptions of the training programs to determine whether high-level service school courses would meet their graduate degree requirements. At its May 1963 meeting, CASE unanimously approved the committee's recommendations and amended its policy regarding the academic levels of commission recommendations to include graduate-level recommendations (CASE 1963b, 8). For the first time in its 17-year history, CASE would evaluate courses at the graduate-degree level. By May 1964, the commission had completed its evaluations of the Air War College and Air Command and Staff College programs at Air University and had received requests to evaluate courses in four other programs (CASE 1964b, 7–8).

The scope of CASE's evaluations broadened again in 1964, when the commission agreed for the first time to evaluate training offered by a nonmilitary government agency. At the request of the Foreign Service Institute, under the Department of State, the commission authorized the evaluation of the institute's language programs and introductory area study courses (CASE 1964a, 1). Gradually, CASE was paving the way for nonmilitary and, ultimately, nongovernment course evaluations.

1966: TWENTY YEARS OF CASE

The years following Turner's first 10 as director of CASE held the promise of even more growth. A new standardization study of the GED Tests was planned with the help of ETS for 1967, and a revised edition of the *Guide* was to be released in summer 1968. The commission had been in existence for 20 years, and there was no question that what had been established as a temporary operation to help returning veterans had become a permanent and important part of adult education in the United States. Neil Turner's leadership was one of the greatest forces behind that transformation.

NOTES

[1] Prior to signing a contract with Ohio State University, USAFI and the Office of Armed Forces Information and Education had discussed the proposed study with the commission and secured its support.

[2] Today, these are the DANTES Subject Standardized Tests.

[3] Because USAFI had developed the Subject Standardized Tests, it did not use the Comprehensive College Subject Tests, which were intended for use by institutions to evaluate students.

[4] In 1966, the commission decided that the large number of evaluations and the passage of the new GI Bill warranted revision of the 1954 *Guide*.

CHAPTER 6

*End of the
Turner Era*

1967–1974

END OF THE TURNER ERA, 1967–1974

LEAVING A LEGACY:
Turner's Final Years as Director

*T*he final years of Cornelius P. Turner's term as director
saw unprecedented growth in the influence of the
Commission on Accreditation of Service Experiences (CASE).
By the time Turner retired in 1973, acceptance of the GED Tests
was at an all-time high; there were two additional publications of
the *Guide to the Evaluation of Educational Experiences in the Armed
Services* (the *Guide*); and the role of the commission expanded to
include the evaluation of nonmilitary courses. This expanded
role resulted in a name change: the Commission on Educational
Credit (COEC). Befitting his dedication to the commission and
its programs, Turner continued to work for the commission as a
staff consultant after his retirement.

A NEW HIGH:
The Growth of the GED Testing Service
Turner's Capstone

The rapid growth of the GED Testing Service (GEDTS) continued during Turner's final years as director. First, there were the
sheer numbers of examinees: In 1967, more than 218,000 people took the GED Tests; by 1974, that number had almost dou-
bled, to more than 430,000 (CASE 1968, 11; COEC 1975c, Tab
7a). The tests also were more widely accepted than ever before:
A 1969 survey of almost 2,000 higher education institutions
revealed that 91 percent accepted satisfactory GED scores for admission to college (CASE 1969c, 9).

An important administrative practice was established during
this period: In 1971, the first GED administrators' conference was
held at the Mayflower Hotel in Washington, DC. Forty-nine of
the 59 administrators attended the meeting, as did other
staff members, for a total of 90 attendees. The purpose of the

meeting was to "discuss and reach a consensus insofar as possible" on issues such as minimum age for issuance of credentials, testing of 17-year-olds, minimum score requirements, and residence requirements. The conference proved an excellent forum for discussing important policy issues and became one of the most important annual GEDTS events (CASE 1970c, 15; 1971b, 11).

But perhaps the most gratifying event for Turner during these years was the long-awaited acceptance in 1973 of the GED Tests by the California State Department of Education. Previously, California state officials had let the governing boards of the local school districts decide whether to recognize the GED Tests, making California the only state without a uniform GED policy. Since the introduction of the tests in 1946, Turner and others' efforts to bring about a change to California's "no-policy" status had been fruitless. According to Turner, California's superintendent of public instruction from 1963 to 1970 was "a strictly conservative person" who didn't support alternative education options such as the GED Tests. When a new superintendent, Wilson Riles, was appointed, Turner invited him to join the commission (Turner Undated, 7) and began a dialogue about how to get California to endorse the GED Tests. In 1972, Riles secured permission from the California State Board of Education to seek legislation that would enable the state to issue equivalency certificates. The following year (the year of Turner's retirement), the state assembly and state senate passed a bill allowing the superintendent of public instruction to issue a California high school equivalency certificate based on the GED Tests. Then-Governor Ronald Reagan signed this bill into law (Quigley 1991, 37). The passing of this law served "as a capstone to the career of Neil Turner" and meant full implementation of the GED Tests in the United States (CASE 1973b, 4).

But perhaps the most gratifying event for Turner during these years was the long-awaited acceptance in 1973 of the GED Tests by the California State Department of Education.

Spanish-language GED Tests

California's acceptance of the GED Tests was not the only important event during Turner's final years as director. In 1969,

Puerto Ricans in New York and New Jersey requested that the commission develop a Spanish-language version of the GED Tests. In 1960, approximately 860,000 Puerto Ricans were living in the United States; by 1969, that number had increased to 1.5 million. The Puerto Ricans who requested the accommodation argued that non–high school graduate, Spanish-speaking adults in the United States could not qualify for jobs or admission to college because the GED Tests were inaccessible—putting them at an extreme disadvantage. Turner agreed, and at the May 1969 meeting, he asked the commission to consider a Spanish-language version of the GED Tests (CASE 1969c, 4, 11).

The Spanish-language tests were intended for use by all Spanish-speaking adults in the United States, but it was made clear that Puerto Ricans would be the primary audience.

Turner told the commissioners that he had met with officials from both the New Jersey and New York State Departments of Education who "tentatively agreed" that if CASE developed a battery of Spanish-language tests and established adequate norms, New Jersey and New York could issue a high school equivalency certificate based on the tests. He also reported that officials at the Educational Testing Service (ETS) were interested in developing the battery (CASE 1969b, 11).

At the following meeting, in fall 1969, John Moe, program director of ETS, presented a proposal to the commission for the development of the Spanish-language battery. He explained that the development process would begin with a revision by ETS of the English-language GED Tests' specifications, "so that they will be appropriate for application within a Spanish-language culture." A committee of Puerto Rican educators would review the new specifications and make changes accordingly. The committee then would contribute test items, which first would be reviewed by ETS and then by representatives of other Spanish-speaking groups, such as Cubans and Mexican Americans. The Spanish-language tests were intended for use by all Spanish-speaking adults in the United States, but it was made clear that Puerto Ricans would be the primary audience. In his proposal, Moe stated, "It should be emphasized that the tests will be developed even though the reviews by Cuban and Mexican-American groups may indicate that the items developed are not appropriate for application within their groups. It is felt that there is sufficient need within the Puerto Rican community alone to warrant the development of the tests." The items created by the Puerto Rican educators would be assembled into pretests, which would be administered to approximately 4,000 high school seniors in Puerto Rico and then compiled into two forms of the tests. The forms would be administered again to Puerto Rican high school seniors for scaling, norming, and equating (ensuring that the items were "psychologically 'indigenous' to the culture of the people") (CASE 1969c, 5–7).

With the commission's approval, ETS began development of the Spanish-language GED Tests (funding was provided by GEDTS), with distribution planned for late summer 1971. Each battery would include six tests: the first five would parallel their English counterparts, and the sixth would be an "English as a Second Language" test. The analysis of Test 6 pretest items showed they were too difficult for Puerto Rican students in the pretest group. Even though states had indicated that they would not use Test 6 for decisions about equivalency certification (rather, it would be used to provide additional information to employers or college officials), Test 6 was revised to reflect a level of difficulty appropriate to the Puerto Rican English curriculum. The first Spanish-language GED Tests were administered on schedule in August 1971. By the end of the year, 2,500 Spanish-speaking residents had been tested, and 22 state departments of education had adopted policies regarding the new version (CASE 1970b, 4; CASE 1970c, 11; CASE 1971c, 2).

At CASE's November 1970 meeting, the commission voted to recommend that Spanish-language GED Tests be administered with the same age and residency requirements as the English-language tests. It also recommended that the name of the equivalency certificates include the word "Spanish" in parentheses, which raised concerns among some examinees. At the fall 1971 meeting, Turner told the commission that he had been visited by representatives of the Spanish-speaking community in New York City who felt that by including "Spanish" on the certificates, the commission had inadvertently "placed a stigma" on them and "downgraded [the certificate's] value." As a result, New York State changed its policy and deleted "Spanish" from the certificates. Acknowledging that it never intended to stigmatize the Spanish-language GED Tests or the examinees, the commission voted to change its recommended policy so that certificates for the English-language and Spanish-language tests would be the same (CASE 1970c, 11; CASE 1971b, 12).

GED in Canada

Another significant event during Turner's final years as director was the introduction of the GED Tests in Canada. Originally, the Minister of Education in Nova Scotia requested permission to use the civilian restricted forms of the tests as the basis for issuing a "Nova Scotia High School Equivalency Diploma" to adult residents who had not completed high school. Much as the GED Tests in the United States grew from the need to accommodate veterans, Nova Scotia first intended to use the tests to accommodate retiring Canadian naval personnel. In a letter to Turner, Turney Manzer, "father" of the Canadian GED Tests and Nova Scotia's first GED administrator, wrote: "We . . . do not have suitable test instruments such as your GED Tests to assess the achievement of [the naval] personnel" (Quigley 1991, 37, quoting Manzer). Curriculum specialists in Nova Scotia determined that the GED Tests were an appropriate measure of educational achievement of English-speaking residents and could be used just as they were. After reviewing the proposed policy and procedures for administration of the tests, as well as the security conditions under which the tests would be stocked and administered, the commission approved the request at its spring 1969 meeting (CASE 1969a, 2). The first Canada GED Tests were administered on 30 September 1969 at the Nova Scotia Institute of Technology (Quigley 1987, 6).

Other provinces soon followed suit. However, the expansion of the GED program in Canada did not parallel its systematic and

rapid growth in the United States. The expansion was less organized and slower—at least in part because of existing Canadian
credentialing programs, and Adult Basic Education programs in
particular. As Allan Quigley explained,

> Provinces and territories entered with an understanding
> of the GED as an alternative to their own curriculum-
> based adult basic education institutional programs . . . .
> Canada entered the GED for reasons of promoting better
> jobs, improved educational access, and personal satisfac-
> tion—similar to the United States. But, at the social pol-
> icy level, the GED was not explicitly seen as a program
> for rehabilitation or transition. It was and still is seen as a
> test of general knowledge as acquired by adults—an
> alternative to adult basic education.

Consequently, adult basic education programs were "much better known and, perhaps as a result . . . [were] often held as more
'valid' than GED Tests among adult educators and secondary institutions." The GED in Canada thus "became known and established through an informal network of communications
among provincial civil servants and politicians" (Quigley 1991,
38, 39–40). This network, though slower, succeeded in getting
the word out to other provinces. In 1970, Saskatchewan was
granted authorization to use the tests (CASE 1970a, 2); in 1971,
Prince Edward Island joined; Manitoba in 1972; British
Columbia in 1973; New Brunswick and Newfoundland in
1974; Northwest Territories in 1975; Yukon Territory in 1976;
and Alberta in 1981 (GEDTS 1993, 65). Ontario and Quebec
were the only remaining Canadian provinces that had not
adopted the GED Tests.[1]

Although most of Canada adopted the GED Tests, it did so with
adaptations. Over the years, several changes were made in the administration and content of the tests to suit Canadian requirements and culture. For example, Canada has a standard minimum
passing score of 45 for every province and territory, whereas in
the United States, each state can set its own minimum passing
scores (as long as they exceed the minimum standard set by
GEDTS). Canada also created a series of grade-level equivalents

to test scores when Nova Scotia adopted the GED Tests in 1969. These equivalents of grade IX, X, XI, and XII were assigned depending on the GED recipient's score. Allan Quigley described these equivalents as "an apparent attempt to accommodate Nova Scotia's desire to meet the lower than XII standards of licensing boards and vocational or technical training schools." Assigning grade-level equivalents meant that GEDTS had to gather lower grade normative data, a practice it eventually discontinued. GEDTS never attempted to stop provinces from using the grade-level equivalents, but it did "discourage the use of grade levels since high school equivalency . . . should mean the equivalent 'sum total' of four years of high school" (Quigley 1987, 7).

Another important adaptation concerned the social studies test. As early as 1972, there was concern that the content of the U.S. social studies test was unfair to Canadian GED examinees (even though Canadian examinees scored higher than their U.S. counterparts on the test). To address this concern, GEDTS originally proposed to revise the exam so it would be appropriate for both Canadian and American test takers. But this idea was readily rejected. As Quigley observed, "Perhaps this notion was doomed as comparing apples and oranges; perhaps it was naïve in its underestimation of Canadian insistence that Canada is unique; or perhaps the Washington attempt to create a one-size-fits-all test for Canada and the United States actually meant a test that suited the United States mostly and Canada only minimally." Regardless of the reason, Canada set out to create a social studies test that was uniquely Canadian. The result was the creation in 1978 of six new forms of the social studies test (Quigley 1987, 13). Without this important change, Quigley observed, the "GED would probably have died out in Canada and surely never would have been taken up by Alberta or Ontario in the form used across the United States" (2000, 3).

Perhaps [revising the social studies test to make it appropriate for both Canadian and American test takers] was doomed as comparing apples and oranges . . . or perhaps the Washington attempt to create a one-size-fits-all test for Canada and the United States actually meant a test that suited the United States mostly and Canada only minimally.

—B. Allan Quigley

By the early 1980s, Canada had nearly completed its nationwide conversion to an all metric system. The science and mathematics tests thus were revised to include metric units. The guidelines for metrication in education that were established by the Council of Ministers of Education were sent to GEDTS with a request for appropriate revisions. By fall 1984, the Canadian series had the first two metric versions of the science and mathematics tests (Quigley 1987, 15).

French-language GED Tests

The introduction of the GED Tests in Canada led to another new development. When New Brunswick requested permission to join the Canadian GED testing program, it did so on the condition that a French-language version of the tests be developed. The rationale was clear: Approximately 25 percent of the New Brunswick population spoke French. In other provinces, such as Quebec, the percentage was even higher (Quigley 1991, 39). If other provinces were to make use of the GED Tests, a French-language version would have to be developed. The commission supported the idea but told the New Brunswick government that the American Council on Education (ACE) could not fund the project. Because a French-language test would not be used extensively in the United States, it would be difficult to "sell" the idea of a French-language version to past sponsors (such as the Veterans' Administration [VA] and the Department of Defense [DoD]). New Brunswick offered to fund the project and ACE accepted, with the understanding that ACE would copyright the tests and assume ownership (CASE 1972a, 17). It was further decided that ETS would develop two batteries of the tests at an estimated cost of $160,810—including standardizing and equating—and deliver them by 1 September 1974. At the October 1972 CASE meeting, the commission unanimously agreed to accept the funds for the project (CASE 1972b, 25). The development of the French-language GED Tests was underway.

A SECOND LOOK:
Studying the GED Tests

Measuring the Success of GED Recipients

As the GED testing program grew, so did the need for closer scrutiny of testing procedures. To guarantee the program's continued success, the commission would have to ensure that it met the needs of both adult learners and educators who relied on the tests as a standard of measurement. Turner and the commission were particularly concerned about whether the GED Tests predicted success in college— especially as increasing numbers of colleges and universities were accepting students with GED equivalency certificates and diplomas. In 1969, a study was proposed that would ascertain whether the tests were valid measures of potential college performance, how the program helped nontraditional candidates, and the impact of nontraditional students on the colleges they attended[2] (CASE 1969b, 8–9).

In 1969, a study was proposed that would ascertain whether the tests were valid measures of potential college performance, how the program helped nontraditional candidates, and the impact of nontraditional students on the colleges they attended.

The study surveyed a sampling of more than 1,300 GED graduates from 19 four-year institutions and 10 junior colleges, using the students' overall grade point averages as the primary measure of success in college. The results were favorable: The tests could be "appropriately used for prediction of college success" (CASE 1971b, 9).

Perhaps more interesting were the in-depth interviews conducted with 30 students who were asked why they had left high school and why they had decided to take the tests, among other questions. Most cited the need to help support their families as their reason for leaving school, and half said they took the tests specifically to gain admission to college. When asked about the impact of the GED Tests on their lives, one student wrote, "The GED was a dream come true. I doubt if I would have given serious thought to attending high school for even the one year required to earn sufficient credit for a diploma. The opportunity to receive a diploma this way has definitely been the ticket to success for many others also" (CASE 1971a, 5).

Changing Specifications

At the April 1973 CASE meeting, Neil Turner questioned whether a shorter version of the GED Tests should be created. At the time, the GED Tests required two days of administration; as

P

95

such, they were the only widely used educational tests that required more than one day of administration. Since the GED
testing program had begun, several state departments of education had requested a shorter version; after all, the Scholastic
Aptitude Test required only about five hours to complete, and
the American College Testing (ACT) battery required four
hours. The possibility of preparing a shorter
version of the GED Tests was to be presented to the state administrators at the an-
ince the GED testing nual GED conference in June 1973. Turner
program had begun, several suggested, and the commission agreed, that
state departments of a committee be appointed to review the
issue after GEDTS concluded the confer-
education had requested a ence and gathered state administrators'
shorter version; after all, opinions. Based on the advice of the admin-
the Scholastic Aptitude Test istrators and testing experts from ETS, the
required only about five committee would make a recommendation
hours to complete, and the to the commission at its fall 1973 meeting
(CASE 1973a, 13).
American College Testing
(ACT) battery required At that meeting, the committee proposed
four hours. that a feasibility study be conducted to determine whether the GED Tests reflected cur-
rent high school curricula and whether the current format was
the most effective method of measuring the "lasting outcomes"
of a high school education. The study would be used to formulate the specifications for construction of the new versions of the
GED Tests (CASE 1973b, 17).

The commission solicited proposals from both ACT and ETS to
conduct individual studies. With information gleaned from these
studies, the committee presented its recommendations at the
commission meeting the following September. Essentially, it proposed to keep the five tests (writing skills, social studies, science,
reading skills, and mathematics) but to shorten each so that most
examinees could complete the battery in about six hours. The
committee's report included detailed specifications for each of
the five tests that were similar to previous specifications. What
was different, however, was the inclusion of an "International
Characteristics" specification that read, in part:

Since the GED testing program has achieved an international stature, it is imperative that the tests be developed with no intentional English-speaking cultural, economic, or political bias. Particular efforts should be directed towards the development of the social studies and reading tests to ensure no alienation of examinees of other countries, especially Canada (COEC 1974c, 24).

Once again, the testing program proved sensitive to cultural diversity—an issue that would become even more significant as the immigrant adult population increased.

As a result of the feasibility study, the commission thoroughly revised the GED Tests. ETS was awarded the contract to develop 12 forms of the new tests; 11 were introduced in 1978 as the second generation of tests (see Chapter 7). The 12th form was converted into the first two forms of the *Official GED Practice Tests,* which were introduced in 1979 to give potential GED examinees the opportunity to pretest their skills and knowledge. Introduction of the practice tests also influenced the curriculum of GED preparatory classes by giving instructors an accurate sample of test questions and a better understanding of the skills measured by the tests (Whitney 2000b, 5).

OUTSIDE INFLUENCES:
Military Evaluations

1968 *Guide*

While GEDTS adapted to the changes in adult education and standardized testing, the Military Evaluations program adapted to the changes in military education. In 1968, the program published a new edition of the *Guide.* Like the editions that preceded it, this *Guide* was prepared in response to outside influences—the 1966 GI Bill, in particular. This legislation provided education assistance to those who served in the post–Korean Conflict era and the Vietnam War era. The program became effective 1 June 1966 and was available to veterans who served after 31 January 1955 (Montgomery 1994, 50). As before, thousands of veterans were expected to return to the classroom. Changing technology was another reason for publishing the new *Guide*. Technological advances had caused rapid changes in service training programs, which necessitated new or revised recommendations for educational credit. Already, many of the recommendations in the 1954 *Guide* were obsolete (ACE 1974, xiii). For these reasons, members of the American Association of Collegiate Registrars and Admissions Officers unanimously adopted a resolution requesting that the commission prepare a third edition of the *Guide* (Wilson 1966, 2–3).

The new edition contained descriptions and recommendations for more than 8,800 programs of instruction, compared to approximately 3,000 programs in 1954 and 1,000 programs in 1946 (CASE 1968, 5). And the recommendations were used. In a 1969 survey of almost 2,000 colleges, 73 percent reported that they granted credit based on CASE's recommendations for learning acquired through formal service school training (CASE 1969d, 3).

Changing Environment and the 1974 *Guide*

The 1966 GI Bill wasn't the only outside influence in the late 1960s and early 1970s to alter the landscape of the military. At the May 1970 CASE meeting, military representatives began presenting concerns about the future of adult education in general and the role of education in the military in particular. That year, DoD announced a move toward an all-volunteer force; by 1 July 1973, the draft would be eliminated. This caused grave concern within the military in terms of recruiting. Essentially, the services would be competing against private businesses and organizations for employees. This new approach presented an uncertain future. As Deputy Assistant Secretary of Defense for Education Richard Rose observed, "We are relying upon competing in the manpower race . . . . We are obligated to play the game according to new rules" (CASE 1973a, 3–4). Surveys of potential recruits consistently indicated the importance of educational opportunities when considering enlistment or a career in the military, with income playing a secondary role. With the cost of tuition increasing, men and women were willing to forgo a high salary if they could offset the expense of education and earn a four-year degree (CASE 1972b, 4). To make the armed forces more appealing, the military therefore had to "provide greater incentives for 'in-service' education"—and it wanted the commission to help (CASE 1970b, 1).

One of the military's primary concerns was CASE's recommendations for vocational and technical courses. In the 1968 *Guide*, rather than recommend specific credit hours for these courses (as it did for other service school training), the commission recommended that students be required to demonstrate their skills in the workshop or laboratory of the college to which they were applying. The college could determine the amount of credit to award based on that demonstration. The military saw this as a significant obstacle to the continuing education of servicemembers seeking credit for vocational-technical courses. The military was particularly concerned because increasingly, it was emphasizing this type of training, as well as associate degree courses (CASE 1972a, 17–18).

When the issue was raised at the May 1972 commission meeting, Neil Turner explained that when the 1968 *Guide* was being prepared, he had discussed with the American Association of Community and Junior Colleges[3] what the appropriate type of recommendations for these courses should be. The question had been raised because credit recommendations in the 1954 *Guide* were almost exclusively for academic courses. Credit was rarely recommended for vocational or technical courses (the bulk of military coursework), so colleges and universities rarely awarded credit for such training (Sullivan 1999). To resolve this situation, a committee appointed by the American Association of Community and Junior Colleges recommended that credit for vocational-technical training be determined based on a demonstration of skills. However, given the tremendous growth since 1968 in the number of community colleges that offered associate degrees in vocational-technical areas, Turner agreed that this

The committee recommended that CASE publish another edition of the Guide, *which would include semester-hour credit recommendations for vocational-technical military training at the community and junior college level, as well as recommendations for new and revised baccalaureate- and graduate-level training programs developed since publication of the 1968* Guide.

policy should be reexamined. A committee was appointed to evaluate the current policy (CASE 1972a, 17–18).

The following October, the committee recommended that CASE publish another edition of the *Guide*, which would include semester-hour credit recommendations for vocational-technical military training at the community and junior college level, as well as recommendations for new and revised baccalaureate- and graduate-level training programs developed since publication of the 1968 *Guide*. The commission voted unanimously to authorize CASE staff to start work on the new edition, which would become the 1974 *Guide*. Eugene Sullivan, formerly program coordinator for academic affairs of the Maryland State Board for Community Colleges, was hired to direct the project, and a contract with DoD, the VA, and the U.S. Office of Education was secured to fund it (CASE 1972b, 21–23).

But the need for vocational-technical evaluations and recommendations was not the only reason CASE decided to prepare another edition of the *Guide*. Many active-duty servicemembers were seeking college credit for formal military courses they had taken soon after completing training. Recommendations therefore had to be kept as current as possible. In addition, CASE already had been made aware of a vast number of additional courses initiated by the military since publication of the 1968 *Guide*. It was clear that ongoing evaluations would be necessary to meet growing demand (ACE 1974, xiii; Sullivan 1999).

Under the direction of Sullivan, a 90-day planning phase and a nine-month evaluation phase were mapped out, resulting in the first system of continuous evaluation of military courses, rather than the "episodic end product" it had been before. Annual supplements would be published using the new technology of "computerized composition," and course information would be stored electronically. The *Guide* had entered the computer age. The 1974 *Guide* also marked the beginning of site visits for all military evaluations. Previously, site visits had been conducted only for the evaluation of high-level service schools. But with the advent of more sophisticated technology and the increasing numbers of students, onsite evaluations became necessary for all courses (ACE 1974, xiii–xiv). ACE thus entered a new era of military evaluations—one that was more comprehensive, more sophisticated, and more responsive to the needs of the military.

At about the same time the military moved to an all-volunteer force, another difficult change was taking place. In 1972, DoD faced a budget crunch that required it to cut back several of its programs. The United States Armed Forces Institute (USAFI) was one of them. As a result, all of the testing, scoring, and transcript services of USAFI were "homeless." At the request of DoD's Richard Rose, the Navy became the executive agency in charge of finding ways to administer the USAFI services. And the Defense Activity for Non-Traditional Education Support (DANTES) was born.

Headquartered in Pensacola, Florida, DANTES contracted out the services previously provided by USAFI to organizations such as ETS, ACT, the College Board, and ACE. It was a difficult time for those involved with education in the military. USAFI had been a cornerstone in the adult education community—and the military—for more than three decades. Although its programs continued through other organizations, USAFI's dissolution marked the end of an era (Geiken 2000).

NEW TENSIONS:
Community College of the Air Force

Prior to publication of the 1974 *Guide*, the Air Force introduced a plan that would prove one of the most difficult challenges to ACE's longstanding partnership with the military. At a May 1972 commission meeting, Robert Quick, an Air Force representative, reported on the establishment of a department called the Community College of the Air Force (CCAF). The purpose of CCAF was to evaluate and make credit recommendations for vocational and occupational types of Air Force training and to publish the recommendations in a book similar to the 1968 *Guide*. The Air Force was seeking approval from the North Central Association of Colleges and Secondary Schools for courses offered at the bases of Lowry and Chanute. It also planned to seek authorization from Congress to issue the associates degree. Regardless of whether CCAF became a degree-granting institution, Quick reported that it would evaluate vocational-technical training and make recommendations (CASE 1972a, 18).

The Air Force had briefed DoD, the U.S. Commissioner of Education, and the National Advisory Council on Education—but not CASE—on the plan. And how did the commissioners react? The minutes from the 1972 meeting state simply, "There was some surprise and concern expressed by commission members at the Air Force plan." This was clearly an understatement. Having worked so closely with all branches of the military for so many years, the commission undoubtedly was dismayed that the Air Force would establish a unit to replicate the functions of the commission without first consulting ACE and CASE officers. Yet at the time of this meeting, the issue of evaluating vocational-technical courses for semester-hour credit had just been raised; it therefore could be argued that the Air Force was simply trying to fill a gap that the commission had not addressed. However, when asked how the Air Force would respond if CASE were to change its policy, Quick replied, "Should the commission decide to issue recommendations with regard to vocational-technical training, the Air Force might report both recommendations to colleges in which Air Force personnel might enroll" (CASE 1972a, 18).

An early indication of Neil Turner's lack of enthusiasm can be inferred from his comments at the next meeting, in fall 1972, at which the commission announced Turner's impending retirement. He used the "Director's Report"—usually a summary of the commission's activities during the previous six months—to recount the rich history of CASE: its establishment, its accomplishments, and its future directions. He talked about the creation in the early 1940s of the USAFI Advisory Committee—predecessor of the commission—and how, at that time, the committee "made one very fundamental agreement with the military concerning the responsibility of civilian education and the military in matters of academic credit." This agreement was that the granting of diplomas or degree credits was

solely the prerogative of the individual high school, state department of education, college, or university; and that "the Armed
Forces, except for their degree-granting institutions, shall not
make credit recommendations or attempt to influence civilian education institutions in the matter of granting credit for service educational experience." Though Turner did not mention CCAF in
his statement, it seems certain that he was subtly reminding the
Air Force that by establishing an evaluation and credit recommendation unit, it was violating a fundamental tenet of the military's agreement with the academic community (CASE 1972b, 7).

Later in the same meeting, Robert Quick presented more detailed
information about CCAF. He explained that, given the advent of
the all-volunteer force, continuing education was an important recruitment tool. CCAF therefore had been established as a base for
recordkeeping—an important component of the guidance and
counseling of personnel in the development of their educational
and military careers. CCAF would issue transcripts that would list
training completed as well as the number of credits awarded.
Quick reported that CCAF already had received the approval of
the Southern Association of Colleges and Schools and that it was
seeking the approval of the North Central Association of Colleges
and Secondary Schools (CASE 1972b, 13).

Following Quick's report, commissioners expressed their
appreciation of the Air Force's need "to undertake the establishment of an educational program to encourage enlistees in
the all-volunteer Armed Forces." But they also expressed their
concern. First, civilian education already had established institutions and programs that provided the necessary educational
opportunities. The commission cited the establishment of the
Servicemen's (later Servicemembers) Opportunity Colleges—
a consortium of colleges and universities created in 1972 by the
American Association of Community and Junior Colleges in
conjunction with DoD "to increase significantly the enrollment
of Vietnam era veterans and active duty service personnel in college programs."[4] This network made special provisions to serve
military men and women—including offering on-base degree
programs, waiving residency requirements, and facilitating the
transfer of credit between institutions when servicemembers

were transferred to other bases (Anderson 1997, 6). Second, commissioners were concerned that if the Air Force evaluated its own programs, it likely would cause confusion and misunderstanding among civilian education institutions. Because CASE had agreed to evaluate vocational-technical training programs for all the services and to prepare a *Guide* for use by community colleges in granting credit for military training, there was "no reason for the Air Force to enter the credit picture" (CASE 1972b, 13).

The commissioners also expressed concern regarding CCAF's proposed transcripts. Quick had presented a sample transcript that listed training programs completed followed by a number of credits. Quick explained that these numbers did not reflect semester-hour recommendations "but merely credits toward the [Air Force's] career education certificate." The commissioners were concerned that college admissions officers would misinterpret the credit notations as CCAF's credit recommendations and therefore "vigorously opposed any entries being placed on transcripts indicating the amount of credit which might be granted by an institution." Further, they said that "the transcripts would, in the end, be a great disservice to Air Force personnel and to civilian colleges by causing confusion and misunderstanding of the prerogatives of granting credit" (CASE 1972b, 13–14).

*C*ASE's objections to CCAF intensified when . . . it was announced that CCAF had submitted an application for institutional accreditation to the Commission on Occupational Education Institutions of the Southern Association of Colleges and Schools.

To allay the commission's fears, Major General Oliver Lewis, of the Air Force's Office of Deputy Chief of Staff for Personnel, assured members that CCAF "would not evaluate or recommend the granting of credit for Air Force training programs or take any action in regard to the matter of credit which would be contrary to the long-standing agreement between civilian education and the military." Yet the conflict was far from over. To formalize its concerns, the commission proposed a resolution to "confirm our objections to the Air Force recommending credit directly or indirectly through transcripts of its community college." The resolution also stated that the commission would "intensify its efforts to provide appropriate service to the military in recognizing and validating military training and experiences . . . and, further, that this commission work with the Air Force to provide appropriate validation and recognition of training experiences in its new role in career education." The resolution was adopted unanimously (CASE 1972b, 13–14).

CASE's objections to CCAF intensified when, at its November 1973 meeting, it was announced that CCAF had submitted an application for institutional accreditation to the Commission on Occupational Education Institutions of the Southern Association of Colleges and Schools. Because the Commission on Occupational Education Institutions recently had been admitted to membership in the Federation of Regional Accrediting Commissions of Higher Education, its accreditation now had the national endorsement of other regional commissions. Essentially, the Commission on Occupational Education Institutions' accreditation of CCAF would make the college a recognized institution. CASE therefore decided to request that the Commission on Occupational Education Institutions and the Federation of Regional Accrediting Commissions of Higher Education clarify the meaning of accreditation for an institution "as different as CCAF." The commission also passed another resolution stating that if CCAF did become accredited, it no longer would evaluate Air Force courses. If CCAF were not accredited, the commission would evaluate all Air Force course offerings but would require that credit-hour recommendations on CCAF transcripts carry a notation that the credit hours were recommended by CASE. This resolution was not unusual or particularly punitive, but the justification for the resolution made the commission's disapproval clear:

> . . . Whereas, CASE has objected to the practice of the Community College of the Air Force circulating its transcripts, because it is an unaccredited institution, and Whereas, CCAF is not an education institution in the traditional meaning of the term, being primarily a record keeping and course conversion system . . .

If there had been any doubt before about the commission's position on the issue, there certainly wasn't now (CASE 1973b, 11).

Despite CASE's disapproval, CCAF was accredited in December 1973 by the Commission on Occupational Education Institutions as an occupational education (non-degree-granting) institution. At its spring 1974 meeting, CASE agreed to accept CCAF's accreditation and, in the 1974 *Guide*, to recommend that colleges and universities use CCAF's catalog and transcript when granting vocational-certificate credit. Because CCAF's accreditation recognized only vocational-certificate courses, the Air Force still needed evaluations of and recommendations for its associate degree– and upper baccalaureate-level courses. Therefore, the commission agreed to evaluate these courses and make recommendations accordingly. The issue was far from resolved, but the Air Force and the commission had reached an amicable resolution—at least for the time being (COEC 1974b, 9–10).

Despite CASE's disapproval, CCAF was accredited in December 1973 by the Commission on Occupational Education Institutions as an occupational education (non-degree-granting) institution.

A BROADER TASK:
The Commission's Expansion

Perhaps the most significant event for CASE during the final years of Turner's directorship was the expansion of evaluations to include nonmilitary courses. In November 1969, the commission discussed at length the idea of evaluating and making credit recommendations for educational experiences gained through training completed by civilians. Turner told the commission that CASE staff had received requests for such recommendations from a few universities and suggested that it might be time to broaden the mission of CASE to include such a service. The commission members agreed and unanimously passed a resolution to recommend that ACE "take whatever steps necessary to ascertain the desirability of changing the mission of the commission from the evaluation of service experiences to the broader task of evaluating for accrediting purposes noncollegial/nonuniversity experiences, including service experiences" (CASE 1969c, 13–14).

Turner wasn't the only one to consider evaluating civilian training programs. The Commission on Non-Traditional Study, which was formed in 1971 under the sponsorship of the College Entrance Examination Board and ETS and which was funded by the Carnegie Foundation, had a similar idea. The "Gould Commission" (its chairman was Samuel B. Gould) closely examined nontraditional education in all its forms and made recommendations for future directions. Published in 1973, the Gould Commission's final report, *Diversity by Design,* proved a seminal work in modern adult education that would serve as a guide to ACE and others striving to promote adult access to higher education. The report contained 57 recommendations on every facet of nontraditional education, including alternate systems and technologies, and became the foundation for the next two decades of change in lifelong learning.[5] Among its recommendations was the proposal that the techniques used by CASE for evaluating and recommending college credit recommendations for military service "be used in other alternate systems to establish credit and other equivalencies for courses offered by government, industry, and other sponsors." It also recommended that ACE "look into the matter, possibly through a broadly representative committee, and produce an organizational and operational plan" (Commission on Non-Traditional Study 1973, 89, 90). ACE already was doing just that.

While the Gould Commission continued to deliberate, Turner promoted the idea of expanding the commission's operation to include noncollegiate civilian evaluations. Turner initiated a grassroots effort by encouraging colleges and universities that had asked the commission to evaluate nonmilitary courses to contact their regional accrediting associations; his hope was that the impetus for change would derive from educators, not from CASE (CASE 1970b, 12).

Turner also informed CASE and ACE leadership of the Gould Commission's deliberations and encouraged ACE's participation.

As Jerry Miller explained, "In keeping the commission and the president and board of ACE abreast of the Gould Commission's activities and advancing his own similar ideas, Turner was in his clever and characteristic way laying the conceptual ground and building receptivity for the expansion of the commission's activities under the direction of his successors" (Miller 2000, 2). In his October 1972 presentation to the commission (after he had announced his retirement), Turner explained that the increased number of external degree programs meant that "one agency in the country must undertake the responsibility for evaluating civilian educational programs." Turner knew which agency this should be: "This commission has the confidence of educators and the know-how to do this job. It would seem to be not only reasonable but essential that the commission be assigned the task of evaluating civilian education programs" (CASE 1972b, 12).

ACE and the commission wanted to make it clear that the commission's new responsibilities did not diminish the importance of the armed services to COEC's future growth.

In May 1973, Turner resigned, and Jerry W. Miller was appointed director of the commission—its third. Previously, Miller had worked for five years for the National Commission on Accrediting (whose director, Frank Dickey, was serving as chair of CASE) and for four years for the Southern Association of Colleges and Schools. A well-respected leader with solid experience in accreditation, Miller was well prepared to continue Turner's legacy (CASE 1973a, 1).

ACE President Heyns directed Miller to study the Gould Commission recommendations and develop a plan for activities to be conducted under the auspices of CASE. The commission would review the plan and then send it to Heyns and the ACE board for approval. In response, Miller wrote a paper outlining the first concrete proposals for the expansion of CASE. Generally, the paper asserted that ACE should "utilize its resources and prestige to enhance and encourage flexibility in learning opportunities" and that the activities and experience of CASE put it in a unique position in terms of the expansion of nontraditional educational experiences. Specifically, it proposed that the commission's name be changed "to more accurately reflect its current and proposed actions." Second, it recommended that formal course evaluation activities be expanded to nonmilitary government agencies that sponsored educational programs. Third, the paper argued that the commission should be given authority to convene committees and task forces to recommend to CASE actions regarding: (1) the evaluation of courses offered by business and industry and other sponsors; (2) responsibility for making national recommendations to colleges and universities regarding policies and procedures for evaluating learning achieved through informal learning experiences; (3) responsibility for the evaluation of certification, licensure, and registration credentials for the purpose of establishing credit recommendations; and (4) responsibility for the evaluation of courses offered by home study schools (Miller 2000, 2; CASE 1973b, 10).

The paper was presented to the commission at its fall 1973 meeting—Turner's first as staff consultant and Jerry Miller's first as CASE's director.[6] The commission approved the paper's proposals, as did the ACE Board of Directors at its January 1974 meeting. Thus, the expansion of CASE officially began (CASE 1973b, 10).

In March 1974, the commission had conducted its first meeting as an expanded organization with a new name. The Commission on Accreditation of Service Experiences became the Commission on Educational Credit (COEC); the CASE staff became the Office on Educational Credit. ACE President Roger Heyns outlined COEC's expanded role, commenting on the Board of Directors' approval of the commission's "gradual expansion" and the unique "delegated responsibility" of COEC with regard to credit recommendations. But Heyns emphasized that the commission would continue to have "a very heavy commitment to serve the military." This was important. ACE and the commission wanted to make it clear that the commission's new responsibilities did not diminish the importance of the armed services to COEC's future growth. The military had been the backbone of the commission for almost 30 years, and ACE had a keen interest in keeping the services as a close ally in the battle to gain increased acceptance of nontraditional learning (COEC 1974a, 3).

At the same meeting, an important project was proposed that would serve as the basis for OEC's evaluation of all civilian, non-collegiate training for the next 25 years and beyond. Jointly sponsored by the New York Board of Regents and ACE, the Project on the Evaluation of Non-Collegiate Sponsored Instruction[7] was intended to determine the types of courses and programs that could be reasonably evaluated, as well as the criteria, policies, and procedures to guide the evaluation process. The project also was charged with making the arrangements necessary among institutions and agencies at the state and national levels to evaluate courses on a national basis. Finally, the project would establish an effective system to inform colleges and universities of evaluation procedures and credit recommendations. This last objective was critical. As when military credit recommendations had been introduced, it was clear that to encourage institutions' acceptance of the civilian recommendations, faculty and other institutional decision makers had to be acquainted with the criteria, policies, and procedures for conducting evaluations (COEC 1974a, 5–6).

At the September 1974 COEC meeting, John Sullivan, project director, presented a set of "Interim Evaluative Criteria and Procedures" for the evaluation of noncollegiate educational programs. It outlined the types of organizations and businesses that could submit programs for evaluation (private industry, government agencies, labor unions, voluntary associations, and professional associations) and the types of programs that would be evaluated (those conducted on a formal basis and with official approval of the sponsoring organization). Essentially, the procedures served as an initial operations manual for the new project (COEC 1974c, 10–13).

BEYOND DETAILS

In looking at the expansion of the commission's responsibilities, it is easy to get lost in the details—particularly given the increasing number of projects. By the end of 1974, and largely because of the efforts of Neil Turner, the commission was responsible for one of the world's largest testing programs, the

nationwide evaluation of military courses and the most comprehensive course guide in the country, and the evaluation of business and industry training. Guiding all of these efforts was the
commission's overarching philosophy to create greater access for
the adult learner.

In a paper on the commission's expanded role, Jerry Miller wrote
that the main objectives of COEC were to:

(1) encourage and promote diversity and pluralism in
postsecondary education; (2) promote a system of education credit which treats all learning, regardless of where it
takes place, as equitably as possible in the system of social
rewards for individual knowledge and competencies; (3)
encourage flexibility in postsecondary learning opportunities; (4) encourage a high level of quality in postsecondary education efforts; and (5) to encourage close
working relationships between traditional and nontraditional education (Miller Undated, 5).

These same principles had guided the commission in 1946 and
continue to guide it today.

NOTES

[1] Ontario adopted the tests in 1996 (see Chapter 8). As of this printing, Quebec
still had not adopted the tests.

[2] The study originally was intended to examine both the GED Tests and the
College Level Examination Program (CLEP), a new program sponsored by the
College Entrance Examination Board that included the Comprehensive College
Tests. The Comprehensive College Tests were developed by ETS in the early
1960s to replace the college-level GED Tests (see Chapter 5). In 1970, the CLEP
portion of the study was canceled because a significant number of students had
not received college credit based on the CLEP exams.

[3] Prior to February 1972, the American Association of Community and Junior
Colleges had been the American Association of Junior Colleges.

[4] The American Association of State Colleges and Universities played a significant
role in the establishment in 1974 of SOC for four-year institutions.

[5] Twenty-five years after the publication of *Diversity by Design*, every one of the
Commission on Non-Traditional Study's recommendations had been "accepted in
one way or another; either completed or in process" (Nolan 1998, 115, quoting
Gould).

[6] As a consultant, Turner's role was important. Jerry Miller remembered Turner's insights and advice during this time as "invaluable." Wrote Miller, "His manner was

totally supportive. He never passed up the opportunity to publicly praise the actions of his successors. He was totally enthused about the burgeoning activities of the office. He was a great help, and it was a real joy to have his continuing participation." [7] This project later would become the Program on Non-Collegiate Sponsored Instruction (PONSI), which evaluated formal training courses offered by business, industry, organizations, and government agencies. Today, it is known as the College Credit Recommendation Service, or CREDIT.

CHAPTER 7

Revolution,
Delicate Relationships,
and New Beginnings

1975 – 1985

REVOLUTION, DELICATE RELATIONSHIPS, AND NEW BEGINNINGS, 1975–1985

REVOLUTIONARY CELL:
The Push for Nontraditional Learning

*I*n 1975, Congress eliminated the educational benefits that the GI Bill had provided for new enlistees.[1] In many ways, this act set the tone for most interactions between the military and the Commission on Educational Credit (COEC) for at least the next five years. When the draft had ended a few years earlier, the services had used the lure of GI Bill education benefits to compete for recruits against higher-salary jobs in the private sector. And although the military branches had tuition assistance plans, the elimination of GI Bill–funded benefits heightened concern that the military would lose recruits. There also was concern that men and women who *were* recruited would not have the same educational opportunities as previous enlistees. The military had made education a priority for its personnel but now was less able to support it. By 1978, the Air Force had experienced a "notable decline" in voluntary education enrollments (COEC 1978a, 6).

*I*t was anticipated that elimination of the GI Bill education benefits in 1975 would result in an average enrollment decrease of 18 to 25 percent between 1980 and 1987.

Higher education officials also were concerned. The GI Bill entitled veterans to 36 full months of education benefits that could be used within the decade subsequent to their leaving the military. Since World War II, more than 15 million people had benefited from the bill. It was anticipated that elimination of the education benefits in 1975 would result in an average enrollment decrease of 18 to 25 percent between 1980 and 1987 (Coldren 1975, 1, 4).

Higher education provided on military installations was under fire as well. A 1977 article in *Change* magazine blasted college and university programs on military bases as being "so poor that they would be classified as diploma mills were they subject to close educational scrutiny." The authors argued that financial incentives encouraged institutions to offer sub-par academic programs at military bases "far from parent campuses" and with little academic oversight. They further stated that the military, concerned primarily with career advancement, allowed these education programs to operate "regardless of substance" (Ashworth and Lindley 1977, 8).

The American Council on Education (ACE), the Council on Postsecondary Accreditation, the Servicemen's (later Servicemembers) Opportunity Colleges (SOC), and the National University Extension Association responded immediately to the charges. In a joint letter, they countered that the article "tries to perpetuate the myth that high-level educational accomplishments can only be attained on campus"—a myth that "ceased to permeate enlightened educational thinking." Although the letter acknowledged "problems of quality control with some on-base programs," it also argued that "keeping the courses on campus or preventing outreach programs at military bases, as the authors appear to suggest, is too harsh a measure, even if it could be depended upon to insure quality"[2] (Young et al. 1977, 1, 2).

More than being about the quality of voluntary education on military bases, the article and response were about the larger debate surrounding traditional versus nontraditional education. Although this debate had been decades long, the expansion of nontraditional education programs in the late 1960s and early 1970s spurred more visceral responses from critics. As with all social movements, the more popular nontraditional education became, the more threatening it was to the status quo, and the more resistance it encountered.

It was this very resistance that the commission faced in 1975—and that earned the Office on Educational Credit (OEC) the distinction of being labeled ACE's "revolutionary cell" by ACE President Roger Heyns. Heyns always had been a strong supporter of the commission's activities and used the "revolutionary" label to get the attention of more traditional higher education leaders. For example, Heyns introduced OEC Director

Jerry Miller to the ACE Board by saying, "Now, you better sit up and listen. You'll find out what revolutionary things are going on down in the basement" (the location of OEC's offices) (Miller 1986, 10). The descriptor was apt as OEC and the commission worked to further open the doors of nontraditional education.

DELICATE RELATIONSHIPS:
Working with the Military

Elimination of the GI Bill did little to ease the tension that had developed between ACE and the military during the previous decade. In addition to the launching of the Community College of the Air Force (CCAF), procurement regulations required that the Department of Defense (DoD) put out to bid the work of the Military Evaluations program. As Jerry Miller wrote in a memo to President Heyns, "The [military's] delicate relationships with higher education can be easily destroyed and the recent actions of DoD can do just that" (Miller 1976b, 2). It was not an easy time for either the commission or the military.

Competitive Bidding for DoD Contract

In March 1976, DoD issued an invitation to professional agencies and education organizations to bid on a contract to make credit recommendations for military service schools and to evaluate and endorse the Subject Standardized Tests of Defense Activity for Non-Traditional Education Support (DANTES), successor to the United States Armed Forces Institute (USAFI). At the commission's June 1976 meeting, Thomas Carr, DoD's director of defense education, was called to speak on the decision. Carr explained that DoD procurement regulations required that the course equivalency review process be contracted out based on bids and that the requirements "precluded further discussion of the decision at the meeting" (COEC 1976a, 3). DoD later informed the commission that the organization that won the contract also would be given sole responsibility for the content and publication of the *Guide to the Evaluation of Educational Experiences in the Armed Services* (the *Guide*). The policy-making body also would come under the purview of the contractor, which would have final say in the selection of members (COEC 1976b, 3). In other words, should another contractor win the

P
—
117

bid, COEC no longer would have authority over the evaluation and recommendation process.

ACE was not pleased. It was primarily concerned that removing evaluation, recommendation, and policy-making authority from the commission would "disrupt and erode the acceptance of an established system of 30 years" that had strong "standing and identity in the academic community" (Heyns 1976a, 4). ACE had spent decades developing the course review process and brokering the support of the academic community. Both ACE and the military stood to lose a lot if ownership of the process were shifted. At the June 1976 commission meeting, Heyns made clear that "higher education is not prepared to negotiate, or to permit the competitive bidding process, to determine the policy-making body for military course evaluations." In addition, he said that higher education institutions "will expect the Commission on Educational Credit, or some other body designated by higher education, to exercise the policy-making function, regardless of the contractor chosen by DoD to conduct the course reviews" (COEC 1976a, 4).

In October, OEC submitted its proposal to DoD, and at the commission meeting the following month, plans were announced to form a high-level ACE/DoD commission that would address the philosophical and operational concerns facing the military and higher education. The idea for this new commission came out of a meeting with members of COEC and representatives from DoD and the military services and was clearly an attempt to mend relations between the two groups and avoid future roadblocks. As it happened, there was little competition, and COEC easily won the contract. Ultimately, ACE was given "sole source" status so that the competitive bidding process was no longer required.

Community College of the Air Force

The conflict surrounding CCAF was ongoing. In 1973, CCAF received accreditation from the Commission on Occupational Education Institutions of the Southern Association of Colleges and Schools as an occupational education (non-degree-granting) institution. However, COEC continued to evaluate and make recommendations for CCAF's associate degree– and upper baccalaureate-level courses. The commission and ACE still objected to CCAF, but they recognized the college's accreditation and worked with CCAF as with any other appropriately accredited institution (see Chapter 6). However, the conflict was renewed when in 1975, the Air Force announced its intentions to seek congressional authority to grant associate degrees.

Responding to a letter from Major General C. G. Cleveland, director of personnel programs with the Air Force, seeking advice and comment on CCAF's intent to seek degree-granting authority, President Heyns wrote that "as a matter of general policy, the American Council on Education has . . . opposed extension of degree-granting authority to agencies of federal government." He explained that ACE was willing to make exceptions to this policy when there was a "clearly demonstrated need that is not being met, or cannot be met, by civilian institutions." He cited the service academies, the Air Force Institute of Technology, and the Naval Postgraduate School as examples. In the case of CCAF, however, Heyns did not see a special need that could not be met effectively by the civilian academic community, particularly given the establishment in recent years of special programs to meet the academic needs of servicemembers; Heyns cited the SOC consortium, which adopted special policies and practices to accommodate military men and women (see Chapter 6). By 1975, SOC already had nearly 350 participating institutions. Given such programs, ACE could not justify CCAF's seeking of degree-granting authority. Rather, Heyns suggested that "closer cooperation between the academic community and the armed services" would be "in the best interests of the society we both serve" (Heyns 1976b, 1–2).

Heyns's letter did little to ease tensions between the military and ACE. In a memo written "for the file," COEC Director Jerry Miller detailed the events of a meeting with DoD and Air Force representatives in which the Air Force requested that OEC delete the commission's policy statement regarding CCAF in the next edition of the *Guide*.[3] The Air Force also requested that ACE publish only upper-level baccalaureate Air Force courses and refer users of the *Guide* to CCAF for associate degree–level credit recommendations.[4] Finally, the Air Force asked OEC to allow CCAF to award credit based on ACE recommendations for other military courses taken by Air Force personnel. Miller responded that removing the commission's policy statement regarding CCAF would "in effect [nullify] the OEC policy and [endorse] CCAF as an associate degree–level institution." Miller proposed instead that the Air Force submit all its formal courses for ACE evaluation for publication in the *Guide*. In exchange, the commission would alter its policy statement in the *Guide* so it would refer institutions to the CCAF catalog for technical training credit recommendations and thereby eliminate any reference to categories of credit. This proposal would afford maximum recognition of Air Force training and would allow institutions to choose between recommendations and CCAF credit awards (Miller 1976a, 1–2).

The Air Force did not accept Miller's proposal. According to Miller's memo, Colonel Lyle Kaapke, president of CCAF, said that such concessions would infringe on the "institutional prerogatives" of the college. The final paragraph of Miller's memo states:

> There being no common ground for continuing the discussions, the meeting drew to a close. Before it did, Colonel [Robert] Boyette [director of voluntary education] and Mr. [Thomas] Carr [director of defense education] indicated that failure to reach an accommodation with the Air Force could end DoD involvement with OEC. Colonel Kaapke remarked that the Air Force would have to seek recognition from other sources such as [the American Association of Community and Junior Colleges] (1976a, 3).

ACE did not take the threat lightly. In a memo to President Heyns, Miller wrote that DoD's decision to accept bids for course equivalency reviews and recommendations "appears to higher education to be a punitive action for the ACE policy on the Community College of the Air Force." No evidence indicates that this was the case, but it illustrates just how tense relationships between the Air Force and ACE had become (Miller 1976b, 2).

In summer 1976, the DoD authorization bill for fiscal year 1977—
which included language granting CCAF degree-granting
authority—was making its way through Congress. Higher education associations and colleges and universities
began to lobby Congress to discourage acceptance of the "CCAF section" of the bill. In June,
representatives from six higher education associations, including ACE, wrote to the Senate
Committee on Armed Services asking members to study the CCAF section and "recede to
the House on this matter so that the educational issues involved can receive appropriate
consideration" (Huitt et al. 1976). This and
other efforts proved unsuccessful. The size and
importance of the bill made the CCAF section seem trivial by
comparison. So in July 1976, Congress approved the DoD authorization bill, giving CCAF the authority to grant associate degrees.

The higher education community. . . moved quickly to unite its efforts against CCAF's authorization to grant associate degrees.

However, CCAF's degree-granting authority was contingent
upon approval from the U.S. Commissioner of Education. The
higher education community therefore moved quickly to unite
its efforts against CCAF's authorization to grant associate degrees. ACE began working with several higher education associations to develop a policy statement regarding the granting of
degrees by federal agencies. The statement would serve as the
foundation for arguments not only against CCAF, but against
the overall proliferation of federal degree-granting authority.
Commission staff—with Jerry Miller and Eugene Sullivan, director of Military Evaluations, taking the lead—drafted a statement that was circulated among higher education associations
and institutions for their input and support. The final version,
"Statement of Principles Regarding Degree Granting Authority
by Federal Agencies," was presented to the ACE Board of
Directors at its 6 October 1976 meeting and was readily
adopted. The statement was endorsed by the American
Association of Community and Junior Colleges, the American
Association of State Colleges and Universities, the Association
of American Colleges, the Association of American Universities,
and the National Association of Land-Grant Colleges and State
Universities. It was a culmination of the arguments that had

been made against CCAF since it was established. Specifically, it stated that permitting federal agencies to award their own degrees threatened to "isolate federal employees from the society they serve" and would "greatly increase the federal role in education generally." For this reason, the decision to grant degree-granting authority to federal agencies should be based first and foremost on need (Heyns 1976c, 1).

ACE had never based its argument against CCAF on the quality of CCAF's educational programs. Rather, it opposed granting degree-granting authority to any federal agency unless it met a need that was not being addressed by the civilian educational community.

With the Statement of Principles completed and approved, ACE began preparing for the U.S. Commissioner of Education's Advisory Committee public hearings on CCAF, scheduled for 8 December 1976. ACE and the other higher education associations were up against significant odds. A seven-member site review team appointed by the commissioner and comprising civilian educators already had submitted a highly favorable report that described CCAF's technical training as "superior to that of similar programs in civilian community colleges" and recommended approval of CCAF's request for degree-granting authority. Furthermore, it stated that "the civilian educational establishment has as much to gain from learning about Air Force technical education as it has to contribute." Aside from a minority opinion submitted by team member Bruce Dearing from the State University of New York, the team was wholly impressed with CCAF's efforts (Dearing et al. 1976, 20, 31, 41; Dearing 1976).

Of course, ACE had never based its argument on the quality of CCAF's educational programs. Rather, it opposed granting degree-granting authority to any federal agency unless it met a need that was not being addressed by the civilian educational community. This was precisely the point made by President Heyns at the Commissioner of Education's meeting, but the argument met with little success. In January 1977, the commissioner approved CCAF's request, and the college began granting the associate of applied science degree (Heyns 1976c; CCAF 1999).

Once CCAF had received authorization to award degrees, the military began to discuss creation of a Community College of the Armed Forces, which would replicate the Air Force's community college model for all of the military branches. In 1977, the Office of the Secretary of Defense solicited input from the other military services. In a decision briefing to the Secretary of the Army, the Army education staff recommended rejecting the idea and suggested instead that the Army ask the Servicemen's Opportunity Colleges to "network colleges that serve the Army into a system that would meet soldiers' education program needs . . . and for the Army, internally, to establish a transcript service"[5] (Anderson 1997, 45). The Navy and the Marines likewise rejected the idea of a Community College of the Armed Forces. In November 1977, the Office of the Director of Defense Education, headed by Thomas Carr, was eliminated, and all responsibilities for voluntary education were transferred to the Program Management Office of the Assistant Secretary of Defense under the direction of Irvin Greenberg, deputy assistant secretary (COEC 1977c, 4). From the perspective of the higher education community, this was a change for the better. At Greenberg's first commission meeting, in May 1978, he told commissioners that working together, "some organizational arrangement could be created whereby the education community and the armed services could have a continuing dialogue on mutual problems." He and ACE's new president, Jack Peltason, then announced plans to create a commission on military–higher education relations to do just that.[6] This good-faith effort on the part of the military would go a long way toward restoring trust between the two organizations.

At the same meeting, it was announced that the Commission on Colleges of the Southern Association planned to take action the following month on whether to award CCAF candidate-for-accreditation status as a degree-granting institution—the final step to becoming a fully accredited community college. The commission voted unanimously to rescind its policy statement about CCAF, should the college achieve candidacy or accredited status. In 1980, CCAF was accredited by the Commission on Colleges to award the associate in applied science degree. Thereafter, ACE's

policy toward the college was the same as toward all other accredited institutions[7] (COEC 1977c, 8; CCAF 1999).

BUSINESS AS USUAL:
The Ongoing Work of the Adult Education Programs

Military Evaluations Program

Despite the turmoil surrounding the bid for the DoD contract
and CCAF, the Military Evaluations program continued to grow.
A 1975 survey of more than 2,300 higher education institutions
revealed that 83 percent granted credit for military courses. Of
that 83 percent, 91 percent used ACE credit recommendations
when granting credit, compared to only 73 percent in 1969
(COEC 1975b, 12; CASE 1969d, 3).

ACE also was finally able to address an issue that had restricted
the commission's work since the beginning: the evaluation of
classified military courses. The problem was best described by
Ruth Cargo Smith, a Military Evaluations staff member:

> On the one hand, thousands of service men and women
> a year are denied the opportunity for postsecondary
> credit for formal military courses because evaluations
> cannot be conducted due to the classified nature of the
> course content. On the other hand, the commission is
> concerned to protect academic freedom by assuring the
> postsecondary community access to the instructional ma-
> terials of all military courses evaluated. Obviously neither
> the principle of national security nor the principle of ac-
> ademic freedom should be violated, and they are appar-
> ently mutually exclusive, which would seem to leave us at
> a stalemate (1975).

Nevertheless, Smith prepared a compromise solution which included the provision that evaluators of classified courses would
go through the security clearance process required by the armed
services, with the result that they would be allowed access to
classified materials. But this did not solve the problem of how to
provide the materials to the civilian institutions that would
award credit.

In March 1976, a five-person committee of the commission visited the U.S. Navy Resident Cryptologic Training School at
Corry Station, Florida, to determine whether ACE should evaluate classified courses. Each member of the committee, including
Jerry Miller and Military Evaluations Director Eugene Sullivan,
was issued a security clearance. The committee found that the security classification system had no substantial bearing on learning
outcomes and therefore was not an insurmountable obstacle
to establishing credit recommendations for classified courses.
While the availability of classified materials would be "useful in
approximating the work environment for the student," the committee determined that "failure to examine the materials in the. . .
evaluation process would not alter a credit recommendation."
Therefore, credit recommendations could be
made by reviewing only the unclassified
portions of the courses. This enabled COEC to
retain its long-standing policy of basing
evaluations and credit recommendations on
unclassified materials while still allowing the
review of classified courses (COEC 1976a, 8).

A 1975 survey of more than 2,300 higher education institutions revealed that 83 percent granted credit for military courses. Of that 83 percent, 91 percent used ACE credit recommendations when granting credit, compared to only 73 percent in 1969.

The review of classified courses wasn't the
only change to course evaluations during this
time. In 1977, Eugene Sullivan brought before
the commission a proposal to change the policy on awarding credit for military service in
physical education, health, and hygiene. The
existing policy was regarded by some to be
"blanket credit" since it recommended that six
months of military service be accepted as meeting the high
school– or freshman college-level physical education, health, or
hygiene requirement. Like the blanket credit of World War I, this
policy seemed to base credit recommendations on length of
service alone, without regard for learning. Sullivan explained that
the policy presented a "philosophical inconsistency with stated
OEC positions on the evaluation of extrainstitutional learning."
In addition, the policy made it difficult to validate the value of
the training. Basic training was different for men and women,
and it was different in each of the military services. How, then,
could ACE justify awarding the same amount of credit for

different training? The staff therefore proposed that credit recommendations be limited to basic and recruit training that could
be validated by the ACE evaluation process. The commission was
not convinced, however, and referred the proposal to the
Subcommittee on Military Affairs (COEC 1977c, 5–6; Suritz
1999; ACE 1968).

The subcommittee agreed with the Military Evaluations staff and
recommended that it conduct evaluations of basic and recruit
training "using the same procedures and criteria as those used for
military courses." Despite the military's concern that this would
result in fewer recommended credit hours, the staff moved forward with its evaluations and presented the results at the commission's December 1979 meeting. As it happened, the majority
of evaluations resulted in the recommendation of more credit
hours than had been recommended under the prior policy.
Pleased with the results, the commission passed a resolution to
rescind the basic and recruit training policy and to subsequently
evaluate this training "in accordance with the commission policies and procedures used to evaluate learning acquired through
military courses and occupations." The Military Evaluations staff
has done so ever since (COEC 1978a, 9; 1979, 4; Suritz 1999).

Military Evaluations expanded its evaluations a third way, as well.
In 1974, the Army approached OEC about evaluating its
Military Occupational Specialty (MOS) system for credit recommendations. The MOS classification system was a method of
grouping soldiers into career management fields based on their
skills and competencies rather than on their formal education.
Within these fields, a specific occupational designation was
given; skill levels were discerned; and a description of the competencies, knowledge, and skills required for adequate performance was developed. This method of classification made the
MOS system an ideal candidate for a model of awarding credit
on the basis of on-the-job learning. The need for such a model
was apparent. Although ACE had been recommending credit for
formal military training, there was no way to recommend credit
for the millions of servicemembers who had "also experienced
high-quality educational opportunities while on active duty . . .
outside the bounds of formal service school courses." In response

to the Army's request, OEC decided to conduct a feasibility study to determine whether the MOS system could be used as a "control point and means of recommending educational credit and advanced standing in apprenticeship programs." It was hoped that evaluation and credit recommendation procedures based on the MOS classification system could be adapted to other military branches and, possibly, labor union or industry apprenticeship programs (OEC 1974, 1–3).

For the first time, OEC would evaluate learning that had not been achieved through formal instruction, thus further opening the doors to higher education for millions of people.

To head the study, which was funded by a $97,500 Department of the Army contract, Jerry Miller appointed Henry Spille, who had developed a national reputation for his work at the University of Wisconsin-Green Bay in the field of nontraditional education. The results of the study showed that an evaluation model based on the MOS classification system could be validly applied to other occupational classification systems and structures as long as the skills, competencies, and knowledge were adequately codified, described, and assessed and the occupational classifications and individual proficiency were adequately recorded. These findings were submitted to the commission in 1975, at which time it readily approved an ongoing evaluation of the MOS system and publication of credit recommendations in the *Guide*. The commission also approved the study of other military classification systems to determine whether the classifications of all branches could be evaluated based on the MOS model (COEC 1975b, 5). By 1976, 260 MOS exhibits were included in the *Guide* for MOS classifications held after 1 October 1973 (COEC 1976a, 21). This was an important step for OEC and adult education. For the first time, OEC would evaluate learning that had not been achieved through formal instruction, thus further opening the doors to higher education for millions of people.

The push to expand use of the MOS model was immediate. In 1976, ACE signed a contract to conduct a feasibility study of the Navy Enlisted Classification system (COEC 1976a, 21), and OEC submitted a proposal to the U.S. Department of Labor to study the feasibility of evaluating apprenticeship programs (OEC 1976, 5). The results of the Navy Enlisted Classification study were similar to those of the MOS study, though a lack of detailed descriptions and reliable assessment instruments prevented the entire Navy Enlisted Classification system from being evaluated. Credit and apprenticeship recommendations were deemed feasible for the occupational standards section of the Navy Enlisted Manpower and Personnel Classification system (Navy Ratings) and the Navy Enlisted Classification systems that were broad in scope and regularly assessed. As with the Army, the commission approved an ongoing evaluation for these Navy Enlisted Classification systems (COEC 1977a, 9).

The proposal submitted to the Department of Labor was to study apprenticeship programs registered with the Bureau of Apprenticeship and Training. It was suggested that these programs met the same criteria of the MOS classification system because they codified and described the various occupations; assessed the skills, competencies, and knowledge required for MOS proficiency; and recorded the assessment results (OEC 1976, 4). However, the Bureau of Apprenticeship and Training did not meet the criteria as expected: Apprenticeship program standards were not administered uniformly at all sites (COEC 1978a, 9). Each program decided autonomously how to administer, implement, and assess apprenticeship programs for the Bureau of Apprenticeship and Training's standards. Without a national standard, OEC could not reliably evaluate the apprenticeship programs. Although this was disappointing, it demonstrated OEC's strict adherence to the policy that it make credit recommendations only for learning outcomes that were measured.

Another outcome of the MOS evaluation system was the development in 1977 of the SOC Associate Degree (SOCAD). Because military men and women were transferred from base to base so frequently, they found it extremely difficult—if not impossible—to complete a job-related associate degree at a civilian college. The Army therefore approached SOC about developing a system that would allow soldiers to earn degrees related to their MOS and guarantee a minimum residency requirement. The Army also requested that the SOC system rotate course offerings at each installation; create schedules that would allow students multiple opportunities to enroll; and, based on *Guide* recommendations, award soldiers as much credit as possible for service experience. Last, the Army asked that the SOC system help soldiers avoid losing credit when transferred to another assignment by offering optimum transferability (Anderson 1997, 51).

To begin this siginificant project, SOC turned to the Office on Educational Credit and Credentials (OECC) to explore development options, with Henry Spille writing the concept paper. On the basis of this proposal, ACE and SOC set out to jointly develop 21 associate degree programs in technical areas that corresponded directly to Army enlisted occupations. First, SOC member institutions offering appropriate associate degree programs were identified and matched to installations that had troop populations sufficient to support the programs. Each institution-installation pair was then linked with other similar paired locations to form a "curriculum network" in a specific associate degree area, making movement within the network—and completion of a degree—easier (Anderson 1997, 52).

To design the curricula, ACE assembled a team of five to eight curriculum specialists (from colleges most likely to participate in SOCAD) and one to three Army warrant officers or senior non-commissioned officers for each of the 21 technical areas. These teams identified the major educational elements in each area and then selected courses based on these elements to be designated as the core curriculum of the degree program. By the end of 1978, 74 institutions were participating in the SOCAD system. The success of the system in significantly expanding educational opportunity for servicemembers seemed inevitable (Anderson 1997, 52 and 56).

Program on Non-Collegiate Sponsored Instruction

The Program on Non-Collegiate Sponsored Instruction (PONSI) also was continuing to grow. Begun in 1974 as a joint project of ACE and the New York Board of Regents, PONSI was the civilian equivalent of the Military Evaluations program, evaluating and making college credit recommendations for courses offered by companies, associations, labor unions, and

P
—
129

other noncollegiate organizations (see Chapter 6). By January 1975—less than a year after its start—the program had reviewed 145 courses, and plans for a PONSI *Guide* were underway[8] (COEC 1975a, 10).

But the program was still new and largely unknown. For PONSI to succeed, it had to encourage participation by organizations in need of course reviews and encourage colleges and universities to accept its recommendations. The best way to do this was to operate PONSI according to a decentralized system of evaluation that ACE coordinated at the national level. Thus, PONSI-affiliated agencies in individual states or regions would conduct course evaluations according to policies and procedures established by ACE. It was believed that this local administration would prove more effective in encouraging organizations to participate in the program and academic institutions to accept the credit recommendations (COEC 1976a, Appendix B). Essentially, this method of operation paralleled that of the GED Testing Service (GEDTS), and the same logic was behind both programs: Local administration facilitates participation and acceptance.

By May 1981, PONSI had evaluated more than 2,000 courses offered by 124 organizations.

In June 1976, PONSI made considerable progress in its effort to establish state-level involvement when the commission agreed to allow the Consortium of California State Universities and Colleges to organize and conduct course evaluations for noncollegiate organizations in California. Now the two largest states in the country—New York and California—were participating in the PONSI program (COEC 1976a, 17).

However, the decentralized model was not without problems. At the February 1977 commission meeting, Jerry Miller reported that the New York Board of Regents was conducting evaluations in several northeastern states. Although the Regents and ACE had worked cooperatively since the establishment of PONSI in 1974, "the persistence of issues arising out of ACE's and New York's differing view of their roles" was becoming problematic (COEC 1977a, 3). New York preferred a "decentralized system that would rely on information sharing among states, rather than on central coordination, to provide coherence and consistency," whereas ACE believed that "without central coordination, states or even individual institutions would develop differing and perhaps inconsistent systems with little chance that their results would travel far beyond the state borders" (OEC 1978, 2). Despite this difference of opinion, the commissioners did not immediately dismiss the Regents' proposal to conduct out-of-state evaluations. PONSI was still a new program, and different approaches to developing it into a successful national program had to be considered, particularly as many smaller states might lack the resources necessary to conduct evaluations on their own (COEC 1977a, 3).

At its following meeting, the commission decided that in those states unable or not choosing to participate directly in PONSI, ACE would conduct evaluations upon request and seek support for the program from appropriate in-state agencies. The New York Board of Regents would be permitted to conduct evaluations in Connecticut, Maine, New Hampshire, New Jersey, Rhode Island, and Vermont until an agency or organization in each of the states entered into an agreement with ACE (COEC 1977b, 3).

However, this arrangement was only temporary. At the commission's November 1977 meeting, Jerry Miller reported that relations with the New York Board of Regents had been terminated as a result of irreconcilable differences concerning the organization and control of PONSI. The commission unanimously ratified the decision to terminate relations with New York but encouraged the staff to "continue to try to work out arrangements whereby New York could reaffiliate" with PONSI (COEC 1977c, 5).[9] Despite this setback, PONSI continued to grow. By May 1981, PONSI had evaluated more than 2,000 courses offered by 124 organizations (PONSI 1982, 1).

GED Testing Service

GEDTS continued to change between 1975 and 1985. But the change was more of a maturing than frenzied growing pains; having survived adolescence, GEDTS was settling into a productive adulthood. An example of this was GEDTS's expanded research capability. In July 1978, Henry Spille was appointed director of GEDTS. Spille accepted the position on the condition that he be allowed to hire a psychometrician to provide the testing expertise he felt GEDTS was sorely lacking, a sentiment he reiterated at the 1978 meeting of GED administrators. At this meeting, he called for expanded research capability to provide GEDTS with a better understanding of GED examinees—and, consequently, better tests[10] (Whitney 2000b, 5; Spille 2000a, 1). Miller agreed with Spille's assessment, and in August, Douglas Whitney was hired as GEDTS's first director of research. Whitney had been a faculty member in the department of psychometrics at the University of Iowa and was well-suited to lead GEDTS's test development and research projects over the next several years (Spille 2000a, 1; Miller 2000, 4). The decision to establish a professional research unit and hire a psychometrician ultimately led to a more sophisticated testing service with significantly more control over test content and delivery. The first outcome of GEDTS's expanded research capability was publication of the *Candidate Study,* or GEDTS Research Study No. 1, in 1981. Using "an unprecedented collection of data from a national sample of GED testing centers," this study provided the first comprehensive description of GED examinees, an important tool in helping GEDTS understand more thoroughly the adults it served (Whitney 2000b, 5).

The decision to establish a professional research unit and hire a psychometrician ultimately led to a more sophisticated testing service with significantly more control over test content and delivery.

The second result of GEDTS's new research capability was ACE's ability to conduct studies of its own tests—something it had relied on other research or testing organizations to do in the past. This was especially important given the introduction in 1978 of the second generation of GED Tests. Based on test specifications defined in the mid-1970s (see Chapter 6), the new tests reflected changes in high school curricula over the past 36 years. Among the major changes were the development of a reading skills test to replace Test 4 (Interpretation of Literary Materials) and the reduction of the reading load in the science and social studies tests.

In addition, one-third of the science and social studies tests were made up of "concept" items, which assumed that examinees had some prior knowledge of the subjects. Another change was the replacement of Test 1 (Correctness and Effectiveness of Expression) with a writing skills test. The mathematics test also included more practically oriented items. The second generation of tests was used through 1987 (GEDTS 1993, 2–3).

But soon after the second generation of tests was introduced, GEDTS received reports that examinees were having difficulty finishing the mathematics and writing skills tests in the allotted time limits. GEDTS partnered with the GED testing centers in Wisconsin to study the issue. GEDTS subsequently decided that the time limits for both tests should be expanded; in 1981, the six-hour battery became the six-and-three-quarters-hour battery. Whitney described this development as noteworthy on two counts: First, by partnering with Wisconsin to study the time issue, GEDTS "established a pattern of cooperative research involving both ACE staff and the GED officials in the state." Partnerships such as these have "marked many of the efforts during the past 20 years and certainly [carry] out Turner's 1958 promise of 'continual appraisal of the GED Tests and the program'" (see page 74). Second, the study ultimately led to the decision to bring the test development process in house. "As we came to understand better the nature of the tests and examinees through our own research," Whitney said, "we came to believe that we could make significant improvements ourselves" (2000b, 5).

The decision to bring test development "inside" attested to GEDTS's growing maturity. Although ACE had taken back responsibility for distributing the GED Tests in 1954, the Educational Testing Service (ETS) had continued to develop the tests under the direction of ACE. However, as GEDTS began to consider developing a new generation of tests, it seemed clear that it would be in the organization's best interest to bring the development process under ACE's control. The decision was based on two factors: The first was lack of data. Because ETS had been developing the tests for so many years, GEDTS did not have complete information about GED examinees' test performance and therefore did not have a complete understanding of

P

examinees' skills. By bringing the test development process under the GEDTS roof, staff would have greater control and more data from which they could derive conclusions and test revisions; consequently, it could create better test items. The second factor stemmed from the belief that if GEDTS were more knowledgeable about test content and examinees' skills, it could influence the curriculum of GED preparation classes. During the late 1970s and early 1980s, the quality of instruction in such courses was viewed as largely inadequate. With the test development process in house, GEDTS could increase awareness of the skills examinees would need to succeed through instructor workshops, manuals, and other publications, and consequently improve instruction (Whitney 2000a).

Once the decision to bring test development in house was made, GEDTS began organizing to make it happen. In 1984, ACE hired five curriculum experts and Richard Swartz, the first GEDTS director of test development, to develop each of the five GED Tests in house. Meanwhile, GEDTS contracted with American College Testing (ACT) to develop seven test forms between 1982 and 1985. These would be the last tests to be developed externally (Whitney 2000a; 2000b, 7).

During this period, GEDTS also implemented a periodic review of the tests' goals and specifications to ensure the continued validity and credibility of the GED Tests. In 1982, GEDTS began a five-year review process of the tests to ensure that they would address and measure the educational outcomes expected of graduating high school seniors during the late 1980s and early 1990s. The process was unique in that it was the first development effort that would be public and "open to comments from a wide variety of stakeholders." It began with formation of a panel of national educators to create the outlines for the new GED Tests. During the panel's deliberations, the seminal publication *A Nation at Risk* was being discussed nationally, providing even more fodder for GEDTS's test development process. As Whitney explained, "Through a fortunate coincidence of timing, many educators were discussing the outcomes of a high school program of study, so we had a lot of useful ideas." GEDTS also hosted a public forum at the first meeting of the newly formed

American Association for Adult and Continuing Education to solicit comments and share information; the forum became a tradition at the association's annual meetings for years to come. GEDTS staff also attended "nearly every state adult education meeting to advise on progress and solicit suggestions," met with publishers of adult education materials to review the basic outline of the new tests, and involved the GED administrators at their annual meeting in sessions devoted to test development (Whitney 2000b, 6–7).

In 1982, GEDTS began a five-year review process of the tests to ensure that they would address and measure the educational outcomes expected of graduating high school seniors during the late 1980s and early 1990s.

Inclusion of the public in the test development process was a significant step in ACE's involvement with the nation's growing adult education community. Although local adult education programs had thousands of participants interested in taking the GED Tests, ACE had "kept its distance from the adult education teachers and publishers." It wasn't until the late 1970s and early 1980s that GEDTS decided the staff could help improve the programs by working with educators and publishers; this collaboration continues today. Examples of the "products" of the collaboration include the introduction of the *Official GED Practice Tests* in 1979 (see page 97), the publication of *What Do the GED Tests Measure?* in 1982 to help adult education instructors understand the skills the tests assessed, and ongoing presentations and workshops conducted by GEDTS staff to help educators better understand and prepare their students to take the tests (Whitney 2000b, 5–6).

Public input and GEDTS's own work in the review process made it clear that any "new" testing program must adhere to the original mission of the GED Tests. Because their primary mission was to provide people who had not graduated from high school the opportunity to earn a high school–level credential, the tests were to be developed so as "to include the major and lasting outcomes of a high school program of study" (COECC 1984a, 9). In 1984, after the first panel's report was released, GEDTS staff appointed a Tests Specifications Committee to develop general recommendations for the content of the new

P

tests. Comprising 26 secondary curriculum and adult education experts, the committee identified five major themes around which redevelopment should be centered. They stated that first, the new GED Tests should require examinees to demonstrate their high-level thinking abilities and problem-solving skills. Second, the tests should include a clear emphasis on the relationship of the skills tested to aspects of the work world. Third, the new GED Tests should represent awareness of the role and impact of computer technology. The tests also should address certain consumer skills and should use settings that adult examinees would recognize. Last, the committee stated that "in all five tests, stimulus materials should relate to aspects of everyday life" (GEDTS 1993, 4).

With the addition of the writing sample requirement, the GED Tests became the first direct assessment of writing ability on a national, continuing basis.

One of the first changes was made prior to completion of the study. At the September 1984 commission meeting, the issue of adding a writing sample requirement to the GED Tests was raised. The commissioners noted that most modern high school curricula included a writing test or assignment to assess students' educational achievement and that the ability to write well was increasingly important to employers. The commission therefore approved at its September 1985 meeting the addition of a writing sample requirement to the writing skills test (COECC 1985, 5). Originally, it had been anticipated that the writing sample would be added during the next test redesign, in 1998. However, Richard Swartz, GEDTS's first director of test development, argued for its inclusion in the third generation of tests, to be introduced in 1988. When Whitney agreed, Swartz brought in experts to design the writing sample and researched the validity and feasibility of grading 800,000 samples each year. (This research could not have been conducted so quickly if GEDTS had not established its own research capability.) Swartz's efforts proved successful, and the new writing sample requirement was introduced in January 1988[11] (Whitney 2000b, 7). With the addition of the writing sample requirement, the GED Tests became the first direct assessment of writing ability on a national, continuing basis (COECC 1985, 5). Once again, the GED Tests set a precedent for other standardized tests to follow.

GEDTS's growing maturity was also demonstrated by its increased development of publications. In addition to the aforementioned research studies, GEDTS published the first Canadian GED candidate study in 1979. Based on a survey of a random sampling of examinees, the study looked at how the GED Tests had affected Canadian examinees; examinees' plans for further education; test preparation; and other pertinent issues. The results demonstrated that, as in the United States, the tests had had a positive impact on examinees. For example, almost 60 percent of respondents who had passed the GED Tests reported that they had gained confidence in their own abilities since receiving their high school equivalency diploma, and more than 63 percent expected the diploma to increase their future earning power. In 1984, the first issue of GEDTS's newsletter, *GED Items,* was published; it soon became an important communication tool for the organization.

The establishment of the GED Advisory Committee was another significant development for GEDTS during these years. As the program and the complexity of related issues grew, it became clear that GEDTS would benefit from the counsel of a cross-section of GED constituents. So in March 1982, a group of 10 committee members—including state administrators, adult education experts, a GED graduate, and Turney Manzer, a Canadian, as the chair— met for the first time. The role of the Advisory Committee was (and is) to review GED policies and make recommendations for change. Typically, most recommendations go to the commission; some continue as far as the ACE Board of Directors. The GED Advisory Committee soon became an integral part of the administration of GEDTS, as well as a model for OEC's other programs, all of which eventually formed their own advisory committees.

NEW BEGINNINGS FOR OEC

Between 1975 and 1985, a number of new and important projects further established the commission's role as a leader in adult education. First, there was another reorganization. In 1978, ACE implemented a five-year plan that included a new set of responsibilities for OEC—namely, "ongoing concern for the meaning and integrity of academic credentials." This new responsibility inspired another name change, from the Office on Educational

Credit to the Office on Educational Credit and Credentials (OECC). The commission's name also was changed accordingly, from the Commission on Educational Credit (COEC) to the Commission on Educational Credit and Credentials (COECC). OECC was made part of ACE's new Division of Institutional Relations, with Jerry Miller as director. Given Miller's promotion, OECC was without a leader, so Henry Spille was named acting director; this soon became a permanent appointment (COEC 1978b, 3).

The ACE Task Force on Educational Credit and Credentials was partly responsible for the expanded responsibilities of the commission and OECC. Begun in 1974, this task force—comprising college and association presidents, faculty, and staff—addressed issues relating to the educational credentialing system and made recommendations for colleges, universities, and other education organizations to improve that system. The task force's final report, which included 15 recommendations, was approved in 1977 by COEC and endorsed by ACE's Board of Directors. In 1978, the final report was published by ACE as *Credentialing Educational Accomplishment*. The recommendations included the push for clearer definitions of degrees and certificates so they might accurately reflect the learning acquired and the suggestion that higher education organizations "work toward common meanings for certificates and for degrees that are in the same area of specialization and at the same level of accomplishment." The task force also encouraged the development of alternative education programs and the acceptance of nontraditional credit. All of these recommendations helped shape the commission's and OECC's work over the next several years (Miller and Mills 1978, xii, 222–41).

> *The committee recommended the evaluation of normative, credit-by-examination programs and developed guidelines and procedures for evaluation similar to the criteria for the review of military and noncollegiate courses.*

Credit by Examination Program

Another new development was the establishment of the Credit by Examination program. Although ACE had been making credit recommendations for the College Entrance Examination Board's

College-Level Examination Program (CLEP) and DANTES's (previously USAFI's) Subject Standardized Tests for many years, it had not evaluated other organizations' tests. In 1975, OEC received an official request to evaluate the New York College Proficiency Exams and the New York Board of Regents External Degree Tests, which ACT administered throughout the country (COEC 1975b, 11). This request was the result, at least indirectly, of ACE's decision in 1964 to recommend college credit for CLEP (see Chapter 5). Douglas Whitney, the first director of the Credit by Examination program, explained, "As a direct competitor of CLEP, ACT and the New York Board of Regents felt that the ACE recommendations gave an advantage to the ETS tests, so they requested recommendations as well." ACE began reviewing the tests in 1978 and completed its review the following year (Whitney 2000b, 8). Other requests soon followed.

COEC appointed a committee to study the possibility of evaluating other tests as well. The committee recommended the evaluation of normative, credit-by-examination programs and developed guidelines and procedures for evaluation similar to the criteria for the review of military and noncollegiate courses. Essentially, the guidelines emphasized the need to evaluate learning outcomes and the importance of institutions' voluntary acceptance of recommendations. The commission approved the committee's recommendations, and ACE's Credit by Examination program was born (COEC 1976a, 9). The evaluation process began immediately, and by 1981, ACE had published the first edition of the *Guide to Educational Credit by Examination* (COECC 1981, 2).

Army/ACE Registry Transcript System and Registry of Credit Recommendations

With the addition of the Credit by Examination program, OEC administered four programs as of 1976: GEDTS (with Jerry Walker as administrator and then Henry Spille as director), the Military Evaluations program (directed by Eugene Sullivan and now including MOS and Navy Enlisted Classification system evaluations), PONSI (directed by John Sullivan), and the Credit by Examination program (directed by Douglas Whitney). With the exception of GEDTS, all of the programs involved credit recommendations for a total of several thousand courses and a few occupational systems. It became clear that what was missing from OEC's range of services was a record-keeping system. ACE recognized that if it could establish a system having national identity, visibility, and acceptance, then higher education institutions would have greater confidence in the recommendations; adults would have an easily accessible tracking system for their noncollegiate and military courses; and institutions would be able to award credit more easily (Miller 1986, 8).

The idea for a registry came first from the military. At the January 1975 commission meeting, the Army announced a proposal to establish the Accrediting Recording Centralized System for its soldiers. The system would provide a record of soldiers' test scores, MOS classifications, formal military training, coursework completed at civilian education institutions, and ACE credit recommendations (COEC 1975a, 4). This proposal evolved into the Army/ACE Registry Transcript System (AARTS).

AARTS began in the late 1970s as the direct result of a survey conducted for the Army by DANTES under the direction of Barry Cobb. The purpose of the survey was to determine to what extent credit recommendations for military training and education were used. The survey found that most servicemembers failed to ask academic institutions to award credit for their learning in the military. In fact, more than 50 percent were not even aware that ACE credit recommendations existed. AARTS therefore was intended to give soldiers a transcript resembling an official college transcript that would include their military learning and ACE credit recommendations. Initially, the Army saw the transcript as a tool for keeping soldiers in the service. Later, when downsizing of the military began, the AARTS transcript became a tool that veterans could use to get jobs in the private sector or to continue their education (AARTS Undated, 1; Fenwick 2000).

While there was no question of the value of such a transcript, there was a question of funding. The project would be massive, including the collection of extensive data from all over the United States and compiling it into a single system. DoD agreed to fund the effort, and by 1979, the AARTS project was underway. ACE hired Dorothy Fenwick of St. Louis University to be its representative on the project. She and John Raines of the Army Continuing Education System began the complex task of determining how to pull together all of the information, what the transcript would look like, and where to house the service. With regard to location, Fenwick and Raines decided on Fort Leavenworth, Kansas, primarily because of the strong leadership of Mimi Stout, an education services specialist and later AARTS manager, and their confidence that she could make this complicated project work (Fenwick 2000).

It became clear that what was missing from OEC's range of services was a record-keeping system.

Having laid the groundwork for the AARTS system, the next step was to create computer systems to run it. The Army hired American Management Systems, a private consulting firm, to complete the system design. By the end of 1983, American Management Systems, working with Fenwick, Raines, and Stout, had developed—and the Army had accepted—the AARTS system software. The following year, the Army and ACE established the AARTS database, and a pilot program at four Army bases began. The pilot proved successful: Not only were the transcripts accurate, but they inspired great interest and enthusiasm among the soldiers who received them. The Army and ACE phased in AARTS at other bases and completed its implementation in 1987 (AARTS Undated, 1–2).

Prior to the development of AARTS, but after the Army had proposed a record-keeping system, OEC had begun work on its own registry. In 1976, OEC staff presented to the commission a proposal for a registry of ACE credit recommendations. The registry, "in its broadest scope," would be a central recording system for GED test scores, student records for courses carrying ACE credit recommendations, and a permanent record of veterans' service-related educational experiences. Because the scope was so broad (and unrealistic in terms of immediate implementation), the Army and ACE decided to first offer the registry to organizations participating in PONSI, with the goal of including other OEC programs later. ACT would operate the registry, in cooperation with ACE and under the policy direction of the commission.[12] The commission accepted the proposal, and by 1978, the Registry of Credit Recommendations was operational (COEC 1976b, 3; 1977b, 4).

Commission on Higher Education and the Adult Learner

Another important development during this period was the creation of the Commission on Higher Education and the Adult Learner (CHEAL). Established by ACE in 1981 and originally chaired by John Sullivan, the purpose of CHEAL was to "address developments in public policy and in college and university operations that would be markedly more productive for the society and more responsive to adults than existing policy and practices." Specifically, CHEAL's mandate was threefold: First, it was charged with proposing public policies at both the state and federal levels that addressed the needs of adult learners; second, it was to facilitate the work of higher education institutions in clarifying their roles and improving their performance in providing education to adult learners; third, it should facilitate effective cooperation and division of labor among adult learner associations (CHEAL Undated, 1).

To accomplish these goals, CHEAL brought together representatives from business, industry, labor, the media, government, and higher education to serve on a 40-member commission.[13] The Council for Adult and Experiential Learning and the University of Maryland University College joined ACE as cosponsors in 1982. These two organizations provided critical financial support through grants and in-kind donations, including the services of Morris Keeton, president of the Council for Adult and Experiential Learning, who succeeded John Sullivan as chair of the commission. Although the University of Maryland University College provided the majority of financial support, contributing more than $200,000 between 1982 and 1989, a federal government agency and other foundations—including the Fund for the Improvement of Postsecondary Education, the W. K. Kellogg Foundation, the Arthur Vining Davis Foundations, and the George Gund Foundation—also provided funding (CHEAL Undated, 1; COECC 1983, 6; Keeton 2000).

Between 1981 and 1985, CHEAL accomplished much. It effectively lobbied Congress to change the language in the reauthorization bill of the Higher Education Act to make financial aid more accessible to less-than-half-time students. In 1984, it published *Adult Learners: Key to the Nation's Future,* which called for a nationwide emphasis on adult learning and suggested specific programs to meet the critical needs of adult learners. In 1985, CHEAL initiated, organized, and cosponsored a national invitational conference for state officials and representatives from business, labor, industry, and higher education to discuss the need for state policies on adult education that complemented federal policies.

CHEAL also published *Postsecondary Education Institutions and the Adult Learner: A Self-Study Assessment and Planning Guide* in conjunction with the National University Continuing Education Association. Underwritten by the Fund for the Improvement of Postsecondary Education, the *Planning Guide* was designed to help colleges and universities evaluate the quality of their adult learner services or their readiness to serve adult learners if they were not already doing so. To aid in the evaluation and implementation process, CHEAL sponsored workshops and seminars for college and university presidents and administrators. In 1984 and 1985, CHEAL conducted nine institutional self-assessment workshops for more than 100 institutional teams (CHEAL Undated, 2).[14]

Diploma Mills

Despite the significant strides of CHEAL and the other OECC programs, higher education in general and adult education in particular were still confronted with a number of complicated issues—including the proliferation of diploma mills.

When the Task Force on Educational Credit and Credentials issued its final report in 1977, it included the recommendation that "the primary responsibility for awarding degrees should remain with the faculties, administrations, and boards of control of accredited institutions that are legally authorized to grant such formal recognition" (Miller and Mills 1978, 223). Consequently, ACE's reorganization in 1978 included the additional responsibility for OEC (later OECC) to monitor and direct policy "for the meaning and integrity of academic credentials." This would become one of the office's most important functions in the 1980s. As nontraditional education gained ground, so did academically deficient and fraudulent enterprises that billed themselves as higher education institutions but that were (and are) little more than mail-order degree programs, or diploma mills. Diploma mills had existed for a long time. They were first mentioned at a commission meeting in 1959 when a representative from the Army spoke of the increasing number of officers who were purchasing degrees and submitting them to their personnel officers (CASE 1959b, 17). Diploma mills had always been a concern of ACE, but their increasing numbers and the sophistication of their operations were cause for alarm.

Diploma mills had always been a concern of ACE, but their increasing numbers and the sophistication of their operations were cause for alarm.

Protecting the Integrity of Academic Degrees, a report written by David Stewart, a staff consultant and former system administration staff member at the University of Wisconsin, was OECC's first step in the fight against diploma mills. Stewart identified four basic problems that threatened the integrity of academic degrees: the lack of a commonly accepted definition of "degree"; the creation of new institutions with administrative structures that diminished the academic decision-making role of faculty; the inadequacy of laws governing the incorporation and authorization of education institutions in some states; and inadequate accreditation processes. Essentially, Stewart wrote, the core question was how to maintain the integrity of academic degrees without discouraging innovation and fostering rigidity (Stewart 1982, Abstract).

To find an answer, the report recommended that the American Association of Community and Junior Colleges, the Association of American Colleges, and the Council of Graduate Schools submit findings and recommendations regarding associate degrees, baccalaureate degrees, and graduate degrees, respectively. The report also recommended that the Education Commission of the States review existing state laws regarding the incorporation and authorization of education institutions, compare the states' laws with the model legislation developed in 1978 by the

Education Commission of the States, and identify any gaps or in-adequacies. Last, the report suggested that OEC staff be author-ized to publish and distribute commission-approved definitions of degrees and related terms and to work with state agencies and education institutions to improve legislation or enforcement re-garding incorporation and authorization (Stewart 1982, Abstract). The report was endorsed, and steps were taken to im-plement its recommendations (COECC 1982, 7–8).

OECC's efforts to organize against questionable unaccredited institutions mounted. In 1983, the commission voted for OECC to establish itself as a clearinghouse of accurate, up-to-date information on diploma mills (COECC 1983, 11). However, the commission's actions did not always support the OECC staff's recommendations. At the March 1984 commission meeting, Spille and Stewart emphasized that the essence of the problem was not organizations that were patently fraudulent but rather those institutions that operated legally under weak state laws and without accreditation recognized by the Council on Postsecondary Accreditation.[15] They proposed that ACE publish the *Directory of Colleges, Universities, and Other Organizations Not Accredited by Agencies Recognized by the Council on Postsecondary Accreditation.*

Many commissioners expressed concern that such a directory would put reputable institutions seeking accreditation and ac-crediting agencies applying for recognition from the Council on Postsecondary Accreditation "in a bad light by including them in the directory along with questionable others." Possible legal risks to ACE of such a directory also were cited as problematic. The proposal failed, with seven members voting against it and five members voting for it (COECC 1984a, 7–8). At the next meet-ing, in September 1984, the proposal was again presented to the commission. Stewart told commissioners that he felt "ACE had an ethical obligation to provide information on unaccredited institutions to adult consumers of education." And this time, Spille and Stewart brought in expert testimony: Sheldon Steinbach, ACE's general counsel, told the commission that the legal risks of publishing such a directory were minimal; James Murray, director of ACE's publications division, reported that representatives of Macmillan Publishing Company had expressed interest in publishing the book; and ACE President Robert Atwell gave his support for the proposal, linking the directory to the need for quality assurance mechanisms in postsecondary education. Nevertheless, a tie vote tabled the issue once again (COECC 1984b, 7–8).

But the proposal came to life in another way. ACE President Robert Atwell thought that because the issue was sufficiently important to ACE and might involve legal risks for the organization, it should be presented to the ACE Board of Directors. The board approved publication of a directory, provided the legal issues could be addressed satisfactorily. An attorney subsequently advised ACE that if it adhered to the protocols it had developed for listing an institution as a diploma mill, ACE could withstand all legal challenges, though it might be mired in court battles for years to come. Spille and Stewart therefore decided instead to write a book that would address the problem as a whole but identify by name only those institutions that had been prosecuted successfully by the Federal Bureau of Investigation, the Federal Trade Commission, or the U.S. Postal Inspection Service. Published in 1988 and sold worldwide, *Diploma Mills: Degrees of Fraud* put ACE and OECC on the front line in the war against unaccredited institutions (see pages 159–61).

THE PUSH AND PULL OF NONTRADITIONAL EDUCATION

Diploma mills were an interesting public contrast to the other work of the commission and OECC. Once heralded as too liberal by traditional educators and as a "revolutionary cell" by supporters, OECC was deemed too conservative in the fight against diploma mills. These contrasting "labels" illustrate the complexity surrounding nontraditional education, then and now. The ongoing push to provide greater opportunities for adult learners and the pull to maintain high-quality standards results in a delicate balance. But through it all, fairness remained paramount. Jerry Miller, recounting his years as director of OECC, said: "One of the girding things in all of this was how to make the American credentialing system . . . more fair" (Miller 1986, 8). This manifested itself in OECC's creation of new services—such as the Credit by Examination program, the Registry of Credit Recommendations, and MOS evaluations—and in the fight against unnecessary or harmful actions by other organizations—such as diploma mills. But the debate as to whether OECC's actions, in fact, made the educational system more fair was far from over. It would continue to surround all of the office's work.

NOTES

[1] In 1984, Congress would authorize another GI Bill, which included educational benefits for new enlistees.

[2] These concerns about on-base military education programs prompted the creation in 1991 of the Military Installation Voluntary Education Review (MIVER), a DoD program administered by ACE that provides independent review of military voluntary education programs (see Chapter 8).

[3] The statement the Air Force was referring to was published in the 1974 *Guide* and read in part: "CCAF duplicates the activities of the American Council on Education . . . .The confusion within the educational community resulting from this duplication and the need to clarify to civilian institutions CCAF's accreditation . . . led the Commission on Educational Credit . . . to adopt the following policy . . . " (ACE 1974, xvi).

[4] The 1974 *Guide* recommended that colleges and universities accept ACE's credit recommendations for technical-associate degree and upper division–baccalaureate credit for Air Force courses (ACE 1974, xvi–xvii).

[5] This brief ultimately led to the creation of the SOC Associate Degree (SOCAD) and the Army/ACE Registry Transcript System (AARTS) (see pages 128–29, 140, 156, and 196).

[6] The first meeting of the Commission on Military–Higher Education Relations was held 16 January 1979.

[7] CCAF became a member of ACE in 1997.

[8] The first PONSI *Guide* was published jointly in 1976 by ACE and the New York State Department of Education and listed 638 courses (OEC 1978, 1).

[9] Today, New York State has its own evaluation/recommendation program through the New York Board of Regents.

[10] Spille was "both booed and hissed" at the meeting for his recommendation to establish a centralized research function at GEDTS. "I was viewed as the new kid on the block making all kinds of brash statements," Spille wrote. Ironically, the GED administrators became active and willing participants in GEDTS's research studies and have played a key role in its research ever since (Spille 2000a, 3; Whitney 2000b, 7).

[11] The third generation of tests included writing skills, social studies, science, Interpreting Literature and the Arts, and mathematics (GEDTS 1993, 4).

[12] In 1985, operation of the Registry of Credit Recommendations was transferred from ACT to ACE (COECC 1985, 6). Joan Schwartz, a former college registrar and senior program associate for the Military Evaluations program, was named director (Spille 1985).

[13] Although its membership included a representative from OECC, CHEAL was a commission of ACE—not OECC—and, as such, worked independently from COECC.

[14] These workshops later would be renamed "Focus on Adults." Conducted by the Office on Educational Credit and Credentials and, later, the Center for Adult Learning and Educational Credentials, the workshops continued through 1995 (see Chapter 8) and were reintroduced in 2000.

[15] The Council on Postsecondary Accreditation (later the Council on Recognition of Postsecondary Accreditation and then the Council for Higher Education Accreditation) is the policy-making body that oversees accreditation agencies.

CHAPTER 8

Leading the Fight for Quality

1986–1995

LEADING THE FIGHT
FOR QUALITY, 1986–1995

MORE THAN CREDENTIALING:
The Center as Policy Leader

*B*etween 1986 and 1995, the Office on Educational Credit and Credentials (OECC) underwent another name change (to the Center for Adult Learning and Educational Credentials) and expanded to include two new programs, the National External Diploma Program and the Military Installation Voluntary Education Review. But the most important development during these years was the Center's growing role as an advocate, policy leader, and quality control body for adult education. Although the Center for Adult Learning (which had been CASE until 1974, OEC until 1978, and OECC until 1987) had long served in these capacities, its work during this time under the direction of Henry Spille—and the work of the Commission on Educational Credit and Credentials (COECC, which retained its name until 1998)—made the Center an undisputed leader in influencing and recommending policy for the adult education community.

The social and political environments of the time demanded increased vigilance among education organizations, not only to ensure adults' access to higher education, but also to ensure high-quality programs.

The Center's leadership was not by accident. The social and political environments of the time demanded increased vigilance among education organizations, not only to ensure adults' access to higher education, but also to ensure high-quality programs. Diploma mills were a growing problem. And the proliferation of poorly designed external degree programs offered by legitimate colleges and universities threatened to sully the reputation of all alternative degrees.

An additional factor in the Center's increased presence as a policy leader was the advent of the high-tech age and the rise of the knowledge-based economy. No longer was a degree earned

10 years ago sufficient to keep pace with rapid change. Even adults with advanced degrees found themselves returning to the classroom for additional learning. As a result, the Center began to shift its focus between 1986 and 1995 toward the importance of linking business, labor, and other providers of education and training to postsecondary education. The Center started working more closely with corporate education organizations such as the American Society for Training and Development, labor unions, and other training-related groups. The emphasis on competency-based education with a focus on learning outcomes—rather than on course length and curriculum—also increased.

CONTROLLING QUALITY:
The Center's Policy Push

Principles of Good Practice

One manifestation of the Center's growing role as an advocacy and policy organization was the development of *Principles of Good Practice for Alternative and External Degree Programs for Adults*. These programs began to proliferate in the late 1970s and early 1980s as colleges and universities began to recognize the needs of adult students and to design academic degree programs specifically for them. Whether it was delivering traditional programs off campus, offering classes after regular work hours, or developing new programs to serve adults, institutions were finding alternative ways to offer traditional degree programs. These became known as "external degree programs" and included a wide range of features, such as flexible scheduling, student-designed majors, prior learning evaluation, onsite instruction, distance learning, and self-directed independent study, among others (ACE and The Alliance 1989, Introduction).

The American Council on Education (ACE) had been involved with external degree education since 1976, when it collaborated with the Bureau of Social Science Research in a National Institute of Education–sponsored study of external degree graduates. A condition of the National Institute of Education's funding was agreement that the Bureau of Social Science Research would disseminate its findings to the public. The bureau sought help from ACE, and in

1978, ACE hosted the first conference devoted to external degree programs. At that time, ACE began publishing the *Guide to External Degree Programs in the United States*[1] (Sullivan 1999).

The external degree conference originally was intended to be a forum for institutions and organizations offering external degree programs to share ideas and program practices. However, in the mid-1980s, the focus of the conference began to shift from information sharing to consensus-building activities—particularly with regard to standards for external degree programs. This shift was a response both to the growing need for colleges and universities to dispel the perception that external degree programs were diploma mills and to increasing national attention to the quality and integrity of postsecondary education. There was also an increased need to assist accrediting agencies in the evaluation of institutions that sponsored external degree programs, as well as a need to help administrators and faculty in their planning, implementation, and program evaluation efforts. Finally, colleges and universities that offered external degree programs felt a need to establish the basis for a "coherent and distinct identity within the broad mosaic of postsecondary education." In short, the external degree academic community needed to establish standards or risk being "perceived as a quasi-legitimate, marginal enterprise by many" (COECC 1988a, Tab iii).

The external degree academic community needed to establish standards or risk being "perceived as a quasi-legitimate, marginal enterprise by many."

—Commission on Educational Credit and Credentials

In 1989, a task force sponsored by ACE and The Alliance (An Association of Alternative Degree Programs for Adults) drafted statements of good practice intended to aid institutions in the delivery of new and existing adult degree programs. Chaired by Eugene Sullivan, director of the Center's Military Evaluations program, the task force included nine people from various colleges and universities across the country (COECC 1989a, Tab ii).

Principles of Good Practice for Alternative and External Degree Programs for Adults established eight principles for the various

components of an external degree program. However, as Henry
Spille observed in the foreword, these principles "aim at the
bedrock of what constitutes quality programs" and so should be
appropriate for traditional programs and institutions "and should
contribute to setting standards not just for alternative and external
degree programs but for programs of all learners." The principles
called for alternative and external degree programs to involve
faculty, administrators, and students in meeting the needs of adult
learners without compromising the quality of the degrees (ACE
and The Alliance 1989, Foreword, Overview).

Workshops

A second manifestation of the Center's expanding role in influencing policy and practice was its development of workshops to
help postsecondary institutions and noncollegiate educational
organizations better serve adult learners. The Center began conducting the workshops in 1987 under the direction of Henry
Spille, David Stewart (the Center's director of program development), and Nancy Schlossberg (an adult learning expert and
University of Maryland faculty member).[2] Called "Focus on
Adults," the workshops were intended to help institutions effectively evaluate their existing adult education programs (or the
environment in which they were planning to introduce an adult
education program) and determine steps for improvement. The
workshops proved a natural venue for promoting the Center's
quality principles. By the workshops' end, in 1995, approximately
400 institutions had participated in "Focus on Adults"[3] (COECC
1988a, Tab VI, 2; Spille 1989, 39; 1999).

The second workshop helped colleges and universities implement the Model Policy on Awarding Credit for Extrainstitutional
Learning. Created in 1987 by ACE staff, the model guided institutions in the development of sound, fair policies relating to extrainstitutional credit, including the maximum number of credits
to be awarded, permissible publications and methods to use in assessment, how to record credits on transcripts, and student fees.
Eventually funded by the Boeing Foundation, the workshop first
was offered in 1988 and continued through the 1990s under the
leadership of Joan Schwartz, director of ACE's Registries
(COECC 1988b, 3; 1988a, Tab VI, 2).

Bill of Rights for the Adult Learner

Another document that aided in the Center's effort to preserve quality in adult education programs was the *Bill of
Rights for the Adult Learner*. Developed by the Board of
Directors of the Coalition of Adult Education Organizations[4]
under the direction of David Stewart, the Bill of Rights was
designed to help organizations develop adult learner advocacy
statements of policy for both internal and external use. The
bill listed 12 rights that "institutions and agencies of a demo-
cratic society will strive to assure . . . are possessed by all who
have adult responsibilities and who seek to learn in any setting." Included were the right to leave employment for education, the right to financial aid and educational services "at
levels comparable to those provided for younger or full-time
learners," the right to have relevant experiential learning evaluated and recognized for academic credit, and the right to
childcare and related social supports (COECC 1991a, 11;
CAEO Board of Directors 1991).

All One System

Center staff also authored several papers that expanded the
Center's role as a policy leader. In 1989, Henry Spille wrote
*Beyond the Rhetoric: Toward a System of Learning and Credentialing
for Adults* in which he proposed an "All One System of Learning
and Credentialing." The proposal was based on Harold L.
Hodgkinson's *All One System,* which emphasized the need to
think of all levels of schooling (elementary, secondary, postsecondary) as a single system rather than as separate and distinct
steps. Spille adapted this concept for the adult learner, proposing a system of learning and credentialing that would be
characterized by "formal working, cooperative relationships
among the various providers of postsecondary-level education
and training." Providers would include corporations, labor
unions, the military, government agencies, professional associations, vocational schools, technical institutes, and colleges and
universities—among others—and would be linked by the
shared "commitment to *formally* recognize the learning their
'students' have acquired." Spille added: "Thus, the system
will not necessarily provide more education and training than is
currently provided, but it will identify more effectively the

P
—
155

education and training needs of the workforce and coordinate
or target the efforts of providers who can meet those needs"
(Spille 1989, 14–15).

Spille proposed that ACE lead the effort to create "All One
System for Learning and Credentialing." His rationale was familiar: ACE had 70 years of postsecondary coordinating experience, already had direct ties to the major providers of
education and training, and had 40 years of experience evaluating nontraditional learning. In addition, ACE had played a
critical role in the development of the Servicemen's (later
Servicemembers) Opportunity Colleges Associate Degree
(SOCAD) program, which, Spille observed, "embodies several
characteristics" of the proposed system (see Chapter 7). ACE
also had developed the *Self-Assessment and Planning Guide,*
which included many of the proposals put forth in the paper
(Spille 1989, 38–39).

Beyond the Rhetoric was on the agenda of a May 1989 conference cosponsored by the National Governors' Association
(chaired by then-Governor Bill Clinton), ACE, the Council
for Adult and Experiential Learning, and the College Board.
Titled "A More Productive Workforce: Challenge to Postsecondary Education and Its Partners," the conference was
organized by ACE's Commission on Higher Education and
the Adult Learner (see Chapter 7) and was the group's penul-
timate accomplishment before being subsumed at the end of
1989 into COECC. "A More Productive Workforce" was
attended by more than 200 registrants organized into action
teams that spent three days developing plans for their states'
adult learners and economic development (CAEL 1989, 1,
4, 5; Keeton 2000).

Quality Assurance Project White Paper

Another important paper published during this period was
"Adult Degree Programs: Quality Issues, Problem Areas, and
Action Steps," also known as the Quality Assurance Project
White Paper. The need for such a project was clear: Enrollments
in adult degree programs were skyrocketing, and the numbers of
institutions offering such programs were increasing sharply. Too

often, the motivation for organizing an adult degree program was to use the income it generated to subsidize a foundering program for traditional students. Such rapid growth threatened the quality of the programs and, in turn, threatened the reputation of adult degree programs as a whole. In response, the Council for Adult and Experiential Learning and the Center for Adult Learning initated the Quality Assurance Project with the goal of developing mechanisms to facilitate the quality control of adult degree programs. Written by David Stewart and co-authored by Laura Winters of the Council for Adult and Experiential Learning, the White Paper was the first step in the project, which was funded by the Lilly Endowment (COECC 1992a, Tab VIII).

Published in February 1993, "Adult Degree Programs: Quality Issues, Problem Areas, and Action Steps" addressed seven problem areas identified on the basis of interviews with administrators of postsecondary institutions offering specialized degree programs for adults, officials at six of the nation's seven regional accrediting bodies, administrators at institutions offering "franchising" and institutions operating franchised programs, and regulatory officials in 17 states that exempted religious institutions from oversight. "Problem areas" related to the relationship between adult programs and the institution's mission; the violation of standards of good practice in prior learning assessment programs; administrative deficiencies; inadequate involvement of faculty; overzealous marketing to consumers; questionable financial management practices; inappropriate curricula, instructional format, and assessment of learning outcomes; and inadequate support services for adult learners. Last, the paper identified improper practices at unaccredited, unregulated, or weakly regulated institutions—including some religious colleges—perceived by the public as "typical" of adult degree programs in general (COECC 1992b, 7–8; 1992c, Tab IV; 1993b, 5–6).

The paper concluded that while these abuses needed attention, action should focus "on quality enhancement measures and on promoting consumer awareness of quality and generally on fostering a climate in which abuse is less likely to occur" (COECC 1992d, 4; 1993b, 5–6).

P

Evaluating Barriers in Military Education

A report analyzing higher education practices and trends relating to the military's voluntary education program was another important effort of the Center in the late 1980s. In 1989, ACE, the American Association of Community and Junior Colleges, the American Association of Collegiate Registrars and Admissions Officers, and the American Association of State Colleges and Universities were awarded a year-long Department of Defense (DoD) contract to analyze, examine, and make recommendations regarding problems encountered by military personnel pursuing a college education. Four reports were produced: "State and Institutional Trends in Accepting Traditional and Nontraditional Educational Credits," by David Stewart; "Transferability of Credits between Institutions," by Meredith Ludwig of the American Association of State Colleges and Universities; "Articulation between Degree Programs," by James Palmer of the American Association of Community and Junior Colleges; and "Designation of Nontraditional Learning on Academic Transcripts," by Wayne Becraft of the American Association of Collegiate Registrars and Admissions Officers (COECC 1988b, 4; 1989b, 9–10).

The reports identified six major factors specific to military service that influenced servicemembers' decision to pursue (or not pursue) postsecondary education opportunities.

The reports identified six major factors specific to military service that influenced servicemembers' decision to pursue (or not pursue) postsecondary education opportunities. The first was the positive climate that exists in the military for postsecondary education; second was the educational attainment of recruits at the time of their joining the military; third and fourth were the ambiguous definitions of nontraditional learning and the low profile of Servicemembers Opportunity Colleges (SOC) programs; fifth was the limited use of credit by exam opportunities; and the final factor was colleges and universities' enthusiastic acceptance of the Army/ACE Registry Transcript System (AARTS). The report also identified three nonmilitary-related factors that had an impact on servicemembers' postsecondary enrollment: the rapid increase in the percentage of adult and part-time students entering colleges and universities; the prevailing assumption at "too many institutions" that the typical student was between 18 and 25 years of age and "following a linear course of study"; and public resistance to nontraditional education programs, which sometimes bore the image of a "diploma mill" (COECC 1990a, Tab III).

Taking into account military and civilian factors, the reports recommended specific actions that postsecondary education institutions and associations, state governments and education systems, and the DoD and military services should take to facilitate servicemembers' participation in education programs. Membership in SOC, the use of transcripts for nontraditional learning, increased use of credit by examination, and more accommodating credit transfer policies were recurring themes (COECC 1990a, Tab III).

Diploma Mills

In 1986, ACE abandoned its plans to publish a directory of "diploma mills" (see Chapter 7) because of the risk of lawsuits that might result. Henry Spille and David Stewart instead wrote a book about diploma mills in a broader sense—describing the problem, identifying laws and policies (or the lack thereof) that exacerbated the problem, and proposing solutions. By educating others and increasing awareness of the issues, Spille and Stewart hoped to get educators and state officials to take notice of how widespread the problems were and to begin to take action. *Diploma Mills: Degrees of Fraud* was published in fall 1988 by Macmillan Publishing Company (COECC 1986b, 8; 1988b, 11).

The effect of the book was far-reaching. In 1989, California passed an institutional authorization bill that incorporated several of the book's recommendations, and laws in several other states subsequently were tightened. *Diploma Mills* drew international attention as well. In 1993, the book was translated into Japanese, and that edition is now in its second printing. Stewart and Spille also were asked to write an article about diploma mills for inclusion in the German journal *DUZ* (COECC 1988b, 11; 1989b, 10; 1993b, 8–9).

But the problem of diploma mills was far from over. In the early 1990s, there was a resurgence of diploma mill activity in the United States and abroad. In 1995, there were 34 extremely active unaccredited institutions, with many more operating less

P
—

visibly. The proliferation of "accreditation mills" also was a growing problem. Accreditation mills would offer "full accreditation" to fraudulent or highly questionable institutions, making it difficult for people unfamiliar with the accreditation process to discern the integrity of the college or university. In addition, more employers were accepting degrees from diploma mills as legitimate because of their lack of knowledge about them. In a report to the commission, David Stewart attributed the increased activity to several factors: "credentialing fever" (the trend that everyone must have a degree); the increased acceptance of distance learning, which sometimes fostered questionable programs; inadequate state laws and inadequate enforcement of laws that were relatively strong; disarray in the accrediting community; a lack of public awareness of the problem; and "religious exemption" clauses that exempted any institution claiming religious affiliation from state regulation (COECC 1995b, 13).

Stewart and Spille therefore proposed that states "appropriately examine" institutions that referred to themselves as colleges or universities to ensure the academic integrity of their educational programs.

Religious exemption had long been a problem, and it gained increased attention from the Center in 1993. The issue was simple: In an attempt to clarify the separation of church and state, many states had no regulatory authority over organizations or institutions claiming to have a religious affiliation. This meant that any diploma mill could escape regulation by claiming to be a religious institution. The only requirements for authorization to operate in states with these exemption clauses typically were a small fee and "articles of incorporation" that stated the organization's mission and goals. In 1993, 19 states had a significant number of religious institutions operating under the "exemption law." In response, and at the recommendation of the ACE Board of Directors, Spille and Stewart began publicizing the problem and working with states to press for appropriate changes to state laws (COECC 1993b, 9; Stewart and Spille 1993, 46–47, 50).

One effort to publicize the exemption issue and effect change was an article published in the Spring 1993 issue of *Educational*

Record. In "Religious Exemptions Threaten Higher Education's Integrity," Stewart and Spille described the scope of the problem:

There are at least three big losers in this situation. The nation's authentic religious community is the most obvious of these: its good name is being taken in vain. Accredited higher education institutions, particularly those with ties to well-established religious bodies, are another victim: the integrity of degrees is being compromised. A third loser is the general public, as its members are exploited and "served" by persons—especially "counselors"—who hold meaningless degrees.

Stewart and Spille therefore proposed that states "appropriately examine" institutions that referred to themselves as colleges or universities to ensure the academic integrity of their educational programs. "The methods used to ensure minimal academic standards," they observed, "have resulted in no great outcry from now-regulated religious institutions." Above all, the academic requirements for obtaining a religious degree should be comparable to those required for a secular degree (Stewart and Spille 1993, 47, 50). The Center's efforts brought attention to the issue, but the political ramifications of doing something about it made it an issue worth ignoring for many legislators. As a result, many states continue to have an exemption clause, and many diploma mills continue to operate unfettered.

First Global Conference on Lifelong Learning

Another significant step for the Center for Adult Learning in the early 1990s was its participation in the First Global Conference on Lifelong Learning. Held in Rome, Italy, in late 1994, the conference was coordinated by the European Lifelong Learning Initiative and the World Initiative on Lifelong Learning, with David Stewart as the chief conference organizer and fundraiser in the United States and Henry Spille and W. Keith Davies (president of the European Lifelong Learning Initiative) as co-chairs. The conference was attended by more than 500 educators, administrators, and policy makers from 50 countries. The purpose of the conference was to "create an 'Action Agenda on Lifelong Learning for the 21st Century' and to disseminate that agenda to appropriate policy makers throughout the world"—which it did. After the conference, the "Chief Rapporteurs"—David Stewart and Sir Christopher Ball, director of learning for the Royal Society for the Encouragement of Arts, Manufacturers, and Commerce—worked together to create the Action Agenda (COECC 1995b, 4).

The Action Agenda included recommendations for individuals, organizations, business and industry, education organizations, universities, governments, the media, and organizers of the First Global Conference on Lifelong Learning on how to encourage and shape lifelong learning through their policies and practices. The agenda also included a list of recommended actions, including the development of an easily understood skill profile; the development of practical personal learning plans; the introduction of a learning passport, benchmarking, and a world learning network; development of the public media in aiding learning; and the support of developing countries (COECC 1995b, Attachment 2). In many ways, the Action Agenda reflected the growing globalization of education. Just as business and technology were blurring their international boundaries, so was education—and adult learning in particular. This conference furthered the Center for Adult Learning's far-reaching influence on the international adult learning community.

MORE OPTIONS FOR THE ADULT LEARNER:
Two New Programs Join the Center
The National External Diploma Program

In addition to the Center's policy involvement, its commitment to build programs that facilitated adult access to education remained strong. In 1990, the commission approved the affiliation of the National External Diploma Program (EDP) with the Center. Developed in 1972 by the Syracuse Research Corporation through a Ford Foundation grant, EDP is a competency-based high school diploma program based on the belief that adults, through a variety of learning experiences, acquire skills and competencies that are equivalent to those achieved by high school students through classroom study. To earn an EDP credential, adults need to demonstrate proficiency in 64 generalized life-skill competencies (in communications,

computation, self-awareness, social awareness, consumer awareness, scientific awareness, and occupational preparedness) and one
individualized competency (occupational, advanced academic,
or special skill). The program is unique in that it is noninstruc-
tional and incorporates a variety of assessment techniques appropriate for adult learners who have acquired academic skills
through life experience or learning outside the
traditional classroom. The techniques include
take-home projects, performance assessments,
interviews, and document reviews (COECC
1990a, Tab VII; 1990b, 8–9).

*or many adults—
particularly older adults
who had been out of school
for some time—the idea of
taking a nearly seven-hour
test was intimidating.
EDP gave these adults
another option—one that
was self-paced and
assessed learning through
life experience.*

Prior to becoming a part of ACE, EDP was a
small program serving approximately 1,200
people each year. Part of the reason for its limited reach was that it was run nationally by vol-
unteers. By affiliating with ACE, EDP would
come under the direction of a paid staff whose
sole responsibility would be to promote and administer the program. For ACE, the addition of
EDP seemed natural. The program's structure
and purpose were consistent with the Center's
mission, and EDP was a good complement to
the GED Tests. Although both programs had the same outcome (a
high school diploma), they served different needs. For many
adults—particularly older adults who had been out of school for
some time—the idea of taking a nearly seven-hour test was intimidating. EDP gave these adults another option—one that was
self-paced and assessed learning through life experience. EDP and
the GED Tests clearly served different populations: The average
age of the EDP graduate was 37 years, whereas the average age of
the GED graduate was 24 years. The commission voted 17 to 1 to
approve the affiliation (COECC 1990b, 9).

With this approval, ACE began developing its own version of the
program. It was clear from the outset that several of the 64 competencies needed updating—a difficult task akin to establishing
the validity and reliability of standardized tests. Until this could
be done, promotion of the program had to be delayed. In 1991,
Florence Harvey, who had administered the program in Fairfax

County, Virginia, was named director of the ACE program. After the competencies were updated, the arduous task of promoting the program and setting up EDP sites in each of the states began. Because of the program's unique design, three partners were required for each site: a community college or other education provider to deliver the program, a school or state department of education to provide the diploma, and several businesses or labor organizations to provide prospective EDP students, tuition assistance, and onsite delivery (COECC 1991a, 7; EDP Undated).

The program got off to a good start. By 1995, 101 EDP sites were in 11 states and the District of Columbia. Partnerships among business, labor, and community colleges were on the rise. Unions were expressing significant interest in the program—in part because it enabled older, skilled workers who lacked formal education to obtain a high school diploma. The involvement of unions received a big push when the United Auto Workers union of General Motors was mandated to offer its members a traditional high school diploma (in addition to the GED diploma) through its 131 skill centers. This meant that the infrastructure would be in place to accommodate a program such as EDP, as long as the other key partners would participate (COECC 1995b, 10; 1995d, 16).

However, whether there was sufficient interest to sustain the program remained unclear. The fact that the program required the participation of three different entities made development a challenge—something that would become more obvious in the months ahead.

Military Installation Voluntary Education Review

In 1991, another program joined the Center for Adult Learning: the Military Installation Voluntary Education Review (MIVER). The idea for MIVER originated in the late 1970s when DoD was seeking ways to address the mounting criticisms of on-base college programs. Over and over again, in meetings, letters, and journals, the quality of military education programs was being called into question. In 1979, the American Association for Higher Education published an essay by former ACE Vice President Stephen K. Bailey titled "Academic Quality Control:

The Case of College Programs on Military Bases." Bailey expressed his concern that "some aspects of one of the largest postsecondary educational systems in America—that associated with voluntary, off-duty opportunities for military personnel—might be getting out of hand." Specifically, he was concerned that "academic institutions have broken the tethers of quality control, have proliferated educational services and academic credentialing at the price of galloping shoddiness." Bailey was not alone. DoD soon realized that something had to be done (Anderson, Meek, and Swinerton 1997, e-i; Bailey 1979, vii).

In 1979, DoD contracted with the Council on Postsecondary Accreditation to conduct a worldwide "case study" of on-base military education programs. The study identified some programs that were laudable and others that needed improvement. In the 1980s, the military services conducted site visits through the various regional accrediting associations to help "refine the questions and concerns about quality and set the stage for a more systematic review process." But it wasn't until 1991 that a "systematic review process" was put into place. That year, DoD awarded a contract to ACE to administer the MIVER project to assess the quality of on-base voluntary education programs and assist in the improvement of these programs through appropriate recommendations to institutions, installations, and the military services (Anderson, Meek, and Swinerton 1997, e-i, e-ii).

With the signing of the contract, ACE—and the Center for Adult Learning in particular—became responsible for coordinating military base visits in cooperation with the Office of the Assistant Secretary of Defense, the military services, and those education institutions that provided degree programs on base (Anderson, Meek, and Swinerton 1997, e-i, e-ii). The Center had to hire an administrator to oversee this imposing new task. (COECC 1991a, 9; 1991b, 4; Stewart 1999).

To fulfill the terms of the competitively awarded MIVER contract, the Center was required to hire an administrator from civilian higher education with a strong background in accreditation policies and procedures and a thorough understanding of external degree programs. It was clear that the administrator also would have to be a strong leader not easily intimidated by authority. Professor E. Nelson "Al" Swinerton of the University of Wisconsin–Green Bay was the perfect candidate. MIVER's subsequent success was due largely to Swinerton, who, according to David Stewart, possessed the "unique combination of academic competence, political savvy, and leadership skills" needed to get the job done (1999).

The DoD contract also required that ACE hire a military educator with a good understanding of DoD's voluntary education program to serve as assistant administrator. Spille chose Clinton L. "Andy" Anderson, who was serving as a consultant with SOC and who previously had served as an education officer for more than six years in the Headquarters Department of the Army staff. Swinerton and Anderson, together with Kim Meek, MIVER's program coordinator, worked closely as a team dedicated to the "implementation of a successful review process that was both fair and substantive in determining quality and making recommendations for education improvement" (Anderson 2000, 5).

MIVER's success also could be attributed to the careful development of two sets of principles of good practice—one for military installations and one for institutions. Written by Anderson and Henry Spille, these principles were intended to help define the parameters of excellence in delivering on-base military education and to dispel misunderstandings about the purpose, legitimacy, and worth of voluntary education programs conducted on military bases. The principles also were intended to stimulate a dialogue on how to improve the quality of on-base education programs and services, as well as how to help these programs evolve as part of the mainstream of adult and higher education. *Principles of Good Practice for Voluntary Education Programs on Military Installations* outlined the necessary components of a successful military education program, including command support, managers who were professional adult educators, a process for identifying and retaining academically qualified institutions to deliver on-base education programs, and instructional, physical, and financial resources. *Principles of Good Practice for Institutions Providing Voluntary Education Programs on*

Military Installations listed similar components but included the need for education programs and services "comparable in quality with those provided on the home campus, even if different in kind and method of instructional delivery" (Anderson, Meek, and Swinerton 1997, B-5–B-8, C-7).

Another important factor in MIVER's success was the review process it established. In a process similar to that of accrediting civilian postsecondary institutions, the administrator selects a team of reviewers from a pool of highly qualified education professionals. The team travels to the military base (selected for review by the military service) and reviews all components of the voluntary education program, including the installation's educational mission statement; command support; personnel; needs assessment; education program planning, acquisition, and administration; student services; instructional resources; physical resources; financial resources; and student assessment and program evaluation. After the visit, the team chair compiles the feedback from the other team members and prepares a draft report detailing the findings of the visit, including the team's commendations and concerns. The draft report is reviewed for errors of fact by base personnel who participated in the visit. Next, the final MIVER report is distributed to members of the MIVER Governing Board and the military base. Between 1991 and 1996, MIVER site teams issued 63 site visit reports. The responses were overwhelmingly positive. Although some military services were initially reluctant to support MIVER, the site teams and reports earned the respect of both the military and the higher education community. Today, MIVER is seen as "an effective review methodology that facilitates improvements in adult and continuing education" (Anderson, Meek, and Swinerton 1997, e-ii, e-xxi).

GED TESTING SERVICE

While these new programs were being added to the Center, its established programs continued to grow. The GED Testing Service (GEDTS)—the Center's largest program by far—went through significant changes and challenges during this decade. In 1985, Douglas Whitney was named director of GEDTS, having served as associate director since 1980 and as director of research

P
—
167

prior to that. He would remain the director until 1991, when Jean Lowe (GEDTS's assistant director) acceded to the position (COECC 1986a, 2; 1991a, 12).

During the administrations of both Whitney and Lowe, GEDTS addressed multiple demands: testing at-risk high school students, outreach, increasing research and media attention, adoption of the GED Tests by Ontario, challenges of the Spanish-language test norm group and standard setting for mainland students, accommodations for the prelingually deaf and hard of hearing, accommodations for GED candidates with specific learning disabilities (SLD), the development of an integrated computer system for item banking, test construction, printing of the GED Tests, and the outsourced distribution of test materials.

Testing Programs for At-Risk, In-School Youths

One of the most challenging issues between 1986 and 1995 was the decision to allow at-risk students still enrolled in traditional secondary schools to take the GED Tests. Since the GED Tests had been established, commission policies had prohibited enrolled students from taking them. In fact, one of the first policies ever adopted by the commission stated that the GED Tests should "not be administered or recognized as a measure of high school equivalence until after the class of which the man [or woman] was a member has been graduated." The policy further stated that "systematic education normally is best obtained by regular attendance in high school."

However, as more states began developing programs in the mid- and late-1980s for youths at risk of dropping out of high school, use of the GED Tests as a way of providing these students another alternative gained support. In 1988, Virginia became the first state officially to request an exemption to allow the testing of enrolled, at-risk high school students "under certain, restrictive conditions." Virginia's proposal included a restriction whereby at-risk youths would not be allowed to take the GED Tests until their classes had graduated. Also, at-risk students would have to be enrolled in the program for at least six months before they would be eligible to take the tests (COECC 1988b, 9).

Commissioners' responses to the request varied. Some suggested that testing at-risk high school students would conflict with the primary purpose of the GED Tests as a program for adults and risked compromising the credibility of the tests. Others stated that testing these students would help them make sound educational decisions and provide them an opportunity to earn a diploma while still enrolled in school— something they were unlikely to achieve otherwise. In the end, the commission agreed to Virginia's request, but only as a three-year pilot program after which the GEDTS staff and the GED Advisory Committee would evaluate its efficacy and present findings to the commission[5] (COECC 1988b, 9).

As more states began developing programs in the mid- and late-1980s for youths at risk of dropping out of high school, use of the GED Tests as a way of providing these students another alternative gained support.

As anticipated, other requests soon followed. In 1989, the Texas Education Agency submitted to the GED Advisory Committee a request to test at-risk high school students and high school students who were under court control. However, this request raised concerns because the Texas program seemed to lack instructional and counseling resources for the students. The commission therefore voted that the GEDTS staff should request additional information from the Texas Education Agency "to show clearly that an adequate instructional program is to be provided and that the GED Tests are the best alternative for assessing satisfactory completion." Assuming this requirement was met, GEDTS staff were given permission to approve the state's request for a three-year pilot program (COECC 1989b, 6–7).

Texas's request spurred the development by GEDTS staff of specific criteria for programs intending to test at-risk youths; the GED Advisory Committee approved these criteria. At the March 1990 commission meeting, GEDTS staff presented the criteria. First, the instructional content of programs for at-risk students must be substantive and the instructional resources adequate. In addition, the criteria for student selection must be sound, counseling services must be provided, and a comprehensive evaluation must be conducted and a written report filed with GEDTS. Last,

P

the state or province official GED testing centers must be able to handle the additional testing activity. The motion was approved. With these criteria in place, more states began requesting—and being granted—permission to test at-risk youths. By 1993, Alabama, Florida, Georgia, Hawaii, Tennessee, Texas, Virginia, and Wisconsin were testing at-risk high school students (COECC 1989b, 6; 1990a, Tab IX; 1993d, 7).

In early 1994, as authorizations of the pilot programs came up for renewal and as more states requested permission to conduct programs of their own, GEDTS staff began to review the testing of in-school, at-risk youths. During this review, concerns arose that testing in-school youths might be inconsistent with the current mission and purpose of the GED Tests (as some had argued earlier) and that the population of at-risk students was so large that it might strain the program's staff and financial resources. For these reasons, GEDTS leadership recommended ending the testing of at-risk youths. This recommendation was presented to the GED Advisory Committee at its February 1995 meeting, but the committee decided to delay a vote until July, when GED administrators would have the opportunity to discuss the issue at their annual conference (GEDTS 1998a, 6; COECC 1995d, 9, Attachment 5).

At the administrators' conference, it was found that 60 percent of the states supported the testing of at-risk youths. Many administrators were "adamant that the pilot program be continued, if not extended." Many also expressed their belief that testing at-risk youths enhanced the credibility and visibility of the GED Tests. The GED Advisory Committee therefore voted at its August 1995 meeting to delay making a decision until another review of the pilot programs was conducted—thus allowing those states that adhered to the program's criteria to continue testing at-risk enrolled students. For the time being, the issue would remain unresolved (COECC 1995d, 9, Attachment 5).

Outreach

At the beginning of the 1990s, GEDTS struggled as the number of examinees and diploma recipients decreased significantly. The testing volume had decreased steadily from 1980 (approximately

816,000 examinees) until 1984 (approximately 706,000 examinees), but it had increased to approximately 758,000 examinees in 1987 before decreasing again to approximately 683,000 in 1989 (GEDTS 1980, 4; 1984, 2; 1987a, 2; 1989, 2). The reasons for the fluctuation were not clear, but something had to be done.

Susan Porter Robinson, appointed in 1989 as the Center for Adult Learning's director of outreach and communications,[6] worked with GEDTS staff to design a far-reaching outreach effort—including public service announcement (PSA) campaigns at the national level and marketing kits for local testing centers to use to increase public awareness (COECC 1990c, 6; 1991a, 11). The public service announcements were perhaps GED's best method of increasing awareness and generating interest in the tests. Several celebrities (many of whom were GED graduates themselves) made television and/or radio PSAs encouraging people to take the tests. The PSAs that featured First Lady Barbara Bush, comedian Bill Cosby, Senator Ben Nighthorse Campbell, Wendy's Restaurant founder and owner Dave Thomas, singers Waylon Jennings, Anne Murray, Johnny Cash, and Vikki Carr (who also recorded a television PSA in Spanish), and President Bill Clinton were particularly effective (COECC 1991a, 11; 1993a, Tab VIII).

The public service announcements were perhaps GED's best method of increasing awareness and generating interest in the tests.

To further bolster the GED outreach effort, the National GED Hotline began operation on 31 July 1991. The hotline provided free information about how to apply to take the tests, locations of testing centers, and answers to other frequently asked questions. The toll-free phone number was added to all of the GED public service announcements. Almost immediately, the hotline began receiving approximately 1,500 calls per month; less than a year later, the hotline had received more than 20,000 calls from all 50 states, the District of Columbia, and Puerto Rico. By 1994, the hotline was receiving approximately 4,000 calls per month. However, the success of the hotline was problematic at times. In January 1994, following a particularly successful PSA campaign and a national GED call-in program sponsored by Kentucky Educational Television Network, calls to the hotline spiked at more than 19,000. With each call costing GEDTS $2, the PSAs had to be pulled from several cable "super stations" so the cost of the hotline would return to an affordable level. But there was no question that the outreach efforts were working and the hotline was being utilized (COECC 1991b, 7; 1994, Tab XII).

Research and Media Attention

The launch of the GEDTS outreach campaign coincided with one of the Center's most difficult public relations battles. In fall 1991, the *Wall Street Journal* and *Business Week* published articles about a study by two University of Chicago economists who compared GED graduates' financial performance to that of individuals who had no diploma, as well as to that of traditional high school graduates. The study indicated that GED graduates on average earned only $500 more per year than high school dropouts. Stephen Cameron and James Heckman argued that the financial gains were minimal (a statement many low-wage earners would dispute) and that the GED failed to really help its diploma recipients. In January 1992, the story was picked up by the *Washington Post* and the Associated Press and was widely circulated in the media (COECC 1992a, Tab iv).

ACE and GEDTS responded by arguing that the Cameron-Heckman study was flawed on several fronts. First, the study sample was extremely limited. In 1991, the GED Tests were administered to more than 750,000 men and women between the ages of 16 and 96, yet Cameron and Heckman's sample included only 209 men between the ages of 25 and 28—hardly representative of the entire GED population. Second, GEDTS argued that the finding that GED graduates earned only $500 more per year than high school dropouts was based on 1967 dollars. When that amount was translated into 1989 dollars (the year of the study), it grew to $2,040—an amount replicated in subsequent studies. Third, the Cameron-Heckman study ignored other important factors that would help explain the income difference (regardless of how large or small it was). For example, the average age of GED graduates was 24 years. This meant that, on average, GED graduates had six fewer years of *comparable* work experience than traditional high school graduates—making an age-based comparison less reliable than, for instance, a comparison of earnings since graduation. Socioeconomic differences between GED graduates and traditional high school graduates were also a factor in the difference in incomes. As Jean Lowe wrote in a letter to the *Des Moines Register,* "Students who stay in school generally come from more advantaged economic and educational backgrounds—qualities that serve them well in the labor market. It is naïve to think that once former dropouts gain their GED diplomas, the playing field suddenly becomes level" (Lowe 1992).

Nevertheless, Cameron and Heckman's well-publicized report needed a coordinated response. GEDTS developed a model media response kit to help testing centers respond to inquiries from local media. Also, several other studies, either already published or in development, bolstered ACE's position. For example, Professor Hal Beder of Rutgers University had conducted a study of GED graduates in Iowa who were interviewed two, five, and 10 years after earning their diploma. His study indicated that GED graduates "gain a substantial advantage which compounded over time on a variety of economic and personal measures." Also, a joint research project between GEDTS and the Educational Testing Service (ETS) to link scores on the GED Tests to the scales of the National Adult Literacy Survey was underway. This study found that passing the GED Tests was a strong predictor of at least moderate levels of literacy proficiency. Similarly, higher literacy proficiency was a strong predictor of passing the GED Tests. The GEDTS/ETS study also found that the average literacy scores of adults who passed the GED Tests fell solidly within the moderate range, regardless of the examinee's age, sex, race, country of birth, or disability status (COECC 1992b, 3; 1992d, 11; ACE 1996).

> *Students who stay in school generally come from more advantaged economic and educational backgrounds—qualities that serve them well in the labor market. It is naïve to think that once former dropouts gain their GED diplomas, the playing field suddenly becomes level.*
>
> —Jean H. Lowe

In 1993, researchers D. Kaplan and R. L. Venezky of the University of Delaware conducted a study to assess whether Cameron and Heckman's finding generalized to literacy skills. They analyzed a sample of more than a thousand young adults who responded to the National Assessment of Educational Progress Young Adult Literacy Survey, dividing the sample into four groups: GED graduates, those who took but did not pass the GED Tests, high school dropouts who did not take the GED Tests, and high school graduates. In comparing the literacy skills of these four groups, Kaplan and Venezky concluded that GED graduates performed significantly better than those who did not pass the tests and only slightly lower than high school graduates (GEDTS 1993, 61).

On the basis of these and other studies, GEDTS formulated four conclusions. First, candidates take the GED Tests to qualify for a job or to be admitted to a postsecondary education institution, and for most candidates, these goals are met. Second, employers and postsecondary institutions accept the GED credential as equivalent to the traditional high school diploma for hiring and enrollment purposes. Third, it is not known whether GED graduates attain employment levels and wages equal to those of high school graduates, but both groups experience a definite advantage in employment over those with neither credential. Fourth, GED graduates do as well in college as high school graduates in terms of grades and program completion rates[7] (GEDTS 1993, 62).

In 1993, GEDTS published the GED Tests' *Technical Manual,* which included technical information regarding the development, norming, scaling, equating, reliability, and validity of the 1988 GED Tests. The manual also included information about the development of the Canadian and Spanish-language GED Tests. Intended for those who selected or evaluated tests, interpreted test scores, or used GED Test results to make educational decisions, the *Technical Manual* became a valuable tool for communicating the test development process (GEDTS 1993, iii).

Ontario Joins the GED

In 1995, the Ontario Ministry of Education requested permission to use the GED Tests as part of a research project on methods of prior learning assessment. The objective was to evaluate the effectiveness of the tests in preparing adults to enter the workforce. This was Ontario's first step toward adopting the GED Tests, something that had eluded GEDTS and GED advocates in Canada for more than a decade. Concern that the GED

Tests were strictly a U.S. exam had hindered all previous attempts to offer the tests in Ontario, Canada's most populous province. As Allan Quigley wrote:

> Turney Manzer and I would bring the Canadian admin-
> istrators together year after year at the parliament build-
> ings or other offices in Queen's Park in Toronto to try to
> get the Ontario civil servants to take this 'American test'
> seriously. We always invited someone from the Ontario
> government as an observer. We lobbied directly and indi-
> rectly for some 15 years (Quigley 2000, 3).

GEDTS eagerly granted Ontario permission to conduct the study. The 18-month project was well-received by citizens and enthusiastically supported by employers—key elements in convincing the government that the GED Tests were indeed more than just an "American test." On 16 May 1996, Ontario adopted the GED Tests, giving thousands more adults access to the program and leaving Quebec as the only Canadian province or territory yet to do so (COECC 1995a, Tab VI; 1996c, Tab XII).

Concern that the GED Tests were strictly a U.S. exam had hindered all previous attempts to offer the tests in Ontario, Canada's most populous province.

Spanish-language GED Tests

Redevelopment of the Spanish-language GED Tests was another major issue during the period from 1986 to 1995. Several states began to express concern that the Spanish-language GED Tests were not as rigorous as the English-language tests, and, consequently, Spanish-language GED graduates did not demonstrate achievement equivalent to that of English-language GED graduates. The discrepancy be-tween the Spanish- and English-language test takers' achieve-ment could be attributed to the different norming populations used during the test development process. Because the Spanish-language GED Tests originally were intended specifically for Puerto Rican adults, the tests had been developed based on the Puerto Rican high school curriculum and learning objectives and had been normed on a sample of Puerto Rican graduating high school seniors. Therefore, the difference in the minimum

P

raw score between the two tests "could stem from either a difference in difficulty between the two versions, a difference in
achievement between the two groups, or both." Regardless of
the reason, many state departments of education were sufficiently concerned that they considered discontinuing use of the
Spanish-language tests altogether (COECC 1992c, Tab VII).

In response, GEDTS outlined several possible solutions, as well
as their pros and cons, and presented them to the commission.
The possibilities were numerous. One option was to continue
the existing system and risk possible lawsuits and the loss of
confidence of several states. Alternatively, GEDTS could discontinue the Spanish-language tests entirely or discontinue
their use outside of Puerto Rico. Yet another option was to
create a new Spanish-language version that would be equated
to the English-language version. GEDTS could keep the
Spanish-language version "as is" and require states to identify
the test language on the score report. States could be required
to administer an English proficiency test to Spanish-language
examinees, or new Spanish-language tests for social studies, science, and math could be equated to the English-language tests,
and the writing skills and literature tests could be administered
in English. Another option was to offer an optional English
proficiency test and require states to identify the language edition on the score report if the proficiency test were not taken.
Or GEDTS could issue a formal policy statement describing
how the Spanish-language tests were developed, outlining
appropriate and inappropriate uses for these tests, and recommending how the test scores should be interpreted. At its
fall 1992 meeting, the commission voted unanimously that
GEDTS should develop a new Spanish-language version
equated to the English-language version "with all due vigor"
and that it should bring a detailed proposal to the next commission meeting (COECC 1992a, Tab VII; 1992d, 8).

As a first step, GEDTS sent a survey to the states that would be
most affected by policy changes related to the Spanish-language
tests. The two options that received the most support were to re-
develop the tests based on the same U.S. curriculum and norm
group as the English-language tests and to develop social studies,

science, and math tests based on the same curriculum and norm group but with the writing skills and literature tests in English (COECC 1993a, Tab IV).

The next step (and the first phase of the redevelopment process) was to conduct psychometric and linguistic feasibility studies to evaluate the appropriateness of the GEDTS equating design. With funding from Defense Activity for Non-Traditional Education Support, two panels were formed to conduct the studies. The Psychometric Feasibility Panel determined that it would be feasible to make the Spanish and English versions more directly comparable through linking. Furthermore, the panel believed that the Spanish-language tests could be revised by using a norm group of Spanish-speaking high school seniors in the United States. The Linguistic Feasibility Panel came to quite a different conclusion. It determined that Spanish-speaking U.S. high school seniors would not be an appropriate norming population because "they are not a full representation of Spanish speakers." The Linguistic Feasibility Panel also asserted that the differences between the norming populations might "pose a threat to score comparability and a serious problem for linking." The panel argued that emphasis should be on equal abilities between the two populations (English speaking and Spanish speaking), not on a linking of mean scores. In the hope of reconciling the differences between the two panels' conclusions, a Combined Feasibility Panel met in October 1995 and agreed to compile a set of recommendations by February 1996. The redevelopment process was just beginning (COECC 1993c, Tab VI; 1995d, 5–6; 1996a, Tab IV).

Accommodations for the Prelingually Deaf

Another test development issue that received increased attention in the early 1990s was accessibility for the prelingually deaf and hard of hearing. There was concern that the existing accommodation—an interpreter to assist with test instructions—was inadequate. Educators argued that prelingual deafness (when hearing is lost before one learns to speak) "is a language disability as much as it is a hearing loss." The presumption that "if someone can see, he or she should be able to read" was incorrect. Consequently, GED examinees who were prelingually deaf perceived that they were at a disadvantage. Many also were concerned that more had been done to help examinees who were blind and visually impaired: GEDTS had constructed three special editions of the tests for candidates who were visually impaired but had not developed any for candidates who were prelingually deaf (COECC 1991b, 5).

GEDTS held its first meeting to address this issue in June 1994. Funded by a grant from the Kellogg Foundation, the meeting brought together individuals holding a variety of perspectives on deaf education and testing—including representatives from ACE's HEATH resource center (a national clearinghouse on postsecondary education for individuals with disabilities), ETS, American College Testing, and a GED administrator to represent the state departments of education. Discussion focused on ways to accommodate deaf examinees so their disability would not put them at an unfair disadvantage while maintaining the same high standards as the other tests'. The task was challenging. Even the deaf community failed to agree on the definition of an appropriate education for the deaf and hard of hearing. As GEDTS Director Jean Lowe observed in her final report to the Kellogg Foundation, "Various schools of thought [on educating the deaf] are both significant and political in nature." She added, "In deaf culture, being deaf or hard of hearing is not considered a 'handicap.' According to this group, deaf or hard-of-hearing people simply are another culture in our multicultural society" (COECC 1994, Tab IX; Lowe 1995).

The committee later agreed that, first, deaf examinees should be allowed extra time—when requested—to take the tests. Second, because of the lack of qualified interpreters in certain parts of the United States and Canada, GEDTS should work with Gallaudet University to produce videos of test instructions in American Sign Language and Signed Exact English that would include answers to frequently asked questions. Third, the committee agreed that GEDTS should work with deaf communication experts to identify an edition of the tests most appropriate for deaf examinees and should screen test items dependent on knowledge acquired through hearing. Finally, policies should be developed that would allow deaf examinees to videotape themselves drafting their writing samples in sign language—in place of written notes or outlines—and then to write the sample from the video playback (COECC 1994, Tab IX).

At its March 1995 meeting, the commission unanimously approved the committee's recommendations to make signed and captioned instructions available on videotape, to allow deaf or hard of hearing examinees to "draft" their writing samples on videotape, and to allow examinees double time (upon request and with the appropriate documentation) to complete the tests. However, the commission deemed the committee's recommendation for the development of a special edition of the tests for examinees who were deaf and hard of hearing infeasible. The committee had considered two possibilities: creating a signed version of the tests and creating a visual format of the tests. Each possibility posed unique obstacles. First, at least five known sign languages and systems exist in the United States, necessitating the development of five different signed versions of the tests—a financial impossibility. The committee agreed that deaf high school graduates, who would be the sample group for the tests' norming study, should be required to read in the five test areas (an impossibility in signed tests). To do otherwise would conflict with GEDTS policy on foreign language test development. The second proposal, to develop a visual format of the tests—which is a way of organizing written English based on what one "sees"[8]—was also denied because of insufficient financial resources. Moreover, no significant base of research yet existed to support the utility of visual formatting. Consequently, the commission determined that developing a special edition of the test for examinees who were prelingually deaf was not feasible (Lowe 1995).

GEDTS recognized that many adults had dropped out of high school because they were hindered academically by learning disabilities.

Accommodations for Candidates with SLD

Another access issue that gained attention between 1986 and 1995 was the testing of people with SLD. GEDTS recognized that many adults had dropped out of high school because they were hindered academically by learning disabilities.

Expecting these examinees to take the GED Tests under standard administrative conditions would be unfair. William Langner, who served in the U.S. Department of Education's Division of Adult Education and Literacy and co-founded the National Association for Adults with Special Learning Needs, was a major advocate for developing SLD accommodations. Langner's involvement with GEDTS began in 1982, when Henry Spille appointed him to the first GED Advisory Committee to "help the committee think through the issues facing [people with disabilities] when they took the tests" (GEDTS 1998b; Spille 2000b).

Due in large part to Langner's efforts, GEDTS in 1988 developed policy to accommodate examinees with SLD. The policy required that, for accommodations to be granted, the GED candidate had to complete an application form for nonstandard test administration that required documentation of the disability from a professional, such as a psychologist, counselor, social worker, or teacher. The completed application would be sent to GEDTS, where staff would review it and decide whether and what kind of accommodations would be granted. Accommodations included extra time (up to double time limits), use of the audiocassette edition and accompanying reference copy of the GED Tests, a scribe or secretary to record answers, individualized rather than group testing, frequent breaks, and, with special permission from GEDTS, the use of a calculator for examinees with dyscalculia. GEDTS began publicizing these accommodations in publications and brochures for both examiners and examinees. The effort proved a success. From 1989 to 1990, the volume of special testing accommodations for candidates with learning disabilities increased from 51 to 330—a sizable gain (COECC 1988a, Tab XIV; GEDTS 1997a, 7.2–2).

As the numbers increased, so did recognition of GEDTS's efforts. In 1994, the Department of Justice used GEDTS's SLD policies as a model for the national bar exam. In 1995, GEDTS received the "Distinguished Service to Adults with Disabilities Award" from the National Association of Adults with Special Learning Needs. Once again, GEDTS was at the forefront of a testing trend (COECC 1995c, Tab XV; 1996a, Tab XI).

Integrated Computer System

Another pioneering effort during this period was the development by Joan Auchter, then director of test development and
later executive director of GEDTS, Paul Messersmith, GEDTS
information systems manager, and Wayne Patience, GEDTS psychometrician, of a computer system that integrated GED item
banking, test construction, and test printing.

The new system combined the word processing and database
functions in one program, allowing editors to view all information related to an item simultaneously. It also allowed users to
manage other aspects of item development and test construction
within the system, eliminating the need for paper trails and multiple files. Graphics, copyright information, and reviewer comments were linked directly to an item and could be accessed
instantly. The system was password protected at several levels, ensuring the security of the items. The new system also eliminated
the pressure and cost of working with an external typesetter in
the printing of the items.

At the time, this merging of item banking, test construction, and
printing was cutting edge in the test development field. As
Auchter later observed, "From a test development industry standard, it showed our commitment to preserving the integrity of
the design and the development of the assessment instruments."
The system proved an important addition to the test development process and remains in use today (Auchter, Messersmith,
and Patience 1991, 1, 18; Auchter 2000b).

Outsourcing Distribution of Test Materials

In 1995, GEDTS made another important operational decision:
to outsource the distribution of secure test materials. Previously,
GEDTS staff had fulfilled the testing centers' orders for materials. GEDTS control was important, but the process was slow and
costly, requiring two full-time staff members and several temporary employees. GEDTS began to consider alternatives.

After significant research and a comprehensive cost analysis,
GEDTS staff decided to outsource the distribution of test
materials to a fulfillment house. This not only saved ACE money,

but also allowed for quicker fulfillment of test material orders (typically within three days of receipt of the order). Outsourcing further streamlined GEDTS's operations and enhanced the organization's responsiveness to constituents' needs (GEDTS 1995).

CONTINUED GROWTH:
PONSI and Registries

Though less beset by change than the GED Tests, the other Center for Adult Learning programs continued to develop from 1986 to 1995. The Program on Non-Collegiate Sponsored Instruction (PONSI) and Registries in particular experienced continued growth, solidifying their place as permanent and important Center programs.

PONSI

PONSI expanded the most of any Center program during this decade. It also was one of the key programs in advancing the Center's goal to link business and postsecondary education. In 1987, PONSI Director Sylvia Galloway reported that several corporations and universities—including the Bell Communications Research and Technical Education Center (Bellcore Tec), Sem/Con Inc. (a South Carolina-based consulting firm), and the Trade Union Program at Harvard University—had approached PONSI with proposals to "play an expanded coordinating role." These requests indicated the growing awareness of PONSI in the business and education communities (COECC 1987, 2).

Nevertheless, PONSI had to work hard to build its base of "sponsors," companies and organizations that contracted with PONSI to review their training courses and make credit recommendations. One way PONSI sought to do this was by illustrating that, for a small initial investment, PONSI recommendations ultimately would save companies and organizations tuition reimbursement dollars. Don Trotter of AT&T and James Ratigan of Thomas Edison College created a cost-benefit model for this purpose. The model was based on the assumptions that the average cost of a three-semester-hour course at a typical college was $720; that a company would have 21 courses evaluated at a total cost of $17,000 (the 1990 fee); and that the company would have

a five-year evaluation for an additional $5,000. Using these fig-
ures, Trotter and Ratigan found that a company would realize
$320 in savings after only 31 students took one of the company's
courses and used the credit recommendations at a college or
university. If 100 students took each course (a conservative esti-
mate for large companies), a total investment
of only $22,000 would net a savings of
$50,000 over a five-year period. This model
soon became an effective part of PONSI's
marketing efforts (COECC 1990c, 4).

*In 1995,
ACE/ PONSI
evaluation teams*

But PONSI's biggest marketing thrust began
in 1993, when Al Swinerton, administrator of
the new MIVER project, and Jo Ann
Robinson became director and assistant director, respectively. Under their leadership,
PONSI became one of the Center's most successful programs. Swinerton and Robinson's
first major project was to establish state affiliate offices at colleges and universities that

*conducted 113 days of
site visits to review
organizations' training
courses—more than
double the 42 days of
site visits conducted
in 1992.*

would promote increased cooperation between local institutions
and employers. Specifically, the PONSI state offices would have
more direct contact—and influence—with potential local
PONSI sponsors and the postsecondary institutions that were
being asked to accept credit recommendations. In 1993, state
offices already existed in New Hampshire, New Jersey, Vermont,
West Virginia, and Wisconsin,[9] and colleges and universities
in 12 other states were being considered for appointment
(COECC 1993d, 9).

When the plan to create PONSI state offices was announced at
the December 1993 commission meeting, some commissioners
expressed concern about the validity of the state office–selection
process. Political and educational ramifications were inevitable. To
ensure that the process was fair, the commission recommended
that a set of criteria be established for identifying colleges and
universities that might serve as PONSI state offices. The following criteria were developed: First, the institution's mission and
history must involve serving adult learners and promoting workforce development. Next, the institution must be willing to pro-

mote acceptance of ACE college credit recommendations by institutions and be accredited by an accrediting agency recognized
by the Council on Postsecondary Accreditation[10] or the U.S.
Department of Education. Last, the institution must be a member of ACE if a higher education institution or a member of an
ACE member association (COECC 1993d, 9; CREDIT 2000a).

With these criteria in place, the effort to establish PONSI state
offices got underway. Within a year, 16 additional state offices
were established. The addition of the state offices seemed to be an
effective marketing tool. In 1995, PONSI eval-
uation teams conducted 113 days of site visits
to review organizations' training courses—
more than double the 42 days of site visits
conducted in 1992 (COECC 1995d, 14).

In 1987, 90 percent of colleges accepted the credit recommendations on the AARTS transcript, and Registries staff were fulfilling between 400 and 600 transcript requests per month. By 1995, that number had increased exponentially, to 2,000 requests per week.

Such significant growth required heightened
organization and coordination. Not wanting
to risk being overwhelmed by the increased
volume of course reviews, Swinerton and
Robinson decided to expand the use of
the National Coordinators program. Carefully
selected and trained, the National Coordinators are highly experienced college
faculty who represent ACE during site
visits, serve as leaders during the course
review process, and deliver course review results to the PONSI
office. By 1999, 26 national coordinators were in 14 states
(CREDIT Undated-b).

Registries

The Registries division of the Center for Adult Learning comprised four different transcript services: AARTS, which provides
transcripts of ACE's Military Evaluations credit recommendations to soldiers; the Registry of Credit Recommendations,
which provides transcripts of PONSI and Credit by Examination
credit recommendations; the National Registry of Training
Programs, which provides transcripts of continuing education
units for employees of various organizations; and the
International Registry of Training Programs, which provides

transcripts of continuing education units for International Association for Continuing Education and Training organizations. All of these services grew under the direction of Joan Schwartz. But use and acceptance of the AARTS transcript (the largest registry of the four) grew the most from the mid-1980s to the mid-1990s. In 1987, 90 percent of colleges accepted the credit recommendations on the AARTS transcript, and Registries staff were fulfilling between 400 and 600 transcript requests per month. By 1995, that number had increased exponentially, to 2,000 requests *per week* (COECC 1987, 4; 1995d, 17).

NEW THREATS AND NEW CHALLENGES

"Quality control" best describes the Center's many activities in the 10 years from 1986 to 1995. The Center for Adult Learning and Educational Credentials' expanded role as a policy leader, the effort to expose diploma mills, and the issues faced by the GED Tests all were related to—if not directly the result of—a quest for improved quality in adult education. As opportunities for adult learners and educators expanded, so did threats. The work of Henry Spille[11] and his outstanding staff during his tenure as director (and particularly during these 10 years) put the Center on the frontlines in the fight to maintain quality in and access to adult education.

NOTES

[1] After the publication of the second edition, this guide was revised and published in 1993 as the *Adult Learner's Guide to Alternative and External Degree Programs*. In 1997, Eugene Sullivan, Henry Spille, and David Stewart wrote a new guide that combined the *Adult Learner's Guide* and *Diploma Mills: Degrees of Fraud* (see pages 144–46 and 159–61), titled *External Degrees in the Information Age: Legitimate Choices*. These three iterations sold more than 10,000 copies in all.

[2] The workshops were based on the Commission on Higher Education and the Adult Learner's (CHEAL's) workshops, titled *Postsecondary Education Institutions and the Adult Learner: A Self-Assessment and Planning Guide* (see Chapter 7), led by William Warren, vice chair of CHEAL.

[3] The workshops were reintroduced in 2000.

[4] The Coalition of Adult Education Organizations later became the Coalition of Lifelong Learning Organizations, which disbanded in 1998.

[5] In 1991, the commission denied Virginia's request to make its three-year pilot program permanent, citing "problems and delays with the implementation of the pilot, the lack of data and information, the low quality of the program evaluation, the low passing rate of program participants, and lackadaisical tone of the report." Instead, the commission granted a two-year extension during which Virginia had to stabilize program implementation, provide more analyzed data

that would give better indicators of program quality, increase program participants' passing rate, and provide written reports each year of the extension
(COECC 1991b, 6).

[6] Prior to becoming director of outreach and communications, Susan Porter
Robinson was the editor of GED Test 4 (Interpreting Literature and the Arts),
the GED newsletter, and the GED special editions for the visually impaired. She
would remain the Center's director of outreach and communications until 1997,
when she would become interim director of the Center and then director and
vice president (see Chapter 9).

[7] GED graduates, however, are more likely to attend junior or community colleges than four-year institutions.

[8] For example, in a visual format sentence, time elements should come first,
nouns should be followed by descriptors or adjectives whenever possible, and a
speaker should be identified before his or her comments (Schreiber 1994).

[9] New York State still has its own evaluation/recommendation program through
the New York Board of Regents (see Chapter 7).

[10] In 1994, the Council on Postsecondary Accreditation became the Commission
on Recognition of Postsecondary Accreditation, which in 1997 became the
Council for Higher Education Accreditation.

[11] Upon his retirement in 1996, Spille was awarded the Department of Defense
Medal for Distinguished Public Service and named the Military Educator of the
Year by the American Association of Adult and Continuing Education.

CHAPTER 9

Going the Distance

1996–2000

GOING THE DISTANCE, 1996–2000

TRANSFORMATION FROM WITHIN:
Reorganization

*I*n 1996, the American Council on Education (ACE) prepared for a new president. Robert Atwell had announced his retirement, and Stanley O. Ikenberry, president of the University of Illinois, had been appointed to take his place. In preparation for this change, all of ACE's programs were reviewed for the purpose of determining their strengths and weaknesses and how they could be reorganized for optimal performance. This review led to significant changes for GEDTS, the External Diploma Program, and the Center for Adult Learning and Educational Credentials as a whole.

Decision to Keep the GED Tests

One of the most important questions raised by the review was whether GEDTS should remain part of ACE. Budget concerns and questions about the mission of GEDTS in relation to that of ACE had the leadership taking a second look at GEDTS's role within the organization. Outgoing ACE President Robert Atwell commissioned an independent management consulting firm, Leibman Associates Inc., to review the management and activities of GEDTS and recommend whether the program should remain affiliated with ACE or be sold to another testing agency, such as the Educational Testing Service or American College Testing.

The review began in May 1996. In September, the much anticipated "Leibman Report" was released. The report confirmed that the missions of ACE and GEDTS were aligned and recommended that GEDTS remain a program of ACE, but not without significant changes. Noting that the GED Tests were serving less than 6 percent of the 12.7 million adults between the ages of 16 and 44 who did not have a high school diploma, Leibman recommended that GEDTS place greater emphasis on marketing to build its testing volumes. To address budget concerns, Leibman recommended that GEDTS outsource its scoring service, restructure its cost of sales model and other financial tools, and adopt an organizational structure based on its four primary functions: test development, marketing, operations, and data management (COECC 1996d, 4; Leibman Associates, Inc. 1996, ES 2–5).

The report was presented to the Commission on Educational Credit and Credentials (COECC) at its fall 1996 meeting and was unanimously supported by the commissioners. But final authority to implement the recommendations rested with the ACE Board of Directors, which would meet in February. Interim GEDTS Director Joan Auchter, who had assumed leadership of the program in November 1996 after the departure of Jean Lowe, recognized that despite the Leibman Report's recommendation that GEDTS remain a part of ACE, the future of GEDTS within ACE would remain questionable unless a clear financial plan were put in place. Within two months, Auchter met with all 50 U.S. GED administrators in six regional focus groups to examine the partnership with ACE and a possible fee increase so GEDTS could remain a financially solvent ACE program. The result was the largest increase in fees and change in partner pricing structure since the program's inception. The testing fee increased by 122 percent, from $3 to $8 per examinee. Although GEDTS didn't want to overburden GED candidates, the increase was the only way GEDTS could meet the program's growing demands and cover its own operational, test development, and security costs (Auchter 2000a).

Within two months, Auchter met with all 50 U.S. GED administrators in six regional focus groups to examine the partnership with ACE and a possible fee increase so GEDTS could remain a financially solvent ACE program.

But financial viability wasn't Auchter's only topic of conversation with the regional focus groups: She also facilitated discussion of GEDTS's role within ACE. Administrators presented many cogent reasons for keeping GEDTS at ACE—for example, that the value of the GED Tests lies in the state's credential, and that strong support of ACE's continued ownership of GEDTS would insure the value of that credential. The positive outcomes of Auchter's meetings with GED administrators won the support of President Ikenberry, but the board would determine the program's fate (Auchter 1997, 2).

It was a tense time for GEDTS and Center staff. Throughout its history, the GED Tests had been the cornerstone of the Center for Adult Learning and Educational Credentials. If the board voted to sell GEDTS, the Center's future would be uncertain. On a Sunday afternoon in February 1997, President Ikenberry, the Center's interim director Susan Porter Robinson (appointed following Henry Spille's retirement), Joan Auchter, and Michael Leibman presented the issue to the board. GEDTS staff members waited in the hallway outside the meeting room, looking through the open doors for a "thumbs up" or "thumbs down" from Robinson and Auchter. Once they received the sign, they would call the other GEDTS employees to let them know whether the program would continue as a part of ACE (Robinson, S. P. 1999).

The GED Tests also were an important offering of many higher education institutions; 686 of them—including 545 community colleges and 141 four-year institutions—conducted the program.

Ikenberry and Robinson presented their argument to the board, emphasizing the program's 50-year history with ACE and plans to extend its reach and make it more financially sound. They also stated that approximately 70 percent of all GED examinees cited the desire to pursue postsecondary education as their reason for taking the tests, thus aligning GED's mission with ACE's: to increase higher education access and opportunities for everyone, including adults. The GED Tests also were an important offering of many higher education institutions; 686 of them—including 545 community colleges and 141 four-year institutions—conducted the program. After President Ikenberry concluded his presentation, there was little discussion. The board voted unanimously for GEDTS to remain a program of ACE. Robinson and Auchter gave their "thumbs up" to the staff waiting in the hall (COECC 1996d, 4–5; 1997b, 4; Robinson, S. P. 1999).

Decision to Sell the External Diploma Program

The National External Diploma Program (EDP) had a different outcome. Adopted in 1991 by COECC as a program of the Center for Adult Learning, EDP was a competency-based high school credentialing program targeted at older adults who did not have a diploma (see Chapter 8). Though a valuable program—and a welcome addition to the Center's portfolio of offerings—the Center lacked the infrastructure to adequately support it. At the March 1996 commission meeting, EDP Director Florence Harvey reported a drop in sales of EDP assessment materials—accounting for half of EDP's annual income. EDP also was unable to recover costs from the establishment of its first community college site. Six EDP sites were closed due to insufficient financial support. As a result, EDP was not expected to meet its 1996 income projections (COECC 1996b, 4–5).

In late 1996, the decision was made to phase out EDP over the next two years. How this would be done was unclear. Many within ACE and the commission believed that the program belonged in the Center, as it was closely aligned with the Center's mission and served an often-overlooked portion of the adult learner population. Many also were concerned that if ACE no longer administered the program, its cost to the sites and to adult learners themselves would increase, access would decrease, and its quality would decline. But it was soon determined that the program was not financially viable at ACE. ACE found a responsible sponsor for the program in 1998, when Madison Area Technical College in Wisconsin was chosen from a pool of 120 organizations to be the next owner and administrator of EDP. The sale became final in March 2000 (COECC 1996d, 14; 1997b, 10; 1997d, 14; Commission on Adult Learning and Educational Credentials 1998d, 19).

STREAMLINING OPERATIONS:
The Center's Reorganization

The GED Tests and EDP were not the only programs feeling the effects of change. Following his review of GEDTS, Michael Leibman was hired in October 1996 by outgoing Center Director Henry Spille to look at the Center for Adult Learning as a whole, including its role within ACE, its programs, and its financial management practices and growth potential. Leibman concluded that all programs had "tremendous growth potential but would benefit from strategic planning and revised organizational structure and staffing," such as a transition from a programmatic structure to a functional matrix to allow for greater flexibility and the more efficient use of resources (COECC 1997b, 9).

At the October 1997 commission meeting, Susan Porter Robinson (who had been named vice president and director of the Center for Adult Learning effective August 1) informed commissioners of the plan to reorganize. In the discussion that followed, commission Chair Gregory Prince recommended that the commission change its name to the Commission on Adult Learning and Educational Credentials to better reflect its relationship to the Center. The proposal was approved unanimously, and the commission acquired its fourth name in its 55-year history[1] (COECC 1997d, 3).

The next six months were spent planning the Center's first major reorganization since 1978. The Center's programs would be consolidated into three functional areas: Military (directed by Eugene Sullivan), Corporate (directed by Jo Ann Robinson), and GEDTS (directed by Joan Auchter). Military would encompass the Military Evaluations program, Military Installation Voluntary Education Review (MIVER), the Army/ACE Registry Transcript System (AARTS), and the Sailor/Marine Corps/ACE Registry Transcript (SMART). Corporate would include the College Credit Recommendation Service (CREDIT, formerly the Program on Non-Collegiate Sponsored Instruction [PONSI]), the Credit by Examination program, and the three civilian registries (National Registry of Training Programs, International Registry of Training Programs, and Registry of Credit Recommendations). GEDTS would be organized into four programmatic operations: Test Development, Program Operations, Partner Outreach, and Special Projects. All programs would continue to be served by the Center's Marketing and Communications Department, directed by Stephen Sattler (Center for Adult Learning and Educational Credentials 1998; Commission on Adult Learning and Educational Credentials 1998b, 12).

Meanwhile, ACE was undergoing a reorganization of its own. While the Center's programs were consolidated from seven to three, ACE's departments were consolidated from 15 to five: the Division of Access and Equity, the Division of Programs and Policy Analysis, the Division of Government and Public Relations, the Division of External Affairs, and the Division of Administration. The Center for Adult Learning and other ACE programs now were included in the Division of Programs and Policy Analysis, headed by Senior Vice President Michael Baer (Commission on Adult Learning and Educational Credentials 1999b, 15).

AND FROM THIS, GROWTH:
The Center Programs

Under the new organization, the Center's programs continued to grow—but now in a more streamlined, efficient manner.

Military Programs: Military Evaluations, MIVER, AARTS, and SMART

By the late 1990s, the Military Evaluations program was conducting hundreds of course and military occupation evaluations each year and providing credit recommendations from which thousands of servicemembers benefited. Although the numbers did not double and triple as they had in the early years, they continued to increase, demonstrating the continued value of the program to military men and women, as well as the military leadership. Between 1998 and 1999, the Military Evaluations program evaluated 478 courses at 14 military bases. In addition, the advisory service provided credit recommendations to 1,672 colleges and universities, 504 education services officers, and 1,372 students. By the late 1990s, approximately 650,000 military men and women had attended Servicemembers Opportunity Colleges and/or had used ACE credit recommendations (Commission on Adult Learning and Educational Credentials 1998c, Tab IX; 1999a, Tab XIV).

The *Guide to the Evaluation of Educational Experiences in the Armed Services* (the *Guide*) continued to serve as the primary resource of educational credit for servicemembers and colleges and universities. In 1999—its 55th year of publication—the *Guide* contained credit recommendations for almost 7,000 courses. To make the publication more accessible, the decision was made to put the

Guide online by the year 2000, giving anyone with Internet access the opportunity to use the *Guide* for free and enabling staff to update the *Guide* continuously.

MIVER also was experiencing considerable success. In 1996, MIVER review teams visited 23 military installations, an increase of more than 43 percent from 1995, when MIVER conducted 16 visits (Anderson, Meek, and Swinerton 1997, e–iv–e–vi). The program was growing not only in terms of the number of visits it conducted, but also in the type of visits. Over the years, it had become clear that simply making recommendations for improvements would not be sufficient to effect change. There had to be some way of assessing whether the recommendations were being implemented and how the military installations were doing so. MIVER therefore began conducting re-visits to review the installations' progress in implementing the initial MIVER teams' recommendations. In 1998, MIVER conducted eight re-visits (Anderson, Newman, and Xenakis 1998, 9). MIVER also began offering consultation visits to installations that needed help with strategic issues related to their voluntary education programs. These additional types of visits expanded the reach of MIVER and further encouraged high-quality standards for on-base voluntary education (COECC 1997d, 17).

Between 1998 and 1999, the Military Evaluations Program evaluated 478 courses at 14 military bases. In addition, the advisory service provided credit recommendations to 1,672 colleges and universities, 504 education services officers, and 1,372 students.

In 1997, the project's administrator, E. Nelson "Al" Swinerton, died of a heart attack while en route to a MIVER review at Aviano Air Base in Italy. Swinerton had been a charismatic, astute, and untiring leader who contributed greatly to MIVER's becoming a well-respected and integral part of military voluntary education. As director of PONSI (simultaneous with his leadership of MIVER), he also was largely responsible for that program's significant growth from a small, unknown operation to a renowned national program that was both academically and financially successful. The loss was difficult for Center staff, but they persevered. The day after Swinerton's death, Anderson flew to Italy to conduct the MIVER visit as originally scheduled. Anderson then served as the interim MIVER administrator through June 1998. During the seven years of the Swinerton and Anderson administrations, one or both of them personally participated in every MIVER visit; they also developed a pool of more than 150 adult and continuing education professionals from throughout the United States who served on the MIVER teams and wrote the MIVER reports (COECC 1997d, 20; Anderson 2000, 5).

In summer 1998, William Xenakis, previously of University of Maryland University College, was named the new MIVER director. Under his leadership, MIVER's presence in the military continued to grow. Gradually, military installations began to view the MIVER site reviews as a helpful quality-control measure rather than as a threat (Commission on Adult Learning and Educational Credentials 1999b, 29).

Like the Military Evaluations program and MIVER, AARTS also had become extremely successful. Each year, approximately 150,000 soldiers utilized AARTS. Further, more and more colleges and universities were accepting the transcripts and credit recommendations. In a 1998 survey of 397 postsecondary institutions, 78 percent reported that they used AARTS transcripts to award credit. (Of those that did not award credit on the basis of AARTS transcripts, most indicated that they accepted credits only from regionally accredited institutions.) Twenty percent of respondents indicated that they granted more credit using the AARTS transcript than they would without it. The average number of semester hours of credit awarded was 14 (AARTS 1998).

The success of AARTS spurred the creation of a new registry: SMART, which took effect on 1 October 1999. Prior to implementing SMART, ACE's Military Evaluations program conducted validation studies at more than 15 Navy and Marine bases across the United States. Data from these studies, as well as feedback from personal interviews with more than 1,000 sailors and Marines, were used to test the efficiency and accuracy of the process. SMART now provides more than 350,000 servicemembers an automated process for assigning college credit for learning acquired through military training. For each servicemember, SMART includes descriptions of military courses completed, occupations held, and test scores. With the implementation of SMART, ACE now provides a transcript service to three of the four U.S. military services (ACE 1999).

Corporate Programs

PONSI grew in terms both of the number of courses it reviewed and the breadth of its evaluations and services. The 1999 *National Guide to Educational Credit for Training Programs* database contained credit recommendations for nearly 10,000 courses offered by more than 300 organizations. Approximately 900 colleges and universities nationwide accepted the recommendations (COECC 1997a, Tab XV). Consider how much this program had grown: In 1992, prior to Al Swinerton and Jo Ann Robinson assuming the leadership, only 29 organizations contracted with PONSI for course reviews. In 1999, 87 organizations had course reviews—an increase of 300 percent in only eight years (CREDIT Undated-a).

The types of courses PONSI was evaluating also were expanding. As increasing numbers of organizations began to use technology to deliver employee education and training, PONSI found itself having to evaluate distance learning—a significantly different education medium that required a correspondingly different evaluation approach. In 1996, PONSI and the Distance Education and Training Council therefore jointly published the *Distance Learning Evaluation Guide,* the companion piece to *Guiding Principles for Distance Learning in a Learning Society* (see page 215). Intended for PONSI course reviewers, the guide identified seven factors that influence the quality of distance learning programs: learning design, learning objectives and outcomes, learning materials, technology, learner support, organizational commitment, and subject matter (COECC 1996d, 15). To further enhance reviewers' ability to evaluate distance learning courses, PONSI began to conduct workshops. The workshops were quickly over-subscribed each time they were offered, indicating the demand for a better understanding of distance learning (COECC 1997a, Tab XV).

PONSI also experienced another, more cosmetic change in the late 1990s. Having considered a name change for years (Program on Non-Collegiate Sponsored Instruction was believed by many to be too cumbersome and not intuitively descriptive), the PONSI Advisory Council proposed that a more descriptive name be chosen. In 1997, just prior to its being brought under the direction of the newly formed Corporate department, PONSI officially changed its name to the ACE College Credit Recommendation Service, or CREDIT (COECC 1997b, 7).

With the new name came the push to expand CREDIT's reach, in terms of the number and types of course evaluations conducted and of its leadership in the corporate education community. One example of CREDIT's expansion of its course evaluation services was in September 1998, when the U.S. Coast Guard selected CREDIT as a Quality Standards System organization. The Quality Standards System enables the Coast Guard to monitor all training, competency, assessment, certification, endorsement, and revalidation activities that are required by the International Convention on Standards of Training Certification and Watchkeeping for Seafarers. This designation made ACE one of only five U.S. Coast Guard–accepted, publicly available organizations worldwide to review and evaluate the quality of basic programs offered by schools specializing in maritime training (CREDIT 2000b).

CREDIT also sought ways to expand its presence as a corporate education leader. One way of doing this was through the creation of the Adult Learner of the Year Award. Initiated in 1999 in celebration of CREDIT's 25th anniversary, the award was designed to recognize the person who best demonstrates a commitment to lifelong learning by using his or her credit recommendations for further education. CREDIT also helped celebrate its 25th anniversary by awarding the first E. Nelson "Al" Swinerton Distinguished Service Award to Celeste Sichenze, an ACE National Coordinator. The award will continue to be presented annually at the State Affiliate Directors and ACE National Coordinators Training Workshop (CREDIT 1999).

CREDIT further asserted its leadership in the corporate education community by surveying ACE member institutions with regard to their corporate partnerships. Conducted in partnership with ACE's Business–Higher Education Forum, the survey was intended to determine the general nature of existing corporate–higher education partnerships and identify successful relationships. Of the 460 institutions that responded, 88 percent reported that they currently were engaged in partnerships with business and industry. The types of partnerships varied widely, but the fact that such a large majority of institutions were involved in partnerships with businesses reaffirmed the importance of continuing efforts to link higher education and industry. On the basis of this survey, CREDIT and the Business–Higher Education Forum decided to launch a web site to showcase college–business partnerships and best practices. At www.acenet.edu/calec/partnerships/home.html, college, university, and business representatives can read about how various institutions have partnered with businesses, what has worked, and what has not worked (Commission on Adult Learning and Educational Credentials 1998a, Tab VI).

The Credit by Examination program was another corporate program that continued to enjoy success in its maturity. The fourth edition of the *Guide to Educational Credit by Examination,* published in 1996, contained credit recommendations for more than 200 national testing programs and professional licensure/certification examinations. The Credit by Examination program also began evaluating the testing programs of professional associations; in 1999, it also began making credit recommendations for a new type of exam: the Military Academic Credit Examination.

Initiated in 1995 by the Marine Corps, the Military Academic Credit Examination project was spurred by preparations for SMART. The Marine Corps wanted to provide a standard assessment for eligible Marines to receive ACE credit recommendations by demonstrating proficiency in their Military Occupational Specialty (MOS). But rather than have the MOSs evaluated by the Military Programs division of the Center, as the Army had done, the Marine Corps decided to develop an exam that would assess Marines' proficiency (the Military Academic Credit Examination project therefore fell under the direction of the Credit by Examination program). In August 1999, the Military Police exam, the first of 55 Military Academic Credit Examinations, was submitted for review and received college credit recommendations (Robinson, J. A. 1999).

Given the tremendous growth in the number of reviews and credit recommendations by CREDIT, it was logical that the corporate registries also should experience significant success. In 1995, the Registry of Credit Recommendations (which tracked CREDIT recommendations) had served 55,000 students; by 1999, that number had more than tripled, to 196,000 students from 564 participating organizations. The other registries also had grown. In 1999, nearly 600,000 courses were in the database of the National Registry of Training Programs, which boasted 375 participating organizations, the Credit by Examination registry, and the International Registry of Training Programs (which tracked continuing education units for the 18 members of the International Association for Continuing Education and Training) (CREDIT Undated-a; Robinson, J. A. 2000).

The GED Testing Service Anew

Once its operational review was complete, the GED Testing Service (GEDTS) began to align its functions to meet the challenges of its new environment. Each of its new operations—Special Projects, Test Development, Partner Outreach, and Program Operations—was headed by its own director and guided by its own mission. Special Projects assists the executive director with the growth and appropriate positioning of the GED program; Test Development develops high-quality assessment instruments; Partner Outreach works with GED administrators in three key areas: policy, security, and accommodations for specific learning disabilities; and Program Operations oversees operational aspects of the program, such as contracting, materials distribution, and outsourced scoring services.

Program Changes

In addition to restructuring its national staff, GEDTS made other important changes as well. Research and environmental

changes in education and the workplace led to two major program revisions: raising of the minimum passing standard and the
creation of four dedicated expert panels.

Raising Passing Standards

One of the most significant program changes came in 1997,
when GEDTS—for the second time in its history—raised the
minimum score required for passing the GED Tests.[2] The decision to make this change had been initiated in 1995, when
GEDTS staff conducted two studies to link external educational
performance measures to performance on the GED Tests. The
first study examined the relationship between grades reported
for high school seniors in content area classes that corresponded
to each of the five GED subtests and selected
values along the GED score scale of 20 to 80.
The study revealed that at a score of 35 on the
GED scale, there was little recognizable difference (less than 5 percent) between the performance of graduating seniors who reported
an overall content grade of A and those who
reported an overall content grade of D. At a
score of 40, the difference in performance between these two groups increased to approximately 14 to 20 percent (COECC 1996a, Tab
IV). The second study was based on an analysis of the 1992 GED/National Adult Literacy
Survey, which compared the performance of
persons at each literacy level with GED standard score ranges (see Chapter 8). Based on

*The study revealed
that at a score of 35 on the
GED scale, there was little
recognizable difference (less
than 5 percent) between the
performance of graduating
seniors who reported an
overall content grade of A
and those who reported an
overall content grade of D.*

the results of these studies, the GED Advisory Committee and
then the commission passed the recommendation of the GEDTS
staff that the minimum score required for passing the GED Tests
be raised from 40 *or* 45 to 40 *and* 45 (COECC 1997a, Tab XV).
Only 67 percent of graduating seniors meet the new standard, as
compared to 75 percent of graduating seniors who met the previous standard (GEDTS 1997c, ii).

As a result of the increase in the minimum passing score, 36 jurisdictions (which can set their own minimum score requirement as long as it is higher than the national minimum

established by ACE) were required to raise their passing standard in 1997. The pass rate subsequently decreased by 3.8 percentage points, from 71.8 percent in 1996 to 68 percent in 1997. However, the rate increased in 1998 by 2.5 percentage points, to 70.5 percent, suggesting that examinees may have increased their level of preparation in the second year of the new passing standard (GEDTS 1997c, ii; 1998a, 29).

Expert Panels
Another important change to the GED program was the addition of four expert panels to guide the testing process. While the new generation of tests was being developed, GEDTS recognized a need for greater breadth and depth of continuous expert guidance than its permanent staff could provide. Thus, four expert panels—psychometrics, workplace issues, research, and learning disabilities—were formed to advise on key areas of the program.

The psychometric advisory panel comprises nationally recognized experts who have extensive practical experience with large-scale, high-stakes assessment programs. The purpose of the psychometric panel is to review the recommended subject area test specifications and design (such as alternate formats, sample design, and standard setting) and to recommend the requisite psychometric procedures and research. The panel also helps write the technical manual that accompanies each new generation of tests (Auchter 1999; Commission on Adult Learning and Educational Credentials 1999a, Tab XIV).

The workplace advisory panel is a group of representatives from corporations, unions, and associations that have a high representation of GED graduates in their workforces. The purpose of this panel is to help GEDTS obtain authentic workplace informational texts to use in the reading, writing, and mathematics tests. It also is charged with examining how the GED diploma and graduates are perceived in the workplace and with shaping, positioning, and distributing the appropriate message for and to various workplace constituents: employers, employees, unions, managers, supervisors, and human resource professionals (Auchter 1999).

The research advisory panel is charged with setting a proactive research agenda, framing appropriate research questions, guiding research discussions, reviewing research findings, and facilitating the promulgation of GEDTS research in the research and policy communities.

The learning disabilities panel advises GEDTS about ongoing issues related to accommodations for specific learning disabilities—particularly the impact of accommodations on test security (Auchter 2000a).

In addition to the program changes described above, the work of GEDTS was streamlined to focus on the core competencies identified in the Leibman Report: test development and test de-livery. In the late 1990s, multiple events related to both of these areas transpired, ultimately making the testing program stronger—both financially and in terms of credibility.

Within test development, there were two main objectives: redevelopment of the fourth edition of the test battery (or GED 2002) and redevelopment and renorming of the Spanish-language GED Tests. Within test delivery, four areas were emphasized: ensuring the security of international testing, accommodating examinees with specific learning disabilities, resolving the continued debate surrounding the testing pro-gram for at-risk high school students, and establishing the Strategic Training and Resource Specialists (STARS) program.

Test Development
GED 2002
Initial discussions about redeveloping the GED test battery began in the early 1990s, with the goal of releasing the new generation of tests in 2000. Phase One of the redevelopment process began in 1994 with a review of the tests' goals by GEDTS staff, administrators, the GED Advisory Committee, and the commission. The review resulted in a vote to reaffirm the purpose of the GED Tests ("to provide an opportunity for adults who have not graduated from high school to earn a high school–level educational diploma") and for the content of the GED Tests to continue to reflect the "major and lasting

academic outcomes of a four-year program of study with increased emphasis on workplace and higher education needs
reflected in the context of test items" (COECC 1996c, Tab VIII).

GEDTS also looked broadly at all of the issues related to the tests
and identified those that were most important to the redevelopment process, as well as the questions each issue raised. The first
set of issues had to do with distribution and its impact on test security, score reporting innovations, and the use of computer
technology. Next were feasibility issues and their impact on the
use of computer technology. Third, GEDTS identified issues
such as college outcomes, college acceptance, the economic impact of the GED credential, employer acceptance, high school
acceptance, and predictive validity. Policy issues and their impact
on accessibility and the development of alternate versions of the
tests also were cited. Last, GEDTS identified test development issues, such as test content, item format, cognitive levels, sampling
design, statistical evaluation, standard setting, the use of computer
technology, the role of calculators, and test administration issues
(COECC 1996a, Tab v).

In 1996, the redevelopment process began in earnest—with a revised release date of 1 January 2002 (thus the project name
"GED 2002"). Phase Two of the redevelopment process involved
review and revision of the content and skills to be included in
the new test series. The GED Test Development unit was
charged with establishing a context for the content specifications
of the 2002 GED Test Series, which it did by evaluating national
and state education standards initiatives and their implications.
Recognizing that this research would be a valuable addition to
the debate about establishing national standards, GEDTS decided
to publish and widely distribute its report as a book. *Alignment of
National and State Standards* (1999) examined standards in language arts, mathematics, science, and social studies (the subject
areas of the GED Tests). This link between national and state
standards and the GED Tests was important. As Auchter wrote in
the book's introduction, "Since the GED Tests are a summative
evaluation of what graduating seniors should know and be able
to do, the standards serve as the goal or blueprint for the tests."
It therefore followed that the blueprint could be used in the

establishment of national standards. By publishing *Alignment of National and State Standards,* GEDTS positioned itself as a leader in the discussion about national standards (GEDTS 1999, 6, 7).

Meanwhile, GEDTS had been working with the U.S. and Canadian Test Specifications Committees to determine the content of the 2002 test series. In December 1996, the Canadian committee (comprising national content experts) met in Toronto to review Canadian content standards (such as critical thinking, information management, and technology) and to define critical skills across content areas. These standards did not differ much from the U.S. standards that had been identified in national and state subject matter efforts. In January 1997, the U.S. committee (comprising secondary curriculum and adult education experts) prepared a set of recommendations for revising the specifications for the new generation of tests (COECC 1996c, Tab VIII; 1997d, 17).

The new tests also would reflect the impact of welfare-to-work legislation and the increased nationwide emphasis in the K–12 education community on academic standards in four areas: language arts (reading and writing), social studies, science, and mathematics.

In terms of specific changes, the GED writing test will place greater emphasis on organization, in both the text editing and writing portions. For the writing sample requirement (a 45-minute direct writing sample), the 2002 test series will include a new scoring guide that rates writing samples on a scale of one to four. This descriptive scale is based on graduating seniors' writing samples ranked from the best to the least well written. The reading test still will require candidates to read and interpret fiction and nonfiction, including prose, poetry, and drama, from a wide variety of cultures and time periods.

The 2002 social studies test will emphasize a candidate's ability to process information presented visually through maps, charts, photos, and cartoons. This represents a notable change from prior test series, which were primarily (70 percent) text-based. The 2002 test also will include an increased emphasis on civics, history, and government.

Items on the 2002 science test will continue to cover a full range of scientific areas, with tasks adopted from the framework of the National Science Education Standards. Questions will be multiple choice, but topics will include designing experiments, interpreting others' experimental results, analyzing experimental flaws, applying scientific conclusions to one's personal life, and applying the methodologies and conclusions of scientists of the past to global science issues of the present.

Recognizing that calculators have become a common tool in everyday life, the Test Specifications Committee decided after almost eight years of debate to permit the use of a solar-powered Casio FX-260 calculator on one of two parts of the 2002 mathematics test.[3] Use of the calculator is intended to relieve the tedium of performing calculations by hand and to permit candidates to concentrate on setting up and solving problems that reflect the use of mathematics in daily life. Items on the mathematics test will emphasize algebra, statistics, and probability.

If the Spanish-language test were to accurately assess an examinee's Spanish writing ability, a direct translation would not suffice. Therefore, an extensive translation process was initiated, resulting in 60 percent direct translation and 40 percent altered— but equally difficult—items.

Spanish-language GED Tests

While the GED 2002 redevelopment process was getting underway, redevelopment of the Spanish-language GED Tests was nearing completion. Ultimately, the new Spanish-language GED Tests proved almost a direct translation of the English-language tests—except for Test 1 (writing skills). If the Spanish-language test were to accurately assess an examinee's Spanish writing ability, a direct translation would not suffice. Therefore, an extensive translation process was initiated, resulting in 60 percent direct translation and 40 percent altered—but equally difficult—items. In fall 1997, the revised Spanish-language GED Tests were administered to a small sample of bilingual students who took half of the test in Spanish and half of it in English to ensure that any difficulty with the items was not the result of poor translation. The following spring, the tests were normed on a sample of bilingual Spanish-speaking high school seniors in New York, California,

Florida, Texas, and Illinois. In March 1999, the tests were administered for the first time across the United States (Commission on Adult Learning and Educational Credentials 1998b, 17; Kentucky Education Television 1997).

Test Delivery
International Testing Security
In 1995, GEDTS closed its overseas testing centers because of security concerns. This left U.S. citizens abroad and foreign nationals who wanted to take the tests with limited options: a handful of secure American embassies and Information Service field offices had agreed to administer the tests, as had the Defense Activity for Non-Traditional Education Support (DANTES) testing centers (for military personnel and dependents only). To expand the testing options available to individuals overseas, GEDTS began to explore computer-based testing as a secure and accessible means of administering the GED Tests. In 1997, GEDTS partnered with Sylvan Learning Systems to deliver the GED Tests overseas through computer-based testing at Sylvan's extensive network of testing centers (GEDTS 1997b, 9).

Accommodations for Specific Learning Disabilities
Expanding access for examinees with specific learning disabilities (SLD) continued to be a priority for GEDTS during the late 1990s. Although policies had been established in the 1980s to grant accommodations (see Chapter 8), the volume of accommodations remained low—in part, it was thought, because of the complicated application process. In 1996, GEDTS convened a panel of experts to review the policies for accommodating GED candidates with SLD. Under the leadership of Fred Edwards, GEDTS director of partner outreach, the panel was charged with making recommendations on how to improve access without compromising the integrity and security of the tests (COECC 1997a, Tab XV).

The panel's efforts resulted in two important initiatives: increased outreach to candidates with SLD and removal of the application process from the national, centralized level to the jurisdictional (state, province, or territory) level. Increased outreach took the form of a brochure, "How to Take the GED Tests If You Have a

P
—
207

Learning Disability," which included information about the accommodation process, a definition of SLD, and information about how to seek funding. The removal of the application process from the national to the jurisdictional level was more complex. The application process for accommodations—although necessary to ensure fairness—was time-consuming and complicated, making access to the GED Tests even more difficult for the population of examinees with SLD. To qualify for accommodations, a GED candidate had to complete a request form that required documentation within the past five years of the disability, to include a psychological evaluation, and a measure of current educational achievement, such as the Woodcock-Johnson Tests of Achievement. Candidates also could use supportive information, such as an existing individual education plan, to define the nature of the accommodation being sought (GEDTS 1997a).

In an effort to streamline the application process (and thereby make it easier for candidates), GEDTS decided to begin transferring the process from the national level to the jurisdictional level. This would speed the approval process and enable administrators and examiners to offer more hands-on help to applicants. However, for the transfer to be successful, GEDTS would have to make the procedure very clear and train GED administrators and examiners in it. To begin, GEDTS incorporated the U.S. Department of Education's definition of a learning disability into its policies and procedures, which it distributed through such publications as the *GED Examiner's Manual*. GEDTS also prepared a draft video training script for examiners and initiated development of a training program and materials for GED administrators. Last, GEDTS sought the advice and counsel of major SLD organizations and advocates (COECC 1997c, Tab XIV; GEDTS 1997a; Commission on Adult Learning and Educational Credentials 1998a, Tab XI).

Training was the most important element of the successful transfer of the application process. Following the panel meeting in 1996, GEDTS contracted with experts from testing organizations, national advocacy organizations, the U.S. Department of Education, and the Civil Rights Division of the U.S. Department

of Justice—as well as attorneys—to develop and review the criteria for granting accommodations. Introduced at the July 1998
GED administrators conference, the new criteria allow GED administrators to process 80 percent of all requests; the remaining
20 percent are forwarded directly to GEDTS for clinical review
by a team of experts. GEDTS also developed a 30-minute video
to augment training. Three-day training sessions were offered beginning in September 1998, and by the end of 1999, the transfer
of the application process was complete (Commission on Adult
Learning and Educational Credentials 1998c, Tab IX).

Testing Program for At-Risk Enrolled Youths
The policy of testing at-risk students enrolled in traditional secondary schools continued to be debated in the late 1990s. The
issue had arisen in 1988, when Virginia received permission from
the Commission on Educational Credentials to become the first
state to administer the GED Tests to enrolled at-risk students.
Other states soon followed suit, and by 1993, eight states had
pilot programs for testing at-risk students. After reviewing the
programs, the GEDTS leadership in 1994 recommended ending
the testing of at-risk in-school youths. But action was delayed
due to support of the program by the majority of GED administrators, who believed in-school GED testing was an important
option for at-risk students. States adhering to the program's
criteria were permitted to continue testing enrolled students
(see Chapter 8).

However, this policy soon changed. In early 1996, GEDTS received an inquiry from Calvert County, Maryland, requesting
permission to use the GED Tests as an exit exam for high school
seniors. Although this request had been made before (by
Oklahoma in 1991), Maryland's request spurred extensive discussions between GEDTS and ACE leadership. The result was
ACE President Robert Atwell's decision to discontinue all administration of the tests to enrolled students. The revised policy
would be implemented over several years, enabling states with
such programs to phase them out while disrupting students as
little as possible. The decision to end the program was based on
several concerns. First, GEDTS was worried that in the long
term, distinguishing between high school students judged to be

P
—

at risk and those judged not to be at risk would result in administrative and credibility problems. Second, there was a prevailing sense that GEDTS should not be involved in high school exit testing, "wholesale" or at all. Third, GEDTS was concerned that testing of this potential magnitude was inappropriate for an agency with limited resources and whose mission was focused on higher and adult education (GEDTS 1998a, 6–7).

At its February 1996 meeting, the ACE Board of Directors supported Atwell's decision. GEDTS and affected jurisdictions created a five-year timetable to phase out the testing of enrolled students. All testing programs for at-risk youths were scheduled to end in 2001 (GEDTS 1998a, 7).

Despite the new policy, states continued to request permission to use the GED Tests. The rationales varied: Some wanted to test at-risk students; others wanted to use the tests as an exit exam or benchmarking tool; still others wanted to use it for remediation or diagnostic testing. In 1998, discussions of the issue resumed. Increasingly, state departments of education were seeking appropriate methods for assessing performance against state standards for the core academic disciplines. As the only national secondary-education assessment instrument, the GED Tests were in a prime position for having their purpose and use expanded. The question was whether ACE wanted to do so.

Increasingly, state departments of education were seeking appropriate methods for assessing performance against state standards for the core academic disciplines. As the only national secondary-education assessment instrument, the GED Tests were in a prime position to expand their purpose and use.

The new ACE leadership, under the direction of President Ikenberry, was willing to explore the possibilities. In March 2000, Auchter and Senior Vice President Michael Baer proposed that the ACE Board endorse the GED testing program for at-risk youths, explaining that GEDTS had examined several states' pilot programs and was confident that with modest refinements, it would remain a valuable and appropriate use of the GED Tests. The board agreed and voted unanimously to continue the program (GEDTS 1998a, 9–10, 19–21; ACE 2000).

STARS

The Leibman Report had identified test security as one of GEDTS's core competencies but had also noted that it was "an acknowledged vulnerability of the program"; it therefore had recommended that GEDTS assume a greater role in implementing security procedures (Leibman Associates, Inc. 1996, ES-3). In December 1996, a task force of GED administrators and chief examiners met to examine security issues and make recommendations for improvement. They made several: that GEDTS establish a monitoring team to evaluate security measures throughout each state, province, and territory; that GEDTS educate high-level administrators—including chief state school officers, college deans and presidents, superintendents, and prison wardens—about the importance of test security; that GEDTS change the way addendum sites were selected, administered, monitored, and evaluated; that each GED testing center be notified of when secure materials would be shipped, to include an estimated time of arrival; that GEDTS expand the production of training materials so examiners and administrators would be familiar with all security policies; that GEDTS develop more specific requirements regarding the storage of secure testing materials at testing centers; and that GEDTS require all newly appointed chief examiners to hold at least a bachelor's degree, regardless of "equivalent experience" (Allin 1997, 1, 9–10, 12).

To implement these recommendations, Auchter appointed a technical assistance manager and technical assistance specialists to the staff and launched the STARS program. This program grew out of a suggestion that GEDTS hire retired administrators to provide field support—including the training of new administrators and examiners—to GED jurisdictions. The need for such a program was clear. Between 1994 and 2000, GEDTS experienced a 70 percent turnover in jurisdictional GED administrators. Training new administrators would require more resources and support than the GEDTS staff could provide and would leave a service gap at the jurisdictional level. By hiring experienced administrators to serve as mentors to new state staff, these problems would be eliminated—or at least mitigated (Malone 1999; Auchter 2000a).

After extensive planning and feedback from the GED administrators, GEDTS hired a field service manager who in 1998
began hiring retired administrators and other GED professionals.
By 1999, 11 "STARS" with 350 years of combined experience
had been hired. Upon the request of jurisdictional administrators, these specialists travel to the testing site at no cost to the
states and provide consulting and training services—with test security being the primary objective—to administrators, examiners, and other staff. In the first six months of the program's
operation, STARS attended 35 meetings in 17 states and four
Canadian provinces (Malone 1999).

Full Circle: The GED and the Military
Another important development for GEDTS during the final
years of the 20th century was a new effort by the Army and Navy
to recruit nontraditional high school graduates. Ever since the
GED Tests had ceased to be strictly a "veteran's test" (in the late
1940s), the relationship between the military and GED graduates
had been inconsistent. Often, the services would limit the number of enlistees with GED diplomas—or refuse them entirely—
because historically, the attrition rates of nontraditional high
school graduates (including GED recipients) had been higher
than those of other recruits. Whereas the traditional high school
graduate had almost an 80 percent probability of completing the
first three years of service, nontraditional graduates had only a
60 percent probability of doing so. To compensate for this higher
attrition rate, nontraditional graduates were required to achieve
higher scores on the Armed Services Vocational Aptitude Battery
to qualify for enlistment. Nevertheless, when the number of
applicants with traditional high school diplomas exceeded military service employment requirements, the services would enlist
only a limited number of nontraditional graduates—typically no
more than 10 percent of the total number of enlistees (Hone
2000, 1; Sellman 1985, 1).

ACE had long taken issue with this practice, asserting that an applicant's educational credential "should not be used as the basis
for enlistment priority and that the practice unfairly discrimi-
nates against the majority of GED graduates who do complete
their first term of enlistment." ACE encouraged the services to

adopt a screening system that did not take into acount the type of credential (GEDTS 1987b, 1). As ACE President Atwell said at the Department of Defense's 1994 Worldwide Education Symposium,

> Potential recruits should be evaluated on their educational attainments and their aptitude—what they actually have achieved and what they are likely to achieve. The military is one of the few large organizations remaining in our society that still accepts the high school diploma as proxy for educational attainment, persistence, and other desirable qualities . . . . The military should end its arbitrary and misleading reliance on the standard high school diploma and move toward the use of other tools to evaluate the achievements and potential of its recruits (GEDTS 1994, 12).

Although the military did not formally change its policy, great strides were made in 1999 and 2000 with the introduction of two Army and Navy programs. The Army's initiative, "GED Plus," was designed to provide the Army with alternative predictors of applicants' success. The pilot program, which was launched in 40 percent of the Army's recruiting areas, requires GED graduates to score in the top 50 percent on the Armed Forces Qualifications Test and in the top 75 percent on the Assessment of Individual Motivation test. The Army then sponsors successful applicants to complete an attendance-based GED instructional program while serving in the Army's delayed-entry program. Through "GED Plus," the Army pledged to recruit as many as 6,000 non–high school graduates each year until the program ends in 2003 (Auchter 2000c, 2). For the first time, rather than changing policy to adapt to low recruitment levels, a military service had implemented a program to predict prospective enlistees' success.

Through "GED Plus," the Army pledged to recruit as many as 6,000 non–high school graduates each year until the program ends in 2003.

The Navy introduced a similar program on a smaller scale. In fall 1999, the Navy's Recruit Training Command, in conjunction with the Great Lakes Navy College Office and DANTES, opened a new GED testing center in Great Lakes, Illinois, as part of its Academic Capacity Enhancement program for recruits without a high school diploma. These recruits must score in the top 50 percent on the Armed Services Vocational Aptitude Battery and are enrolled in the Academic Capacity Enhancement program prior to the start of boot camp. At the end of the program, they are given the option of taking the GED Tests over a two-day period. Of the 90 percent who choose to take the tests, 82 percent pass (Dermody 2000, 4). Although not as large an effort as the Army's, the Navy's program nevertheless demonstrates a commitment to providing equal opportunity to non–high school graduates.

Looking Ahead

With test development and test security firmly established as core competencies, GEDTS has begun work toward accomplishing three key strategic objectives: to develop and deliver the 2002 series of the GED Tests; to communicate the value of the GED diploma to the public; and to build the testing volume to 1 million examinees annually. All programs, test development, and test delivery initiatives will fall within this framework.

THE DISTANCE LEARNING REVOLUTION:
New Opportunities and New Challenges

One of the most important educational developments in the late 1990s was the explosive growth of distance learning. Online classes, computer-based training, videoconferencing, and satellite feeds became common offerings at most colleges and universities, not only in continuing and adult education programs, but also in "traditional" programs for "traditional" students. Distance learning had entered the mainstream. In 1998, only 5 percent of U.S. students were in distance learning programs; by 2002, 15 percent are expected to be enrolled, not including the untold numbers who will take web-assisted traditional classes (COECC 1996d, 9).

Although distance learning is the culmination of a century's work on the part of adult educators to increase access, it has its risks. Even as it invites access, it invites fraud and lower quality programs that can be delivered at less cost and greater profit.

The Center for Adult Learning recognized this. In 1993, with funding from Jones Educational Network, the Center convened a task force to develop *Guiding Principles for Distance Learning in a Learning Society.* Completed in 1996, the principles define distance learning as "a system and a process that connects learners with distributed learning resources" and identify the "central qualities that should characterize all effective learning activities, regardless of setting or purpose, but that are of special relevance to the practice of distance learning." These qualities include learning design, learner support, organizational commitment, learning outcomes, and technology—the same qualities adopted by PONSI when it developed the *Distance Learning Evaluation Guide* (see page 197). The commission readily endorsed *Guiding Principles for Distance Learning in a Learning Society.* Like *Principles of Good Practice for Alternative and External Degree Programs for Adults,* it became a valued resource for colleges and universities (COECC 1996a, Tab iii).

In 1998, only 5 percent of U.S. students were in distance learning programs; by 2002, 15 percent are expected to be enrolled, not including the untold numbers who will take web-assisted traditional classes.

Publication of *Guiding Principles* was only the beginning of the Center's involvement in the distance learning revolution. On the recommendation of the commission, Center Director Susan Porter Robinson commissioned an independent consultant to analyze the current distance learning environment and explore possible roles for ACE and the Center to play in its expansion. In 1998, consultant Neil O'Farrell presented to the commission "Distance Learning and the American Council on Education: An Agenda for Leadership and Action." In this paper, O'Farrell examined the socioeconomic and demographic trends and emerging technologies that influence distance learning, as well as the role of higher education in its delivery and ACE's relationship to it. As O'Farrell observed, "ACE must represent not only its members, but in fact the highest aspirations of its members in a time of shifting forces. If the academy is to survive the dawn of the Knowledge Age, and flourish in the future, it must begin the process of reinventing itself" (O'Farrell 1998, 17).

The commission subsequently decided to develop its own distance learning agenda—namely, to facilitate the sharing of resources among educational providers, focus on the education of users and students, maintain quality assurance, and promote access (Commission on Adult Learning and Educational Credentials 1998d, 7).

Complementing the commission's work, the Center established a three-pronged action plan to address distance learning issues: writing and disseminating publications (such as *Guiding Principles for Distance Learning in a Learning Society*); evaluating corporate and military distance learning courses; and training faculty in how to develop and evaluate effective distance learning programs. The Center also became a frequent participant in conferences and leadership councils related to distance learning. For example, in October 1995, the Center participated in a meeting of the Global Alliance for Transnational Education. One of the key action items to come out of the conference was the decision to develop guiding principles for transnational education based on ACE's distance learning principles. The following year, the Center participated in the International Council on Distance Education's Standing Committee of Presidents of Open and Distance Learning Institutions. The Center also sponsored sessions on distance learning at ACE's annual meeting in each of the last four years of the 20th century. Through these and other initiatives, the Center for Adult Learning began taking a more active leadership role in the distance learning revolution (COECC 1996a, Tab XI; 1996c, Tab XII; 1997a, Tab XV).

NOTES

[1] From 1942 until 1974, it was the Commission on Accreditation of Service Experiences; in 1974, it became the Commission on Educational Credit; in 1979, it became the Commission on Educational Credit and Credentials.

[2] The first change was in 1981, when the minimum score of 35 was increased to 40 on each test in the battery.

[3] Part I permits use of the calculator while Part II does not; a candidate's final score will be a compilation of the two scores. All GED candidates will be allowed to practice using the calculator before the test begins.

AFTERWORD

*T*he span of the Center's history has been wide and deep—and those of us who continue the work of the Center's founders are humbled and grateful to be part of it. What began in 1942 as a single program to help veterans earn high school diplomas has evolved into a national organization devoted to increasing adult access to further education. And quality assurance has been a continuous element throughout that evolution.

Since 1949, an estimated 14 million adults have received GED diplomas. Additional millions have earned college credit through the Military Evaluations, College Credit Recommendation Service (CREDIT), and Credit by Examination programs. And now there are other measures. As we enter a new century, the Center for Adult Learning's web site (www.acenet.edu/calec) hosts more than 50,000 user sessions each month: some 4,000 for Military Programs, nearly 7,000 for Corporate Programs, and 42,000 for GEDTS. By the time you read this, those numbers will be even higher.

*S*ince 1949, an estimated 14 million adults have received GED diplomas.

But numbers are only half the story. Through its advocacy efforts, the Center for Adult Learning has helped change the way in which Americans view adult education. From Neil Turner and Thomas Barrows's national tour in the 1940s to promote the GED Tests, to the Center's exposure of diploma mills and its call in the 1980s and 1990s for higher standards in distance education, the Center has helped make adult education a more integral part of American higher education—rather than the afterthought it had been for so many years.

The passage has not always been easy. The growing pains of the GED Tests and the controversy surrounding them, occasional conflicts with various external partners, and missteps along the way have provided numerous lessons on the importance of diplomacy, clear objectives, and open communication. But these lessons have helped guide the Center's mission, and learning has been lifelong for us, as well.

Now, as we begin to move into the years ahead, the Center for Adult Learning and Educational Credentials will continue the twin missions of its founders: quality and access.

GEDTS, through the development of the 2002 series GED Tests, heightened test security, and the testing of adults with disabilities, has become a benchmark for quality and access in the assessment and measurement fields. The Military Programs division of the Center is further expanding access by making the *Guide to the Evaluation of Educational Experiences in the Armed Services* available online. This in turn will serve as a template for the CREDIT *Guide*, which is scheduled to be made available online by 2001. The Military Programs division also is expanding to evaluate many more Navy courses, and it expects to increase its number of course evaluations for the other services, too. The Corporate programs' work in evaluating distance learning courses has made the Center a leader in this growing arena. Corporate programs continue to offer workshops on how to evaluate distance learning courses—and they're consistently overbooked.

As it has since World War II, the Center continues to be a steward—bridging the world of nontraditional learning and guarding the credentialing opportunities of the adults it is called to serve.

It is not only at the programmatic level, however, that the Center persists with its mission. The Center also has become a leader in the lifelong learning community—both nationally and internationally. It has been a privilege to represent the Center at the White House, at the Pentagon, on Capitol Hill, and at the United Nations. More and more, our voice—and that of all adult learners—is being heard.

The Center is increasing its services by embracing technology. In addition to making two *Guides* available online, the Center recently revamped its newsletter, *CenterPoint* (formerly *Update*), to be an entirely electronic publication. By visiting the American Council on Education's web site (www.acenet.edu), readers can access *CenterPoint* and learn about national trends affecting adult education. Insights on adult learning, opinion pieces, updates on Center programs, and links to related web sites are also provided.

In these and numerous other ways, the Center for Adult Learning continues the promise of its founders. Today, the mission of access may appear very different as distance learning continues its significant and sweeping changes. And measures of quality assurance—new tests, new standards, new initiatives—now have a different look as well. But the passion for helping adult learners still carries the original flame. As it has since World War II, the Center continues to be a steward—bridging the world of nontraditional learning and guarding the credentialing opportunities of the adults it is called to serve.

In closing, I would like to pay tribute to my forebears and colleagues. I began this afterword by saying that the legacy of our founders leaves us humble and grateful. But that extends beyond our original founders—Neil Turner, Thomas Barrows, and others. It extends to everyone who has been part of the Center and helped lay the foundation upon which its work has risen. For every history, no matter how thorough, has its unsung heroes. I commend all of them—including the 58 men and women who currently work for the Center. Their names may not be mentioned individually here, but they, too, are part of this legacy. And through them, and *their* successes, that legacy will continue—for generations to come.

Susan Porter Robinson
Vice President and Director,
Center for Adult Learning and Educational Credentials

REFERENCES

Allin, Cathy. 1997. Task force considers improvements to test center security rules. *GED Items.* January/February: 1, 9–10, 12.

American Council on Education (ACE). 1943. Sound educational credit for military experience: a recommended program. Washington, DC: American Council on Education.

_____. 1954. History of the development of Veterans' Testing Service. American Council on Education, Center for Adult Learning, file H-10. Unpublished.

_____. 1968. *Guide to the evaluation of educational experiences in the armed services.* Washington, DC: American Council on Education.

_____. 1974. *Guide to the evaluation of educational experiences in the armed services.* Washington, DC: American Council on Education.

_____. 1996. Literacy skills closely linked to ability to pass GED Tests, new ACE study finds. Press release. 26 January.

_____. 1999. ACE, Navy, and Marine Corps unveil SMART transcript. Press release. 4 November.

_____. 2000. American Council on Education board of directors summary and follow-up. Memorandum. 18 March.

American Council on Education (ACE) and National Association of Secondary School Principals. 1943. School and college credit for military experience: answers to questions. Washington, DC: American Council on Education and National Association of Secondary School Principals.

American Council on Education (ACE) and The Alliance. 1989. Principles of good practice for alternative and external degree programs. Washington, DC: American Council on Education.

Anderson, Clinton L. 1997. *Servicemembers Opportunity Colleges: 1972–97 (submitted as part of SOC final FY 96 report).* Washington, DC: Servicemembers Opportunity Colleges.

_____. 2000. Letter to the author, 8 May.

Anderson, Clinton, Kimberly Meek, and E. Nelson Swinerton. 1997. *Military Installation Voluntary Education Review (MIVER) final report, fiscal years 1991–96.* Washington, DC: American Council on Education.

Anderson, Clinton L., Nilla Newman, and William A. Xenakis. 1998. *Military Installation Voluntary Education Review Project (MIVER) end-of-year report, fiscal year 1998.* Washington, DC: American Council on Education.

P

Army/American Council on Education Registry Transcript System (AARTS). 1998. The results of the annual AARTS college survey. American Council on Education, Center for Adult Learning, AARTS files. Unpublished.

_____. Undated. AARTS. American Council on Education, Center for Adult Learning, file H-W. Unpublished.

Ashworth, Kenneth H., and William C. Lindley. 1977. The disgrace of military base programs. *Change.* February: 8, 61.

Auchter, Joan. 1997. GEDTS—alive and well with ACE. *GEDItems.* March/April: 2.

_____. 1999. Executive director's report: mission possible. Report read at the GED advisory committee meeting, 23 September. American Council on Education, Center for Adult Learning, GEDTS files.

_____. 2000a. Electronic mail to the author, 2 March.

_____. 2000b. Electronic mail to the author, 11 March.

_____. 2000c. New opportunities for GED candidates in the military. *GED Items.* March/April: 2.

Auchter, Joan, Paul D. Messersmith, and Wayne M. Patience. 1991. Description of an integrated Macintosh and IBM-compatible item banking, test construction, and test printing system. Paper read at the annual meeting of the National Council on Measurement in Education, April. American Council on Education, Center for Adult Learning, GEDTS files.

Bailey, Stephen K. 1979. Academic quality control: the case of college programs on military bases. Washington, DC: American Association for Higher Education.

Barrows, Thomas N. 1947. Accreditation of service experiences. Paper read at the annual meeting of the American Council on Education, 7 May. American Council on Education, Center for Adult Learning, file H-20.

_____. 1948. Letter to Dr. George F. Zook, 14 January. American Council on Education, Center for Adult Learning, file H-10. Unpublished.

_____. 1949. Letter to Dr. George F. Zook, 21 December. American Council on Education, Center for Adult Learning, file H-R. Unpublished.

_____. 1950. Letter to Dr. John Dale Russell, 12 May. American Council on Education, Center for Adult Learning, file H-R. Unpublished.

Bennett, Michael J. 1994. The law that worked. *Educational Record.* Fall: 8–10.

Cates, C. B., General. 1950. Letter to Thomas N. Barrows, 23 March. American Council on Education, Center for Adult Learning, file H–R. Unpublished.

Center for Adult Learning and Educational Credentials. 1998. The reorganization of the Center for Adult Learning and Educational Credentials. Report presented at the 1–2 April meeting of the Commission on Adult Learning and Educational Credentials. American Council on Education, Center for Adult Learning. Unpublished.

Coalition of Adult Education Organizations (CAEO) Board of Directors. 1991. A bill of rights for the adult learner. American Council on Education, Center for Adult Learning, file H-CC. Unpublished.

Coldren, Sharon L. 1975. Memorandum re: termination of GI educational benefits, 25 September. American Council on Education, Center for Adult Learning, file H-43. Unpublished.

Commission on Accreditation of Service Experiences (CASE). 1946a. Accreditation policies of state departments of education for the evaluation of service experiences and USAFI examinations. Washington, DC: American Council on Education.

_____. 1946b. Minutes of 7 January meeting of CASE. American Council on Education, Center for Adult Learning. Unpublished.

_____. 1946c. Minutes of 6 April meeting of CASE. American Council on Education, Center for Adult Learning. Unpublished.

_____. 1946d. Minutes of 4 May meeting of CASE. American Council on Education, Center for Adult Learning. Unpublished.

_____. 1946e. Minutes of 14 September meeting of CASE. American Council on Education, Center for Adult Learning. Unpublished.

_____. 1946f. The bulletin, number 1, 18 October. Washington, DC: Commission on Accreditation of Service Experiences.

_____. 1947a. Commission on Accreditation of Service Experiences of the American Council on Education progress report. American Council on Education, Center for Adult Learning, 7 March 1947 CASE Minutes file. Unpublished.

_____. 1947b. Minutes of 7 March meeting of CASE. American Council on Education, Center for Adult Learning. Unpublished.

_____. 1948. Minutes of 16 January meeting of CASE, American Council on Education, Center for Adult Learning. Unpublished.

_____. 1949a. Review of commission activities reported at 7th meeting. American Council on Education, Center for Adult Learning, 10 May CASE Minutes file. Unpublished.

_____. 1949b. Minutes of 10 May meeting of CASE. American Council on Education, Center for Adult Learning. Unpublished.

_____. 1949c. Minutes of 10 November meeting of CASE. American Council on Education, Center for Adult Learning. Unpublished.

_____. 1949d. Report of a subcommittee to the Commission on Accreditation of Service Experiences on policies and procedures relating to accreditation. American Council on Education, Center for Adult Learning, file H–R. Unpublished.

_____. 1950. Policies and procedures relating to accreditation. American Council on Education, Center for Adult Learning, file H–R. Unpublished.

_____. 1951a. Minutes of 26 January meeting of CASE. American Council on Education, Center for Adult Learning. Unpublished.

_____. 1951b. Minutes of 17 May meeting of CASE. American Council on Education, Center for Adult Learning. Unpublished.

_____. 1952a. Minutes of 18 January meeting of CASE. American Council on Education, Center for Adult Learning. Unpublished.

_____. 1952b. Minutes of 26 September meeting of CASE. American Council on Education, Center for Adult Learning. Unpublished.

_____. 1953a. Minutes of 20 March meeting of CASE. American Council on Education, Center for Adult Learning. Unpublished.

_____. 1953b. Minutes of 26 October meeting of CASE. American Council on Education, Center for Adult Learning. Unpublished.

_____. 1954a. Introducing our newsletter. *Newsletter.* 1: 1.

_____. 1954b. GED testing program. *Newsletter.* 1: 3–4.

_____. 1954c. Minutes of 2 April meeting of CASE. American Council on Education, Center for Adult Learning. Unpublished.

_____. 1954d. Minutes of 5 November meeting of CASE. American Council on Education, Center for Adult Learning. Unpublished.

_____. 1954e. Plans to continue *Newsletter. Newsletter.* 2: 1.

_____. 1955a. Minutes of 18 May meeting of CASE. American Council on Education, Center for Adult Learning. Unpublished.

_____. 1955b. Second Meeting, Policy Committee of the Commission on Accreditation of Service Experiences of the American Council on Education, 22–23 September. American Council on Education, Center for Adult Learning, file H-26. Unpublished.

_____. 1955c. Minutes of 21 October meeting of CASE. American Council on Education, Center for Adult Learning. Unpublished.

_____. 1955d. Evaluating reserve training programs. *Newsletter.* 4: 1–3.

_____. 1956a. The 1955 GED normative study. *Newsletter.* 5: 2–6.

_____. 1956b. Minutes of 3 May meeting of CASE. American Council on Education, Center for Adult Learning. Unpublished.

_____. 1956c. Minutes of 2 November meeting of CASE. American Council on Education, Center for Adult Learning. Unpublished.

_____. 1957a. Summary of annual report of activities of VTS official agencies. *Newsletter.* 7: 2–3.

_____. 1957b. Minutes of 3 May meeting of CASE. American Council on Education, Center for Adult Learning. Unpublished.

_____. 1957c. Minutes of 22 November meeting of CASE. American Council on Education, Center for Adult Learning. Unpublished.

_____. 1957d. Modification of policy to allow administration of GED Tests in state and federal health and penal institutions. *Newsletter.* 8: 2.

_____. 1958a. VTS to move to Washington. *Newsletter.* 9: 4.

_____. 1958b. Minutes of 19 May meeting of CASE. American Council on Education, Center for Adult Learning. Unpublished.

_____. 1958c. Minutes of 8 December meeting of CASE. American Council on Education, Center for Adult Learning. Unpublished.

_____. 1959a. Minutes of 1 May meeting of CASE. American Council on Education, Center for Adult Learning. Unpublished.

_____. 1959b. Minutes of 6 November meeting of CASE. American Council on Education, Center for Adult Learning. Unpublished.

_____. 1959c. Analysis of annual report of VTS agencies. *Newsletter.* 12: 1.

_____. 1960a. Advisory service. *Newsletter.* 13: 4.

_____. 1960b. Minutes of 6 May meeting of CASE. American Council on Education, Center for Adult Learning. Unpublished.

_____. 1961. Minutes of 5 May meeting of CASE. American Council on Education, Center for Adult Learning. Unpublished.

_____. 1962. Minutes of 4 May meeting of CASE. American Council on Education, Center for Adult Learning. Unpublished.

_____. 1963a. Transcript of proceedings: committee on graduate credit for specialized training meeting, 26 February. American Council on Education, Center for Adult Learning, file H-37.

_____. 1963b. Minutes of 3 May meeting of CASE. American Council on Education, Center for Adult Learning. Unpublished.

_____. 1963c. Minutes of 1 November meeting of CASE. American Council on Education, Center for Adult Learning. Unpublished.

_____. 1964a. Evaluation of the language programs of the Foreign Service Institute. *Newsletter.* 21: 1.

_____. 1964b. Minutes of 8 May meeting of CASE. American Council on Education, Center for Adult Learning. Unpublished.

_____. 1964c. Comprehensive College Tests replace college-level GED Tests. *Newsletter.* 22: 1–2.

_____. 1965. Minutes of 7 May meeting of CASE. American Council on Education, Center for Adult Learning. Unpublished.

_____. 1966a. GED testing of the visually handicapped. *Newsletter.* 25: 2–3.

_____. 1966b. Minutes of 4 November meeting of CASE. American Council on Education, Center for Adult Learning. Unpublished.

_____. 1966c. Activity reports of CASE, 1956–66. American Council on Education, Center for Adult Learning, file H–U. Unpublished.

_____. 1966d. GED testing at state institutions. *Newsletter.* 26: 4.

_____. 1967. Annual report of Official GED Test Centers. *Newsletter.* 27: 3.

_____. 1968. Minutes of 6 May meeting of CASE. American Council on Education, Center for Adult Learning. Unpublished.

_____. 1969a. Use of GED Tests by province of Nova Scotia. *Newsletter.* 31: 2–3.

_____. 1969b. Minutes of 5 May meeting of CASE. American Council on Education, Center for Adult Learning. Unpublished.

_____. 1969c. Minutes of 3 November meeting of CASE. American Council on Education, Center for Adult Learning. Unpublished.

_____. 1969d. Policies of institutions for granting credit for service school and USAFI courses and for admission based on GED Test scores. *Newsletter.* 32: 3–5.

_____. 1970a. Use of GED Tests by province of Saskatchewan. *Newsletter.* 33: 2.

_____. 1970b. Minutes of 4 May meeting of CASE. American Council on Education, Center for Adult Learning. Unpublished.

_____. 1970c. Minutes of 2 November meeting of CASE. American Council on Education, Center for Adult Learning. Unpublished.

_____. 1971a. Minutes of 24 May meeting of CASE. American Council on Education, Center for Adult Learning. Unpublished.

_____. 1971b. Minutes of 1 November meeting of CASE. American Council on Education, Center for Adult Learning. Unpublished.

_____. 1971c. Introduction of Spanish editions, GED Tests. *Newsletter.* 36: 2.

_____. 1972a. Minutes of 15 May meeting of CASE. American Council on Education, Center for Adult Learning. Unpublished.

_____. 1972b. Minutes of 30 October meeting of CASE. American Council on Education, Center for Adult Learning. Unpublished.

_____. 1973a. Minutes of 30 April meeting of CASE. American Council on Education, Center for Adult Learning. Unpublished.

_____. 1973b. Minutes of 5 November meeting of CASE. American Council on Education, Center for Adult Learning. Unpublished.

Commission on Adult Learning and Educational Credentials. 1998a. Agenda materials for 1–2 April meeting of Commission on Adult Learning and Educational Credentials. American Council on Education, Center for Adult Learning. Unpublished.

_____. 1998b. Minutes of 1–2 April meeting of Commission on Adult Learning and Educational Credentials. American Council on Education, Center for Adult Learning. Unpublished.

_____. 1998c. Agenda materials for 7–8 October meeting of Commission on Adult Learning and Educational Credentials. American Council on Education, Center for Adult Learning. Unpublished.

_____. 1998d. Minutes of 7–8 October meeting of Commission on Adult Learning and Educational Credentials. American Council on Education, Center for Adult Learning. Unpublished.

_____. 1999a. Agenda materials for 21–22 April meeting of Commission on Adult Learning and Educational Credentials. American Council on Education, Center for Adult Learning. Unpublished.

_____. 1999b. Minutes of 21–22 April meeting of Commission on Adult Learning and Educational Credentials. American Council on Education, Center for Adult Learning. Unpublished.

Commission on Educational Credit (COEC). 1974a. Minutes of 15 March meeting of COEC. American Council on Education, Center for Adult Learning. Unpublished.

_____. 1974b. Minutes of 6 May meeting of COEC. American Council on Education, Center for Adult Learning. Unpublished.

_____. 1974c. Minutes of 16 September meeting of COEC. American Council on Education, Center for Adult Learning. Unpublished.

_____. 1975a. Agenda materials for 20 January meeting of COEC. American Council on Education, Center for Adult Learning. Unpublished.

_____. 1975b. Minutes of 18–19 May meeting of COEC. American Council on Education, Center for Adult Learning. Unpublished.

_____. 1975c. Agenda materials for 29–30 September meeting of COEC. American Council on Education, Center for Adult Learning. Unpublished.

_____. 1976a. Minutes of 21–22 June meeting of COEC. American Council on Education, Center for Adult Learning. Unpublished.

_____. 1976b. Minutes of 18–19 October meeting of COEC. American Council on Education, Center for Adult Learning. Unpublished.

_____. 1977a. Minutes of 22–23 February meeting of COEC. American Council on Education, Center for Adult Learning. Unpublished.

_____. 1977b. Minutes of 20–21 June meeting of COEC. American Council on Education, Center for Adult Learning. Unpublished.

_____. 1977c. Minutes of 21–22 November meeting of COEC. American Council on Education, Center for Adult Learning. Unpublished.

_____. 1978a. Minutes of 3–4 May meeting of COEC. American Council on Education, Center for Adult Learning. Unpublished.

_____. 1978b. Minutes of 4–5 December meeting of COEC. American Council on Education, Center for Adult Learning. Unpublished.

_____. 1979. Minutes of 10–11 December meeting of COEC. American Council on Education, Center for Adult Learning. Unpublished.

Commission on Educational Credit and Credentials (COECC). 1981. Minutes of 27–28 May meeting of COECC. American Council on Education, Center for Adult Learning. Unpublished.

P

_____. 1982. Minutes of 25–26 January meeting of COECC. American Council on Education, Center for Adult Learning. Unpublished.

_____. 1983. Minutes of 28 February–1 March meeting of COECC. American Council on Education, Center for Adult Learning. Unpublished.

_____. 1984a. Minutes of 26–27 March meeting of COECC. American Council on Education, Center for Adult Learning. Unpublished.

_____. 1984b. Minutes of 24–25 September meeting of COECC. American Council on Education, Center for Adult Learning. Unpublished.

_____. 1985. Minutes of 23–24 September meeting of COECC. American Council on Education, Center for Adult Learning. Unpublished.

_____. 1986a. Minutes of 24–25 March meeting of COECC. American Council on Education, Center for Adult Learning. Unpublished.

_____. 1986b. Minutes of 8–9 September meeting of COECC. American Council on Education, Center for Adult Learning. Unpublished.

_____. 1987. Minutes of 28–29 September meeting of COECC. American Council on Education, Center for Adult Learning. Unpublished.

_____. 1988a. Agenda materials for 26–27 September meeting of COECC. American Council on Education, Center for Adult Learning. Unpublished.

_____. 1988b. Minutes of 28–29 March meeting of COECC. American Council on Education, Center for Adult Learning. Unpublished.

_____. 1989a. Agenda materials for 27–28 March meeting of COECC. American Council on Education, Center for Adult Learning. Unpublished.

_____. 1989b. Minutes of 25–26 September meeting of COECC. American Council on Education, Center for Adult Learning. Unpublished.

_____. 1990a. Agenda materials for 26–27 March meeting of COECC. American Council on Education, Center for Adult Learning. Unpublished.

_____. 1990b. Minutes of 26–27 March meeting of COECC. American Council on Education, Center for Adult Learning. Unpublished.

_____. 1990c. Minutes of 24–25 September meeting of COECC. American Council on Education, Center for Adult Learning. Unpublished.

_____. 1991a. Minutes of 25–26 March meeting of COECC. American Council on Education, Center for Adult Learning. Unpublished.

_____. 1991b. Minutes of 30 September–1 October meeting of COECC. American Council on Education, Center for Adult Learning. Unpublished.

_____. 1992a. Agenda materials for 27–28 April meeting of COECC. American Council on Education, Center for Adult Learning. Unpublished.

_____. 1992b. Minutes of 27–28 April meeting of COECC. American Council on Education, Center for Adult Learning. Unpublished.

_____. 1992c. Agenda materials for 29 September meeting of COECC. American Council on Education, Center for Adult Learning. Unpublished.

_____. 1992d. Minutes of 29 September meeting of COECC. American Council on Education, Center for Adult Learning. Unpublished.

_____. 1993a. Agenda materials for 29–30 March meeting of COECC. American Council on Education, Center for Adult Learning. Unpublished.

_____. 1993b. Minutes of 29–30 March meeting of COECC. American Council on Education, Center for Adult Learning. Unpublished.

_____. 1993c. Agenda materials for 6–7 December meeting of COECC. American Council on Education, Center for Adult Learning. Unpublished.

_____. 1993d. Minutes of 6–7 December meeting of COECC. American Council on Education, Center for Adult Learning. Unpublished.

_____. 1994. Agenda materials for 26–27 September meeting of COECC. American Council on Education, Center for Adult Learning. Unpublished.

_____. 1995a. Agenda materials for 27–28 March meeting of COECC. American Council on Education, Center for Adult Learning. Unpublished.

_____. 1995b. Minutes of 27–28 March meeting of COECC. American Council on Education, Center for Adult Learning. Unpublished.

_____. 1995c. Agenda materials for 27–28 September meeting of COECC. American Council on Education, Center for Adult Learning. Unpublished.

_____. 1995d. Minutes of 27–28 September meeting of COECC. American Council on Education, Center for Adult Learning. Unpublished.

_____. 1996a. Agenda materials for 27–28 March meeting of COECC. American Council on Education, Center for Adult Learning. Unpublished.

_____. 1996b. Minutes of 27–28 March meeting of COECC. American Council on Education, Center for Adult Learning. Unpublished.

_____. 1996c. Agenda materials for 2–3 October meeting of COECC. American Council on Education, Center for Adult Learning. Unpublished.

_____. 1996d. Minutes of 2–3 October meeting of COECC. American Council on Education, Center for Adult Learning. Unpublished.

_____. 1997a. Agenda materials for 2–3 April meeting of COECC. American Council on Education, Center for Adult Learning. Unpublished.

_____. 1997b. Minutes of 2–3 April meeting of COECC. American Council on Education, Center for Adult Learning. Unpublished.

_____. 1997c. Agenda materials for 8–9 October meeting of COECC. American Council on Education, Center for Adult Learning. Unpublished.

_____. 1997d. Minutes of 8–9 October meeting of COECC. American Council on Education, Center for Adult Learning. Unpublished.

Commission on Higher Education and the Adult Learner (CHEAL). Undated. The Commission on Higher Education and the Adult Learner: a report of phase I: 1981–85. American Council on Education, Center for Adult Learning, CHEAL file. Unpublished.

Commission on Non-Traditional Study. 1973. *Diversity by design.* San Francisco: Jossey-Bass Publishers, Inc.

Community College of the Air Force (CCAF). 1999. http://www.au.af.mil/au/ccaf/. Public affairs: the facts: history.

Council for Adult and Experiential Learning (CAEL). 1989. Executive summary: a more productive workforce: challenge for postsecondary education and its partners. American Council on Education, Center for Adult Learning, CAEL file. Unpublished.

CREDIT. 1999. Adult learner of the year award. Description. American Council on Education, Center for Adult Learning, CREDIT files. Unpublished.

_____. 2000a. Criteria for affiliate offices. Description. American Council on Education, Center for Adult Learning, CREDIT files. Unpublished.

_____. 2000b. Quality Standards System. Description. American Council on Education, Center for Adult Learning, CREDIT files. Unpublished.

_____. Undated-a. ACE college credit recommendations. Description. American Council on Education, Center for Adult Learning, CREDIT files. Unpublished.

_____. Undated-b. ACE national coordinators. Description. American Council on Education, Center for Adult Learning, CREDIT files. Unpublished.

Dearing, Bruce. 1976. Letter to Dr. Jerry Miller, 22 November. American Council on Education, Center for Adult Learning, file H–V. Unpublished.

Dearing, Bruce, Walter M. Hartung, Barbara H. Knudson, J. Warren Perry, Richard C. Richardson, Jr., John Roueche, and Victor Hurst. 1976. Report of the site review team which visited the Community College of the Air Force to review a proposed associate degree program, 25–29 October, San Antonio, Texas. American Council on Education, Center for Adult Learning, file H–V. Unpublished.

Dermody, Bill. 2000. Navy reports high GED pass rate for new recruits at Illinois "boot camp." GED Items. March/April: 4.

Detchen, Lily. 1947. The United States Armed Forces Institute examinations. Reprint, Washington, DC: American Council on Education, Educational Record, October 1947.

Dobbins, Charles. 1968. American Council on Education: leadership and chronology 1918–1968. Washington, DC: American Council on Education.

Dressel, Paul L., and John Schmid. 1951. An evaluation of the Tests of General Educational Development. Washington, DC: American Council on Education.

External Diploma Program (EDP). Undated. Community colleges and the External Diploma Program, a high school diploma option. American Council on Education, Center for Adult Learning, file H-AA. Unpublished.

Fenwick, Dorothy. 2000. Telephone interview by author, 6 January.

Geiken, Duane. 2000. Telephone interview by author, 1 August.

General Educational Development Testing Service (GEDTS). 1980. GED statistical report. Washington, DC: American Council on Education.

_____. 1984. *GED statistical report*. Washington, DC: American Council on Education.

_____. 1987a. *GED statistical report*. Washington, DC: American Council on Education.

_____. 1987b. Military recruiting and the adult student. *GED Items.* March/April: 1, 4.

_____. 1989. *GED statistical report*. Washington, DC: American Council on Education.

_____. 1993. *The Tests of General Educational Development: technical manual*. Washington, DC: American Council on Education.

_____. 1994. Overhaul of military education urged. *GED Items.* March/April: 12, 10.

_____. 1995. GEDTS distribution project: distribution team recommendations (5 December). American Council on Education, Center for Adult Learning, GEDTS files. Unpublished.

_____. 1997a. *GED examiner's manual*. Washington, DC: American Council on Education.

_____. 1997b. Sylvan Learning Systems goes to bat; will deliver international testing for GEDTS. *GED Items.* November/December: 9.

_____. 1997c. *Who took the GED? Statistical report*. Washington, DC: American Council on Education.

_____. 1998a. Uses of the GED Tests with students enrolled in traditional accredited secondary schools: discussion paper (July). American Council on Education, Center for Adult Learning, GEDTS files. Unpublished.

_____. 1998b. Death of Bill Langner. *GED Items.* September (archived text).

_____. 1999. *Alignment of national and state standards*. Washington, DC: American Council on Education.

Grattan, C. Hartley. 1955. *In quest of knowledge: a historical perspective on adult education.* New York: Association Press.

Harrington, Fred Harvey. 1977. *The future of adult education.* San Francisco: Jossey-Bass Publishers.

Heyns, Roger W. 1976a. Letter to chief of naval education and training, Naval Air Station, 25 March. American Council on Education, Center for Adult Learning, file H-43. Unpublished.

_____. 1976b. Letter to Major General C. G. Cleveland, 4 February. American Council on Education, Center for Adult Learning, file H-V. Unpublished.

_____. 1976c. Statement presented to the U.S. Commissioner of Education's advisory committee on accreditation and institutional eligibility. 8 December. American Council on Education, Center for Adult Learning, file H–V. Unpublished.

Hone, Lisa Richards. 2000. Army pilots GED program in two-fifths of United States recruiting areas. *GED Items.* March/April: 1, 4.

Houle, Cyril O., Elbert W. Burr, Thomas H. Hamilton, and John R. Yale. 1947. *The armed services and adult education.* Washington, DC: American Council on Education.

Huitt, Ralph K., Roger W. Heyns, Rev. Msgr. John F. Murphy, Frederic W. Ness, Charles V. Kidd, and Allan W. Ostar. 1976. Letter to the Honorable John C. Stennis, 3 June. American Council on Education, Center for Adult Learning, file H-V. Unpublished.

Keeton, Morris. 2000. Telephone interview by author, 10 January.

Kentucky Education Television. 1997. Spanish version of GED Test to promote access without changing standards. *KET Quarterly.* Fall: 1.

Knowles, Malcolm S. 1977. *A history of the adult education movement in the United States.* Malabar: Robert E. Krieger Publishing Company.

Leibman Associates, Inc. 1996. A management review of the GED Testing Service. Report presented at the 2–3 October meeting of the Commission on Educational Credit and Credentials. American Council on Education, Center for Adult Learning. Unpublished.

Lindquist, E. F. 1944. The use of tests in the accreditation of military experience and in the educational placement of war veterans. Paper presented at the meeting of the National Association of State Universities. Reprint, Washington, DC: American Council on Education, *Educational Record,* October 1944.

_____. 1968. Interview by William J. Feister and Douglas R. Whitney. In *Epsilon Bulletin: Epsilon Chapter—Phi Delta Kappa College of Education,* edited by William J. Feister. Vol. 42, 17–28. Iowa City: University of Iowa Press.

Lowe, Jean H. 1992. Letter to the *Des Moines Register,* 13 March. Agenda materials for 27–28 April meeting of Commission on Educational Credit and Credentials. American Council on Education, Center for Adult Learning.

_____. 1995. Letter to Dr. Betty Overton, 21 February. Agenda materials for 27–28 March meeting of Commission on Educational Credit and Credentials. American Council on Education, Center for Adult Learning. Unpublished.

Malone, Kyle. 1999. Interview by author at the American Council on Education, Washington, DC, 9 November.

Miller, Jerry W. 1976a. Memorandum for the file, 24 February. American Council on Education, Center for Adult Learning, file H-43. Unpublished.

_____. 1976b. Memorandum to Roger W. Heyns re: forthcoming meeting with Mr. Taylor, assistant secretary of defense, 23 July. American Council on Education, Center for Adult Learning, file H–V. Unpublished.

_____. 1986. Interview by Ruth Cargo at Miller's office at the Association of Independent Colleges and Schools, transcript, 11 November. American Council on Education, Center for Adult Learning, file H–Z.

_____. 2000. Letter to the author, 18 April.

_____. Undated. Expanded role of the Commission on Educational Credit, American Council on Education. American Council on Education, Center for Adult Learning, file H-E. Unpublished.

Miller, Jerry W., and Olive Mills, eds. 1978. *Credentialing educational accomplishment: report and recommendations of the task force on educational credit and credentials.* Washington, DC: American Council on Education.

Miscampbell, Floydine. 1946. Letter to E. J. Smith, 26 April. American Council on Education, Center for Adult Learning, file H-19. Unpublished.

_____. 1947. The advisory service of the Commission on Accreditation. Paper presented at the meeting of the American Association of Collegiate Registrars. Reprint: American Association of Collegiate Registrars, *Journal of the American Association of Collegiate Registrars,* July 1947.

Montgomery, G. V. "Sonny." 1994. The Montgomery GI Bill: development, implementation, and impact. *Educational Record.* Fall: 49–54.

National Association of Secondary School Principals (NASSP). 1943. *Secondary school credit for educational experience in military service: a recommended program by a national committee for secondary schools.* Washington, DC: National Association of Secondary School Principals.

National Center for Education Statistics (NCES). 1996. Fall enrollment in colleges and universities surveys and integrated postsecondary education data system (IPEDS) surveys; and U.S. Department of Commerce, Bureau of the Census, unpublished tabulations. http://nces.ed.gov/pubs/pj/P97t08.html

Nolan, Donald J. 1998. *Regents College: the early years.* Virginia Beach: The Donning Company/Publishers.

O'Farrell, Neil. 1998. Distance learning and the American Council on Education: an agenda for leadership and action. Report presented at 1–2 April meeting of the Commission on Adult Learning and Educational Credentials. American Council on Education, Center for Adult Learning. Unpublished.

Office on Educational Credit (OEC). 1974. Proposal to study feasibility of using military occupational classification systems as a means of recognizing learning (April). American Council on Education, Center for Adult Learning, file H-48. Unpublished.

_____. 1976. Proposal draft for feasibility study of Department of Labor (23 September). American Council on Education, Center for Adult Learning, file H-48. Unpublished.

_____. 1978. Discussion paper: plans and requirements for the Program on Non-Collegiate Sponsored Instruction, 1978–82 (18 January). American Council on Education, Center for Adult Learning, PONSI files. Unpublished.

Patterson, William F. 1946. Letter to Thomas N. Barrows, 29 January. American Council on Education, Center for Adult Learning, file H-21. Unpublished.

Program on Non-Collegiate Sponsored Instruction (PONSI). 1982. Overview. American Council on Education, Center for Adult Learning, file H–W. Unpublished.

Quigley, B. Allan. 1987. The Canadianization of the GED: the history and development of the General Educational Development testing program in Canada. GED Testing Service Occasional Paper, Number 1. Washington, DC: American Council on Education.

———. 1991. Exception and reward: the history and social policy development of the GED in the U.S. and Canada. *Adult Basic Education.* 1: 27–43.

———. 2000. Letter to the author, 24 April.

Robinson, Jo Ann. 1999. Electronic mail to Susan Porter Robinson, 31 August.

———. 2000. Electronic mail to the author, 11 January.

Robinson, Susan Porter. 1999. Telephone interview by author, 5 October.

Rose, Amy D. 1989. The dilemmas of equivalency: American colleges and the evaluation of armed services training in the 1940s. *Journal of the Midwest History of Education Society.* 17: 18–29.

———. 1990. Preparing for veterans: higher education and the efforts to accredit the learning of World War II servicemen and women. *Adult Education Quarterly.* 42: 30–45.

Schreiber, Elizabeth J. 1994. Letter to Jean H. Lowe, GED Testing Service, 8 December. Agenda materials for 27–28 March 1995 meeting of Commission on Educational Credit and Credentials. American Council on Education, Center for Adult Learning. Unpublished.

Sellman, Wayne S. 1985. Military adaptability screening: a manpower management perspective. *GED Items.* July: 1–2.

Sewell, Walter E. 1947. Letter to Paul E. Elicker, 8 July. American Council on Education, Center for Adult Learning, file H-21. Unpublished.

Smith, Ruth Cargo. 1975. Memorandum to Eugene Sullivan re: evaluation of classified military courses, 7 August. American Council on Education, Center for Adult Learning, file H-43. Unpublished.

Spille, Henry A. 1985. Letter to Colonel Bruce T. Battey, 12 June. American Council on Education, Center for Adult Learning, AARTS/Registries file. Unpublished.

———. 1989. Beyond the rhetoric: toward a system of learning and credentialing for adults (5 April). American Council on Education, Center for Adult Learning, file H–DD. Unpublished.

———. 1999. Telephone interview with the author, 5 October.

———. 2000a. Electronic mail to the author, 16 May.

———. 2000b. Electronic mail to the author, 14 August.

Stewart, David W. 1982. Protecting the integrity of academic degrees: a report to the Commission on Educational Credit and Credentials, American Council on Education, for final recommendation and action at meeting on 20–21 September 1982. American Council on Education, Center for Adult Learning, file H–Y. Unpublished.

_____. 1999. Electronic mail to the author, 30 September.

Stewart, David W., and Henry A. Spille. 1988. *Diploma mills: degrees of fraud*. New York: Macmillan Publishing Company.

_____. 1993. Religious exemptions threaten higher education's integrity. *Educational Record*. Spring: 46–50.

Stubblefield, Harold W. 1988. *Towards a history of adult education in America*. New York: Croon Helm.

Stubblefield, Harold W., and Patrick Keane. 1994. *Adult education in the American experience*. San Francisco: Jossey-Bass Publishers.

Sullivan, Eugene. 1999. Interview by the author at the American Council on Education, Washington, DC, 5 November.

Suritz, Penelope. 1999. Interview by the author at the American Council on Education, Washington, DC, 9 November.

Turner, Cornelius P. 1945. A report on the development of the Central Clearing Agency of Accreditation in its relationship to the evaluation of military training, military experience, and educational achievement of service personnel during World War II with recommendations for the continuance of this work through a peace-time USAFI accreditation service and the Commission on Accreditation established by the American Council on Education. American Council on Education, Center for Adult Learning, file H-7. Unpublished.

_____. 1947. Letter to E. G. Williamson, 25 June. American Council on Education, Center for Adult Learning, file H-21. Unpublished.

_____. 1956. Letter to Charles W. McLane, 31 May. American Council on Education, Center for Adult Learning, file H-21. Unpublished.

_____. 1958a. Letter to Brigadier General Sidney F. Giffin, 11 August. Minutes for 8 December meeting of CASE. American Council on Education, Center for Adult Learning. Unpublished.

_____. 1958b. Memorandum to Dr. Arthur S. Adams, 15 August. Minutes for 8 December meeting of CASE. American Council on Education, Center for Adult Learning. Unpublished.

_____. 1986a. Interview by Ruth Cargo at Turner's home in Alexandria, VA, transcript, 25 August. American Council on Education, Center for Adult Learning, file H–O.

_____. 1986b. Interview by Ruth Cargo at Turner's home in Alexandria, VA, transcript, 19 November. American Council on Education, Center for Adult Learning, file H–O.

_____. Undated. Mr. Turner's tape on the history of GED, transcript. American Council on Education, Center for Adult Learning, file H–J.

Tyler, Ralph W. Undated. A summary of the findings of the fact-finding study of the testing program of the United States Armed Forces Institute. American Council on Education, Center for Adult Learning, file H-5. Unpublished.

United States Code. 1946. Title 10, Section 1176, 13 June 1916.

Veterans' Testing Service (VTS). 1947. VTS form 65: VTS plan I discontinued 30 June 1947 (1 July). American Council on Education, Center for Adult Learning, file H-10. Unpublished.

_____. 1948. To agents of Veterans' Testing Service (10 April). American Council on Education, Center for Adult Learning, file H-10. Unpublished.

Whitney, Douglas. 2000a. Telephone interview by the author, 12 January.

_____. 2000b. Letter to the author, 21 April.

Williamson, E. G. 1947. Letter to T. M. Barrows, 18 June. American Council on Education, Center for Adult Learning, file H-21. Unpublished.

Wilson, Logan. 1966. Letter to Dr. Lynn M. Bartlett, 30 August. American Council on Education, Center for Adult Learning, file H–C. Unpublished.

Young, Kenneth E., Lloyd H. Davis, James F. Nickerson, and Jerry W. Miller. 1977. Letter to *Change,* 16 February. American Council on Education, Center for Adult Learning, file H-43. Unpublished.

OTHER PUBLICATIONS FROM THE CENTER FOR ADULT LEARNING

Distance Learning Evaluation Guide
Available from ACE Fulfillment Service (Code W),
Department 191, Washington, DC 20055-0191;
(301) 604-9073.

External Degrees in the Information Age
By Eugene Sullivan, David W. Stewart, and Henry A. Spille
Available from Oryx Press, 4041 North Central Avenue,
Suite 700, Phoenix, AZ 85012-3397; (800) 279-6799.

*2000 Guide to the Evaluation of Educational Experiences in the
Armed Services*
Available from Oryx Press, 4041 North Central Avenue,
Suite 700, Phoenix, AZ 85012-3397; (800) 279-6799.

2001 Guide to Educational Credit by Examination, Fifth Edition
Available from ACE Fulfillment Service (Code W),
Department 191, Washington, DC 20055-0191;
(301) 604-9073.

*Guidelines for Computerized-Adaptive Test Development and Use in
Education* (ACE Credit by Examination Program)
Available from Credit by Examination, American Council on
Education, One Dupont Circle NW, Suite 250,
Washington, DC 20036-1193; (202) 939-9434.

Guiding Principles for Distance Learning in a Learning Society
Available from ACE Fulfillment Service (Code W),
Department 191, Washington, DC 20055-0191;
(301) 604-9073.

2001 National Guide to Educational Credit for Training Programs
Available from ACE Fulfillment Service (Code W),
Department 191, Washington, DC 20055-0191;
(301) 604-9073.

Pocket Guide to College Credit and Degrees
Available from ACE Fulfillment Service (Code W),
Department 191, Washington, DC 20055-0191;
(301) 604-9073.

GLOSSARY OF ACRONYMS

AARTS   Army/American Council on Education Registry Transcript System (Center for Adult Learning and Educational Credentials)

ACE   American Council on Education

ACE/PONSI   American Council on Education's Program on Non-Collegiate Sponsored Instruction (also known as PONSI; predecessor of CREDIT; Center for Adult Learning and Educational Credentials)

ACT   American College Testing program

CASE   Commission on Accreditation of Service Experiences (predecessor of COEC; American Council on Education)

CCAF   Community College of the Air Force

CHEAL   Commission on Higher Education and the Adult Learner (American Council on Education)

CLEP   College-Level Examination Program (College Entrance Examination Board)

COEC   Commission on Educational Credit (predecessor of COECC; American Council on Education)

COECC   Commission on Educational Credit and Credentials (successor to CASE and COEC; American Council on Education)

CREDIT   (not an acronym) College Credit Recommendation Service (Center for Adult Learning and Educational Credentials)

DANTES   Defense Activity for Non-Traditional Education Support (successor to USAFI)

EDP   National External Diploma Program (Center for Adult Learning and Educational Credentials)

ETS   Educational Testing Service

GED Tests   Tests of General Educational Development (Center for Adult Learning and Educational Credentials)

GEDTS   General Educational Development Testing Service (Center for Adult Learning and Educational Credentials)

GI Bill   General Infantryman Bill of Rights

MIVER   Military Installation Voluntary Education Review (Center for Adult Learning and Educational Credentials)

MOS   Military Occupational Specialty (Army)

OEC   Office on Educational Credit (predecessor of OECC; American Council on Education)

OECC   Office on Educational Credit and Credentials (predecessor of Center for Adult Learning and Educational Credentials; American Council on Education)

PONSI   Program on Non-Collegiate Sponsored Instruction (also known as ACE/PONSI; predecessor of CREDIT; Center for Adult Learning and Educational Credentials)

SLD   specific learning disabilities

SMART   Sailor/Marine Corps/ACE Registry
Transcript (Center for Adult Learning and
Educational Credentials)

SOC   Servicemembers Opportunity Colleges (formerly Servicemen's Opportunity Colleges)

SOCAD   Servicemembers Opportunity Colleges
Associate Degree

STARS   Strategic Training and Resource Specialists
(GED Testing Service)

USAFI   United States Armed Forces Institute (predecessor of DANTES)

VA   Veterans' Administration

VTS   Veterans' Testing Service (predecessor of the
GED Testing Service)

INDEX

B

D

E

Age requirements, 29–30, 59–60, 88
Alignment of National and State Standards, xxxviii, 204–205
California, testing in, xxxii, 30, 88
Cameron-Heckman study, 172
Canada, testing in, xiv, xxxii, 91–94, 111, 168, 174–175, 205
Candidate study, 132, 137
College-level, xxxi, 4, 22, 30, 51, 56–57, 76–78, 111 (see also
    Comprehensive College Tests and College-Level
    Examination Program [CLEP])
Computer-based testing, xxxvii, 207
Decision to keep with the American Council on Education,
    xxxvii, 189–191
Distribution of test materials, xxx, 56, 168, 181 (see also
    Educational Testing Service [ETS])
Enrolled high school students, testing of/testing at-risk
    students, xiv, xxxv, xxxvii–xxxviii, 168–170, 203, 209–210
Foreign, see GED, overseas/international
French-language, xiv, 94
hospitals and institutions, testing in, xxviii, xxx, 24–25, 35,
    60–62, 73
Hotline, 171–172
Item banking, 181
Items newsletter, 137
Military acceptance of, 212–214
Minimum score requirements/passing standards, xxxiv, xxxvii,
    28, 68, 88, 201, 216
New York, testing in, see New York High School Equivalency
    Testing Program
Norming/standardization/restandardization, xxvi, xxx, 4, 23,
    27–28, 62–64, 74, 83, 90, 97, 136, 174–175, 177, 179
Outreach and publicity, 168, 171, 172, 193, 200, 207
Overseas/international, xxxi, 73, 203, 207
Practice Tests, 97, 135
prisons, testing in, xxx, 25, 60–62, 72–73
Research, xxxiv, 132–133, 136, 168, 172–174
Research Study No. 1 see *Candidate Study*
Residency requirements, 90, 103
Security, 22, 62, 203–204, 211–212, 214, 218
Shorter version, see GED, Test development, second
    generation (1978)
Spanish-language, xiv, xxxii, xxxviii, 88–91, 168, 174–177,
    203, 206
Standardization, see GED, Norming/standardization
Strategic Training and Resource Specialists (STARS), xxxvii,
    203, 211–212

H

I

J

M

S